The Reward Society

By Dr Tom Manion

Best Wishes

Tom.

ISBN: 978-0-9534415-3-2

Biography

Dr. Tom Manion was born in Birkenhead and began his working life – as did his father and grandfather Thomas Manion Snr (who was killed at Dunkirk in 1940) – as a Crane Driver with British Steel in Shotton.

Tom was appointed Chief Executive of Irwell Valley HA in 1997. Since then, the Association has more than trebled in size and achieved international status across Europe and the USA as a frontrunner of modern methods and innovation in business practice, customer service, property and neighbourhood management.

Under his tenure Irwell Valley has collected over 25 awards, including the prestigious Landlord of the Year and Outstanding Achievement in Housing in the United Kingdom – the highest professional accolade from the Chartered Institute of Housing. In 2004, it was identified as the best company in the north-west by the *Sunday Times*. The *Financial Times* has listed Irwell Valley in the top 50 Companies in the UK since 2005 and it appeared in *The Guardian*'s Top Employers for 2007.

The Office of the Deputy Prime Minister produced a report on Irwell Valley in November 2003. Professor Hill's report in 2007, *The Future of UK Housing*, cited Irwell Valley for innovative approaches.

Tom is a Distinguished Professional Fellow of the Chartered Institute of Housing, a fellow of the Royal Society of Arts and in 2003 he was awarded the Cabinet Office's Public Servant of the Year. In the same year, *The Independent* newspaper identified him as one of the top 10 influential people in housing in the UK. This was followed a year later with recognition from *The Guardian*, which cited him as one of the Top Ten Innovators in the UK, describing him as "a charismatic pioneer".

He also collected the National Customer Services Lifetime Achievement Award which in his own words was "unexpectedly premature but a fantastic honour (he) would accept on behalf of his colleagues".

Tom's followed his first degree, an Upper Second Class Hons, with a doctorate – a study of British housing policy – from the University of Lancaster in 1982. During this time Tom worked at Memphis State University and on housing projects in Tennessee. He also worked in the House of Commons, as a front bench adviser on the 1988 Housing Act.

Tom chaired the Greater Manchester Community Foundation for six years until November 2009, raising its turnover from £60,000 per annum to over £6 million (a 10,000% increase). He advises the Moss Side Fire Brigade's Boxing Club and the Community Change Foundation. He has served on the National Council of the Chartered Institute of Housing. Tom swims every day, plays and sings in the Tomahawks and performs crooning and cabaret. He's been a steelworker, a bin-man, ice cream seller, turf accountant, head sacristan and a roofer, scaffolder, lifeguard and teacher.

He has been a Drug Commissioner of the North West Regional Assembly, a Director of the *Big Issue* and Director of High Peak Housing Trust. He has worked for European housing associations, particularly in the Netherlands, housing authorities in the USA and worked with housing providers in Hong Kong and China. Tom was presented with NAHRO's John D. Lang International Award in the US, which recognises a person in the housing and community development field who has made an outstanding contribution towards international understanding and exchange of international experience. This Award, presented in San Diego in October 2009 was the first time it has ever been presented to a UK housing professional.

Acknowledgements

I would like to thank many people for inspiring me to write this book. My mother and father, Josephine Valentine and Dennis Edward, provided me with a great start in life and taught me the importance of working hard, learning, being responsible and being kind. I hope I've lived up to their expectations.

Family is very very important to me: the love and support I have received from Brigette, Colette and Anouska has helped me through the ups and downs of parenting and life. We've challenged and learned from each other and we know how strong our love is.

My Auntie Beryl features extensively in this book and I'm grateful to her, my Uncle Brian and Uncle Jim for the unswerving support and wisdom they have passed on to me over many years.

During my working life two people in particular have greatly influenced me. Graham Eades and John McHale have given me frank and honest guidance and professional advice. Rob Brown has also been a force for good in my life and a great soul mate.

Board members at Irwell Valley, particularly Nigel H. Neary and Lynne Garsden have provided courageous leadership when we needed it and reined me in when I needed it.

My colleagues at Irwell Valley have shown unbelievable flexibility, innovation and tremendous energy to cut through the crap, enjoy work and treat people with dignity and respect.

Angela Garvin has worked with me since day one and she constantly amazes me with her quiet, efficient effectiveness and wisdom.

Bob Armstrong from Nebraska provided me with the inspiration and much needed confidence to do what was right, often in the face of adverse criticism. Gerrit Teunis helped us go European and translated our ideas into the Dutch housing scene.

Lynne Shaw gave the best interview I have ever experienced and is a fantastic, loyal supporter, who has truly helped me get where I am today.

Kate Miller has provided tremendous advice and direction. Thank you Kate.

What can I say about Julian Richer? He came into my life through an article in a Sunday newspaper and we have developed an enduring professional and personal relationship. He introduced me to his wife Rosie who is a beautiful friend. I would definitely not have written this book had it not been for his enthusiasm, persistence and confidence in my ability, often beating me up (metaphorically) for missing endless deadlines. I apologise to you Jules for over promising and under delivering, but I hope that you're happy and proud of the finished article!

Finally I'm eternally grateful to the Ballerina Girl and to all of you who have helped, supported and been kind to me throughout my life.

What the people say ...

Striving for the best... best company, best neighbourhood and best society is something we can all applaud. Tom Manion's vision of 'how to' gives us plenty of food for thought and rightly challenges some long-held assumptions. – **David Orr** Chief Executive – National Housing Federation

The Reward Society explores a business model to deal with our housing crisis but also many other social issues. It is extremely topical, and written by a man who has made a difference to social housing in the UK... a must read.' – **Professor Cary L. Cooper CBE** Distinguished Professor of Organisational Psychology and Health, Lancaster University Management School

Tom Manion has revolutionised the way housing agencies should operate. His methods have been used in many housing authorities in the United States of America. Thousands of people have benefited from his unique approach and management style. – **Robert L Armstrong** President of AVI Consulting, Omaha, Nebraska

You can have the best strategy in the world but if you don't have the people to execute it, it is worthless. The performance of your people plays a crucial role in any business and the approach outlined here by Tom has proven to be an extremely successful method for getting the best out of your colleagues and therefore maximising overall business success. – **Allan Leighton** Going Plural

It's an explosive concept and some will shed teardrops. – **Wayne Hemingway** Hemingway Design

Tom can legitimately claim to have introduced new ideas which have become embedded in the working practices of other organisations. – **Ross Fraser** CEO, Housemark

It is undeniable that Dr Manion's management philosophy is compelling and his organisation achieves results in one of the most deprived areas of the country. – **Stuart MacDonald** Editor, *Inside Housing*

Tom raises some uncomfortable truths that need to be addressed and proposes a new paradigm if we are to improve economic productivity and social cohesion and morale. – **Tom Bloxham MBE** Chairman Urbansplash Group Ltd

Tom's belief in the rights of every human being to fair play, justice and equality have left me astounded (his knowledge and passion have always left me in awe for the tenacity and resilience he shows to an issue which is very important and never more so than in the world at this very moment). He truly cares about the freedom, responsibilities and welfare of people everywhere whilst sharing his tenet with American Civil Rights Leaders in the battle to achieve equal moral, civil and human rights. – **Simon Weston OBE**

Tom is bright and capable, his enthusiasm is infectious. – **Professor Ian G. Cook** Emeritus Professor of Human Geography, School of Humanities and Social Science, Liverpool John Moores University

Dr Manion practices what he preaches, his high-octane, no-nonsense style captured readers' attention. – *Inside Housing*

Under his tenure, the association has won acclaim for its commitment to improving the lives of tenants. – *The Independent on Sunday*: The Top Brass

Tom Manion Chief Executive, Irwell Valley housing association – charismatic and maverick pioneer of a new system of managing affordable housing that is widely copied and is being endorsed by government. He introduced Gold Service, which rewards tenants who behave and pay rent on time with cash and a better service than those who do not. – *The Guardian*: The Top 10 Innovators

I have worked with some of the greatest achievers in modern society, Beckham, Keegan and Van Der Saar from the world of sport, and industry giants such as Coca Cola, Johnston & Johnston, Microsoft, Heinz etc. I have been privileged to meet Tom who is the very embodiment of all that can be accomplished through self belief. He is a perceptive thinker and visionary who converts thoughts into inspirational actions. If you never meet Tom Manion – the very next best thing is to read his book. – **Watt Nicoll**

Tom has shown how social housing should be delivered and how to reward those who deliver it and also the customers who help. Revolutions are events, they come and go. Tom's is an "evolutionary revolution", a process starting with a vision and its transformation into functioning reality. – **Akhtar Hussain** Chair IV Golden Foundation, Historian and Newspaper Columnist

Tom's ability to strip a problem down to its bare bones and do away with all sidetracking and red tape is a recipe for all aspects of work and, indeed, for life itself. – **Janet Benzie** Resident and Board Member, Irwell Valley

Tom's tough exterior conceals a dedicated multi-talented, but above all, compassionate man. It is a privilege to know him and I commend his book to you and the nation. – **Ted Robbins** Actor, Broadcaster, Radio DJ, Voice-over Artist and Television Personality

One may love Tom Manion or not. There is nothing in between! Nevertheless you should definitely get to know his ideas. Ten years ago Tom's revolutionary approach was ridiculed in Holland; now it's fully accepted and practised by housing associations in urban and rural areas. – **Gerrit Teunis** Chief Executive – Chief Executive, Beter Wonen Vechtdal, The Netherlands

Innovation, energy and passion, these words sum up Tom Manion's commitment to delivering excellent front line customer services. His ideas have transformed the way many housing organisations in the UK work. – **Alasdair McKee** Chief Executive – Glen Oaks Housing Association Limited, Scotland

Tom caught the zeitgeist and succeeded, no longer lampooned but applauded by government and imitated by others. He's a polymath in leathers. – **The late Gaynor Asquith** Director - arc⁴ Limited

I found Tom inspirational and truly believe that I have never met anyone with such charisma and zest for life and my life has been richer for having met him. Thank you Tom. – **Derek Clark** Former Chair of Audit Irwell Valley

In Washington, I had the opportunity to spend the morning with Tom to witness the routine that he undertakes leading up to his speaking engagement. It began at 5am with an across town cab ride to a local YMCA for a 45 minute swim. This was followed with voice exercises and finally some cardio to get the heart rate up to optimal level just prior to his address. I then observed the result of this preparation as an audience member during his Keynote. Tom is a consummate professional whose knowledge of his subject matters leaves audiences standing in applause. – **Dave Eddy** Chief Executive – Vancouver Native Housing Society, Vancouver, Canada

I have the utmost respect for him. – **Lynne Garsden** Chair of Irwell Valley & MD of Guest Garsden, Manchester

Dr Tom Manion is a man of vision who knows how to translate vision into reality – I would love to work for him. The best way to describe Tom: a true leader. – **Father Joseph P. Parkes S.J.** President, Cristo Rey New York High School, New York, USA

Tom is honest and trustworthy and a leader. It is a privilege to work with him. – **Nigel H. Neary** Judge

He was the first person I met who really knew how to fill in the word 'empowerment'. – **Dolf Becx** Chief Executive – Becx & Van Loon, Tilburg, The Netherlands

Tom has the rare ability to develop a vision for improvement and then to share that vision with those around him, to create buy-in and ownership of what quickly becomes a shared sense of direction. His work is innovative and regularly challenging for those working with him. – **Phil Riley** Head of Estate Strategy, Ministry of Justice

Tom was "doing" respect, tough rights/tough responsibilities and "really making a difference to people's lives" long before these phrases became popular mantras in the world of social housing. – **Annie Hopley** Chair, Threshold Housing Group

He is a radical thinker who encourages new ideas and gives you confidence and support to implement those ideas and his powers of persuasion are very sophisticated. After having attended one of Tom's seminars you really will feel that you can walk on water afterwards.' – **Sue Lock** Chief Executive – Wulvern Housing

A great, forward-thinking leader. – **Rob Brown** Stakeholder Engagement Officer, Manchester City Council

This is an exciting and important book. Tom dissects the rather smug and uncritical attitudes, structures and processes that have produced poor quality outcomes in 21st century Britain and shows why we are under-performing and what we need to do to improve. He ranges over psychology, behaviour, housing, health, education, benefits, employment, productivity, crime, fear social interaction and much more, but everything is rooted in a belief that we can all live happier, healthier lives if we alter the way we do things. His focus on a meritocratic society, rewards, unintended consequences and ditching as much as possible of bureaucratic, unintelligent process is a refreshing and welcome approach to problem solving that will improve the lives of over 60 million citizens. – **Professor John Whitelegg** Professor of Sustainable Development, Stockholm Environment Institute Sweden

Contents

Introduction

The history and future of human kind has been shaped by the endeavours, beliefs and values of exemplary and despicable people.

For every Ghandi, Martin Luther King, Einstein and Mother Teresa there has been an Adolph Hitler, Joseph Stalin, Robert Mugabe and Idi Amin.

Without doubt iconic leaders have had an incredible impact on nation states, colonies, empires and humanity itself.

We live in an increasingly interdependent world which is the sum total of thousands of years of human innovation, enterprise and ability to deal with uncertainty and catastrophe.

History shows that extreme forms of society, be they totalitarian, fascist, communist, sectarian or anarchic are unsustainable. In recent years we have seen that unbridled casino capitalism produces wealth, but also human fallout, and is a flawed economic system in terms of social justice.

Equally, extreme fascist and communist regimes characterised by oppression, fear and lack of choice and fulfilment have failed almost everywhere on the globe.

Humans have an infinite capacity to achieve good and bad in almost equal proportions… contrast Neil Armstrong's bouncy jumps across the lunar landscape with Pol Pot strolling across his Cambodian killing fields.

Our society needs a radical overhaul. There is no doubt that our health and material wellbeing has dramatically improved over generations. However in terms of behaviours, social conditions, values and beliefs, there is a noticeable and measurable deterioration in our nation's cohesion, most markedly since the 1950s.

Globally, contemporary societies face enormous challenges: demographic, climatic, economic and energy-related. Rising expectations, coupled with a heavy emphasis on rights rather than responsibilities, supported by European humanitarian legislation, has widened freedom but created paradox, injustice and hypocrisy.

Protest movements and civil disobedience in the West and the revolutionary overthrow of North African and Middle Eastern societies yet again illustrate the need for extreme caution in social, welfare and public policy.

The growth of social media and access to knowledge and information, which human beings now have, is arguably greater than any other epoch. We are now better informed than ever before and expectations have risen accordingly.

Since 1945, state provision in health, education, welfare and numerous other aspects of social and economic life has grown to mammoth proportions. It now results in one in four workers being employed in the public sector and 44% of our gross domestic product being spent on public services and benefits.

As traditional extended family structures have been largely replaced by nuclear or lone parent households, so has the requirement grown for more sophisticated welfare and public policies to deal with demographic outcomes, for example the provision of accommodation tailored to meet the needs of an ageing population who no longer have traditional family support.

The increasing dependence of many people in the UK on welfare benefits is an unintended consequence of the true spirit in which Aneurin Bevan and his colleagues founded our world renowned and respected welfare state.

Bevan, like many others since, understood the need to put in place safety nets, checks and balances to mitigate the market failures of capitalism and to provide support to citizens who either temporarily or permanently need help. But welfare dependency was never intended to be a way of life. Equally, it was never envisaged that the national health service would be increasingly required to deal with what I call lifestyle illnesses, arising from irresponsible and excessive drinking, eating, smoking, drug taking and lack of exercise.

The UK has one of the most sophisticated and advanced state sectors in the world. Its productivity, however, is low compared with many European nations. Our ability to sustain high levels of public sector investment in return for low levels of positive behavioural outcomes – such as lower rates of teenage pregnancy, falling prison population, reducing dependency on welfare, rising educational achievements and health expenditure focused on disease and illness rather than lifestyle issues – will decline sharply in future years. The financial crisis which recently ripped through the heart of almost every western economy has brought the increasing debt burden of those economies under careful scrutiny and has triggered the International Monetary Fund to call for reduced borrowing and deficit reduction plans.

The UK for example is scheduled to cut public expenditure by £80 billion from 2010 to 2015. The impact of such reductions can be seen by the redundancy notices given to 75,000 public sector employees over the past 18 months and there are further redundancies in the pipeline. More is required from fewer people in the public sector, whose morale, productivity and self worth has been dealt a hammer blow and sent already high sickness rates spiralling upwards. The fact that bringing public sector sickness levels down to private sector levels would save £5.4 billion a year and, moreover, if reduced to the record low that my organisation has achieved would save £17.2 billion (almost a fifth of the planned public spending cutbacks) should not be ignored.

Traditional, some may say, tired and old fashioned public sector approaches have run their course. A new paradigm is needed to address the societal challenges we and other nations face and also to ensure that scarce and diminishing public expenditure is used to the greatest effect.

In this book I will explore what I term a meritocratic approach to society, business, neighbourhoods, indeed most forms of human organisation. I'm proposing a meritocracy based on rewarding, encouraging and motivating people to achieve positive outcomes which are beneficial to themselves, to their economic activities, their neighbourhoods and the wider society.

My emphasis is on personal responsibility, within a framework which creates the conditions in which human beings seek to find and fulfil their potential and enjoy enlightenment and fulfilment.

I look at health, welfare benefits, housing, education and prisons in the context of a business model we have developed over the past decade. It is also based upon the experiences of Julian Richer, one of the UK's most enlightened ethical entrepreneurs, my work in America with Bob Armstrong and in Europe with Dr Gerrit Teunis.

I am confident that what we need is an approach to society, which recognises and emphasises the need to encourage people to live healthy, responsible and happy lives where hard work is rewarded, paying your way is seen to be virtuous and where positive human values, such as politeness, kindness and respect are given high esteem.

The iniquities and injustices which frustrate people in their social and working lives need to be tackled, eliminated and replaced by incentivised reward systems which encourage and amplify dignity and respect. If we want a happy, healthy, wealthy, low benefit dependent, low crime, well-educated, loyal nation then we need to have policies, programmes, tax incentives and punishments which support these outcomes.

If a society wants loyalty from its citizens it must demonstrate loyalty to them first. There are many people in our society, who through no fault of their own, are unable to play an active role. Public services, welfare benefits, healthcare and so on are in part designed to be a safety net which cushions the blow for anybody who temporarily needs support and care. There will always be a need for temporary or permanent support for those who are incapable of looking after themselves.

It's not a question of whether our society can pay out the expenditure needed to tackle the nation's ills. We already know that current levels of expenditure are unsustainable and that if they continue to go unchecked, negative social outcomes will accelerate to unimaginable proportions. A reduction in dependency and an emphasis on self sufficiency amongst our population is essential. A new, radical, meritocratic approach to personal contribution must be applied to all walks of life in order to achieve a socially just and equitable society.

With regard to work, we need to ditch bureaucratic, hierarchical, controlling employment and remuneration practices and replace them with a meritocracy which embraces the lessons that I describe in this book. The aim must be to produce new, refreshing and stimulating workplaces where people feel rewarded, recognised and respected. Contemporary employees place sophisticated demands on companies. Turning up, going through the motions and going home are the employment practices of the Ice Age. Personal fulfilment and development are increasingly being demanded. A meritocracy which has as its core value an expectation that human beings will strive to be successful, self sufficient, healthy, motivated — and not benefit dependent, poorly educated, incarcerated and a unnecessary burden on the health service — would save our nation incalculable amounts of time, money and frustration... and make us all a lot happier!

Chapter 1

Creating a happier society

What are we rewarding? At a time of continuing economic and financial crisis in the world, and social unease and unrest in the UK, we should be asking this question above all else.

To see why, we can take two examples: the banking crisis that brought Western economies to the brink of chaos in 2008 and is still with us; and the phone hacking scandal at News International, which not only revealed the grubby depths to which newspapers sank to get so-called exclusives, but also the questionable relationship between certain members of the Metropolitan Police and those newspapers breaking the law.

In both cases, actions were not being taken by crazy mavericks or rogue elements (despite what the public was first told). The bankers, traders and journalists did what they did because they were rewarded for it. It was only as the facts emerged that it became apparent that people were being rewarded – and very generously – for actions that were reckless, often illegal, and altogether inimical to a just and decent society.

These are two examples of how rewarding the wrong actions is hugely damaging. So when we look around at the things that are wrong in society, we need to ask: what are we rewarding that is creating this situation? Only then will we start to find answers to the problems.

In the UK, as in most of Western Europe, we devote a lot of money to what could be broadly described as "creating a just and decent society": in other words, we put public money into health, education, police and the justice system, and in general there is public support for this. The UK spends around £700 billion a year in public expenditure – which represents around 41% of the country's GDP. Nearly a third of this – a staggering £200bn – is soaked up by the welfare benefits system alone.

The current cutbacks mean that between 2010 and 2015 there will be an £80bn reduction in public expenditure. Nevertheless, by 2014 the UK will still be spending amongst the highest proportions of GDP on public expenditure in Western Europe.

Given the vast sums involved, to which we make a direct contribution as tax-payers, we are surely entitled to expect positive improvements in our society. Are we getting the just and decent society we want? If not, why not?

The war on waste

"Government declares war on waste in public sector." These were the head-lines when Chancellor George Osborne revealed his spending review in Oc-tober 2010. He declared that £6bn of wasteful spending would be cut from government departments, while local authorities were to make "efficiency sav-ings" to cover the deep cuts in their funding.

The trouble is, every British government of the past 30 years has pledged to eliminate waste, improve productivity in the public sector and create a health-ier, better educated, happy, safe society – yet somehow the problems remain. In 1983 Margaret Thatcher's government set up the Audit Commission pre-cisely to check on local authorities (and later health authorities) to ensure they got value for money from their spending; in 2010 the government decided the Audit Commission itself was a waste of money and announced its aboli-tion.

No-one seriously claims our public services are models of efficiency, least of all the people who use them (nor, probably, the people who work in them). So why doesn't the search for waste ever produce any real and lasting savings? The assumption seems to be that 'improving efficiency' is a worthwhile and painless way to save money, as if councils and government departments were employ-ing expensive teams of paper-clip counters, whose jobs can be cut and large amounts of money saved, without the authorities having to sack, say, social workers or police officers. Yet somehow the paper-clip counters are never found, and frontline workers do lose their jobs.

By February 2012, 42,000 workers had already left local government, in a mixture of compulsory and voluntary redundancies. Local authorities needed to make these staff savings in order to balance their budgets, and ultimately the reduction in personnel will have to go much further. The Local Government Association estimates about 140,000 jobs in all will be lost in councils as a result of the cuts.

Does that mean councils will be less wasteful and deliver better value for money? Not necessarily. No doubt some services will have been overstaffed and needed to be slimmed down, but inevitably many of those leaving local authorities will be people delivering front line services to the public, and the public will feel the diminution in service. You also have to ask whether a demoralised workforce, fearing redundancy, is best placed to deliver greater productivity.

As part of the war on waste, in October 2010 the coalition government announced a "bonfire of the quangos" to get rid of unnecessary bureaucracy. But after a few months of supposed reorganisation of nearly 200 non-elected public bodies, MPs on the Commons public administration select committee said the whole process was so badly thought-through that the reorganisation would probably cost more than it would save.

I believe we are going about things the wrong way. Getting value for money out of our public spending is not about job cutting and reorganisation. It is no good looking at a public sector job simply as a "cost". We should be asking whether or not that job contributes towards a better society, or detracts from it. It is all about the attitudes, states of mind and feelings of the people doing those jobs. The best way to prevent waste and create value for money is to ensure that people have a sense of pride and purpose in what they do – attributes which engender high commitment and positive behaviour.

If we want to eliminate waste and negativity, we have to look at things differently. "Energy and persistence conquer all things," Benjamin Franklin said. We have to ask some important questions, such as, why do we have more social workers than bricklayers? (There were 100,882 registered social workers in England alone in 2010, compared with around 82,470 bricklayers in the UK).

I'm not decrying social workers: I'm saying that what really costs this country money is dysfunctional families – and producing dysfunctional families and teenage pregnancies are two of the few areas in which the UK is a world leader. Preventing these societal problems has to be the goal, not rehabilitation or taking enforcement action against them.

A huge source of waste in the public sector is absenteeism. The 2010 CBI survey of absence in the workplace showed the continuing difference between the public and private sectors: the average public sector employee took 12 days off sick in a year, compared with the private sector worker who took six days.

Can anything be done to change that? Suppose people are genuinely ill? They can't all be malingerers. No, but there's a good chance that most of them are not very motivated in their job and that they work in a culture where a high rate of absence is accepted as the norm. Absenteeism is more contagious than flu, swiftly creating a sickness sub-culture in vulnerable organisations. But this does not occur when people are highly motivated and committed to what they do.

Currently, more than 600 Greater Manchester police officers (7% of all bobbies on the beat) are on what are described as "restrictive or recuperative duties". Responding to these figures, Graham Stringer, former Leader of Manchester Council and a local MP, said: "Whilst sympathetic to police injured in the course of their duties the sheer scale of these numbers indicates that some people are taking the mickey. I just don't believe that all these officers cannot do their jobs because of injury."

The Chief Constable of Greater Manchester Police, Peter Fahey, admitted that the sheer numbers on light duties was difficult to defend and that it caused resentment amongst colleagues performing full duties. His suggestion was that those on full duties should get a pay enhancement. Right on Peter!

Absenteeism can be reduced, if you take the right approach to motivating people: we've done it in our organisation. I believe we now have a world record low sickness levels, at only 0.4%. The CBI calculated that if public sector absenteeism rates could be brought down to the private sector average, around £5.5bn could be saved over the next five years. If such rates came down to my organisation's level then savings of £17.4 bn would be achieved.

What about the amount government and local government spend on chasing unpaid taxes? In a sense this is not money 'wasted,' because every pound recovered boosts the public coffers, yet think how much fatter the coffers would be if people paid in the first place. There is the huge level of (apparently legal) tax avoidance by corporations and rich individuals. People used to say, "I pay my taxes" with a certain amount of pride, showing that they made a contribution to society and had the right to a say in how society is run. Now it seems that attitude is treated with derision. If people at the bottom and the top end of society consider that paying tax is 'just for mugs,' where does that leave the people in the middle?

Changing behaviour

These issues are all about attitudes, values and behaviour. We certainly are wasting money in Britain, at a time when we can ill afford it, because of the kinds of behaviour that pervade society. Compared with 50 years ago, we are a wealthier society, even during a recession, but we are also an impolite society in which there is more dishonesty, idleness and lack of thought for others. This is an urgent social issue as well as a moral one: these problems are actually costing us money, as well as reducing the quality of life for everyone.

Life in Britain has changed in a relatively short timescale. Behaviours are now tolerated and accepted as normal, which were unthinkable and unacceptable only 15, even five, years ago. Unchecked downward spirals produce terrifying behaviours and norms. The latest form of street robbery is testimony to this. Robbers have realised that being caught in possession of a gun will get them a straight prison sentence; possessing a knife is not as clear-cut but nevertheless likely to lead to a custodial sentence. However, threatening someone with a hypodermic filled with tomato ketchup and pretending it's HIV positive blood instils mortal terror in the victim and enables the perpetrator, if caught, to walk away scot free. How? The script goes like this: "I carry a hypodermic with me because I am a recovering heroin addict on methadone and I like tomato ketchup with my chips!"

Yet behaviours can change, in a positive as well as a negative way. Compared to the 1970s, we see a lot more drunkenness on the high street in the evening, but people no longer think it's cool to drink and drive, while "gay bashing" is no longer seen as acceptable.

To really make a difference to life in Britain, we have to change our culture and behaviours. Psychologists know that behaviour is fuelled by values and beliefs and to improve behaviour we must influence what people believe and value, in a positive way. I'm not talking about re-programming people or the psychological saturation propagated by Antonio Gramsci in his work on ideological hegemony. It is simply a question of rewarding, promoting and encouraging the types of behaviours which we know build positive relationships, strong communities and societies.

The very idea of changing behaviour is bound to raise objections. It sounds hopelessly idealistic, or perhaps old-fashioned and moralising. Some people will regard it as unwarranted social engineering. Some will say it is paternalistic and interfering, proffering that an individual's behaviour is their own business.

I strongly disagree. Every person's behaviour affects innumerable people around them and has consequences for their community. Certainly, every person's behaviour affects what I would call their neighbourhood – be it residential, workplace, town centre, personal space, Facebook, Twitter and so on.

Lecturing and moralising does little. There are more effective ways to change behaviour for the better, using what is known about the psychology of human behaviour, together with what has been learned by experience. These principles should be used in an intelligent way in the public realm, in order to build a positive society.

Changing the way individuals behave may seem like an impossible task. But changing the way public bodies behave ought to be within our grasp, and the two are interlinked. The policies and rules governing public services, the way those services are delivered, the way our public spaces look and function – all affect behaviour, for good or bad (often for bad). If people's behaviour costs society money and erodes the quality of public life, then society should carefully examine how its decisions affect behaviour. The welfare benefits system is perhaps the prime example here.

I would argue this is common sense. It is achievable and I can point to specific changes my organisation has brought about in some of the most troubled areas of urban Britain. Equally my experiences of working with people throughout Europe, America and China give me confidence that things can improve, through clever and enjoyable approaches to changing people's behaviours.

We need to tackle these issues immediately; they are not an irrelevance.

British society has been slipping down a long slope for decades. There is no official way of measuring the robustness of a society but we all know when things are wrong. Look at what has increased, even just over the past 20 years: anti-social behaviour, fear of crime, divorce, depression, personal debt, teenage pregnancy, drug taking, obesity, domestic violence and street robbery. A survey carried out by The Young Foundation found that in the 1950s, a majority of people (60%) thought other people could be trusted. By the early 1980s, the figure was down to 44% and now it's 29% and falling. This is not a sign of a thriving society.

The reaction of politicians to statistics of decline is to look for someone to blame. Governments habitually blame the previous government, whose wrong-headed policies are deemed to be responsible for the mess we're in. They then promise to implement policies that will sort it all out.

The public at large are probably vague about individual government policies but they have an idea about the trends and developments in society that are to blame. The list of popular scapegoats is long but includes: the police (not enough bobbies on the beat); the education system (exams are too easy); immigration (anybody can come over here and get a council house); the welfare state (too cushy for the work-shy and for single mothers); drugs; guns; computer games; feminism (held responsible for the permissive society); women going out to work (neglecting their families); women not going out to work (living on benefits); lax parenting (allowing anti-social teenagers to roam the streets)... The list could go on and on.

The law of unintended consequences

I am not a politician but it seems clear that successive governments, of all colours, over the years have been unable to stop the deterioration in many aspects of society. However, this is usually not for lack of trying. No-one draws up a policy designed to create a worse society; most of the policies that have gone wrong over the years were set out with the best of intentions. The law of unintended consequences generates many of the problems we grapple with.

Take the example of high rise blocks, with which I'm all too familiar, having lived in two in Salford.

Le Corbusier's vision of high density streets in the sky, surrounded by good quality open spaces fostering social interaction and strong communities, was a fine concept. Sadly, it was a million miles away from the monstrosities actually created in the 1960s. The need was real: there had never been enough decent, affordable housing in Britain and after the war the situation had become desperate. In response to this demand, cost effective, system-built high rise blocks shot up all over the UK. These residential edifices became sources of civic virility: in Glasgow Red Road Flats were trumpeted by the council as the highest tower blocks in the UK. Shortly after people moved in, it rapidly became one of the most difficult places to live in

Very quickly tower blocks became synonymous with crime, alienation, 'high rise blues', vandalism, urine-fouled lifts and poor communal facilities, all of which combined to bring high rise living into disrepute in the UK. This was not necessarily so in Europe and the USA... one person's dysfunctional nightmare is another person's Trump Tower! In locations where apartments were well built and (most importantly) well maintained, high rise living was desirable – similar buildings, similar concepts but radically different outcomes.

Planners and architects ignored the seminal works of people like Jane Jacob who urged the need for "eyes on the street" to encourage personal informal surveillance by residents to avoid creating crime havens. Academics studied what had gone wrong, though the people living in tower blocks knew very well. A community protest song of the time expresses it exactly:

> *A fella from the Corpy straight out of planning school*
> *Has told us that we've got to get right out of Liverpool*
> *They're sending us to Kirkby, Skelmersdale and Speke*
> *Don't wanna go from all I know in Back Buchanan Street.*

> *I'll miss the foghorns on the river and me Da will miss the Docks*
> *And me Ma will miss the wash-house where she washed me Granddad's socks*
> *There's lots of other little things like putting out the cat*
> *'Cos there's no back door on the 14th floor of a Corporation flat.*

The Ronan Point disaster in 1968 was the last nail in the tower block's coffin. When a gas explosion caused a corner of this east London tower block to collapse, killing four people, system building was shown to be unsafe and few high rise blocks were built after that. But hundreds remained, deteriorating rapidly and building up severe social problems for the communities in them.

Tower blocks were not deliberately designed to be difficult places to live. They were supposed to give people a good standard of housing, from which residents could lead fulfilling lives. In the 1960s and 70s they failed miserably, largely because of bad management, poor maintenance, inappropriate allocation policies, insecurity and anonymity. This left social landlords with the headache of poor quality buildings, housing unhappy people.

Tower blocks are an apt example because, leaving aside the physical condition of the buildings, where they went wrong is that their design failed to take into account people's behaviour and the way people tend to live their lives. Design failure was compounded by management failure, because local authorities and housing associations did not either understand or consider sufficiently how people behave. It's very hard to get to know your neighbours in a tower block – much harder than in a suburban street, where people see each other go in and out of their houses and walk up and down together to the shops or the station. The simple fact of people not knowing each other leads to all sorts of problems, which landlords failed to tackle, or tackled in the wrong way, for example by relying on CCTV.

So the law of unintended consequences created a disastrous situation for the residents of tower blocks. The communities in this housing deteriorated over time, becoming less cohesive, more insecure, economically worse off; anti-social behaviour and crime flourished in this environment.

Barbarians in the kitchen

But behaviour throughout society has deteriorated over the years. I don't just mean politeness, though that is a factor. Nor am I referring only to the behaviour of some sort of 'underclass.' People rarely say hello, good morning, please, thank you, good night God bless or give up their seats for seniors on buses. Fundamentals such as dishonesty, meanness and lack of thought for others go right the way through society. In poorer parts of our cities the deterioration often goes so far that they become crime hotspots, no-go areas, with difficult to let, difficult to live in (and difficult to get out of) housing.

I witnessed one of the worst examples of barbaric behaviour when I lived in a tower block in Salford on a floor of 30 properties. Only two flats were occupied, one by me and the other by 78 year old Sadie. We were there for 14 months awaiting rehousing, because our 'homes' were being demolished to make way for a Sainsbury's and a retail park.

One morning I noticed that Sadie wasn't around and found out from her daughter that she had passed away. Shortly after the undertakers arrived to take Sadie to the Chapel of Rest, I heard a commotion in her flat. The door was wide open and I smelt bacon being cooked. All of her personal belongings were stacked up by the front door. In the kitchen were two young robbers, who had clearly watched the undertaker take Sadie away and seized the opportunity to burgle her flat before she was barely cold. Unbelievably they were helping themselves to a bacon butty before they stole her lifelong belongings! Needless to say, although I felt like giving them a good hiding, as an upstanding citizen I suggested that they contact their Social Worker, Probation Officer, Youth Offending Officer, Social Inclusion Co-ordinator, Anger Management Coach, Attention Deficit Syndrome Worker, Child Protection Officer, Floating Support Worker, Drugs Counsellor, Anti-Bullying Officer, Solicitor or any other state professional who was doing the job that their parents should be doing.

However, without an understanding of why things get so bad, and without an appreciation of what makes people behave in certain ways, any reactive policies, strategies and action plans are doomed to further failure, piling more mistakes on the mistakes of the past.

Conversely, with a good understanding of human motivation, and a willingness to take tough decisions and to see actions through, it is possible to change behaviours. The roughest housing estates, filled with burnt-out cars and boarded-up windows, can be turned into places in which people are queuing up to live. I know – we've done it, and we did it without turfing out residents wholesale but instead changing the attitudes and behaviours of the people who lived there. On these estates, life has improved: people have become more confident and healthy, more children have gone to college and university and overall, the places have stopped slipping downhill and started moving steadily uphill.

It takes time, but this turnaround is possible. We have transformed many areas and many people who might seem to have given up on life. We operate under a maxim of self power, that is, we enable and facilitate the individual to achieve their potential. Importantly, we take the view that anyone and any organisation that can't help with this process should just get out of the way.

Rewards and penalties

What I want to explore in this book is: what are we rewarding? This is the crucial question that gets to the heart of what is wrong with our current society and, more specifically, with our public services. Humans respond, consciously or otherwise, to reward, recognition and respect. This applies to groups and organisations as well as individuals. They do not necessarily respond in a direct and predictable manner. Nevertheless, when people are acting in ways that are undesirable, we should ask: what reward do they get – or what penalties do they avoid – by behaving in that way?

In September 2010 there was outrage in government and the media when a report by Ofsted suggested that schools had been claiming pupils had special needs when they did not, in order to get extra funding for them. The evidence that this was happening wasn't altogether conclusive, though the percentage of children designated 'with special needs' was shown to have risen from 14% in 2003 to 18% in 2010. But even if it were the case that schools were 'playing the system,' why would this be surprising? And was it wrong? Schools are always looking for extra resources for their pupils. When a route to funds opened up, they responded quite rationally and took it, gaining the rewards on offer. By all accounts it worked. Certain pupils' attainments improved when they had the intensive tuition paid for by the extra funds.

It is disingenuous for the authorities to be surprised and outraged by this. It is back to the law of unintended consequences: every policy has effects other than the intended ones. When government comes up with measures to tackle a particular problem, it should always consider how people, or organisations, might respond to the rewards or penalties on offer. It is no good indulging in recrimination afterwards when it turns out the measures had no effect, did not benefit anybody, or did not benefit the people the authorities had in mind, or simply backfired.

A longstanding feature of our welfare system is the cohabitation rule. Put simply, a single mother will have her benefits reduced or removed if it is judged she has a man living with her. The consequences of this are well known and frequently complained about by authorities, policy makers and the general public. When I visit tenants who are lone mothers, I often see men's trainers in the hall and men's jeans drying on the line. Of course they have boyfriends living with them. Why wouldn't they? And of course they are not going to declare that to the Department for Work and Pensions. Why would they? This is not an attack on lone mothers: my paternal Nana became a single parent with four young children on 1st June 1940 (five years before the advent of the welfare state) when her husband Thomas Manion Snr was killed on HMS Basilisk during the Dunkirk evacuation. She successfully brought up her children by working hard and being responsible and she never accepted any state benefits.

Single mothers are sometimes deemed 'benefit cheats,' but their behaviour is no different to those high-flying financiers who brought global capitalism to its knees. The women respond to the few pounds a week that is the reward for staying 'single.' The financiers too were motivated by personal reward. As former Prime Minister Gordon Brown puts it in his book *Beyond the Crash*, they were driven by "a perverse system of incentives that maximised rather than minimised risks." To take the example of Lehman Brothers, Brown says, "Executives said openly that they did not want to hear "too much detail" about the risks they might face in case it held them back from making the high-risk deals on which the biggest bonuses depend."

Lone mothers face a legal system of penalties and fines if they are found to be cheating, whereas the reward structure for financiers remains largely unchanged, despite political pressure put on a few high-profile individuals to renounce their bonuses. As Brown puts it, "Even as taxpayers all around the world were losing out as a result of their recklessness, the bankers continued to claim that the grotesque rewards they enjoyed were essential to the banking sector and the public interest" and so casino capitalism flourishes.

The banker bonus proliferation flies in the face of a proper rewards culture by, at worst, rewarding persistent irresponsible financial behaviour and, at best, rewarding people for simply doing the job they were hired to do in the first place. Action Aid in October 2011 reported the extraordinary lengths that banks like HSBC, Barclays and Lloyds TSB go to in order to avoid tax. Action Aid pointed out that our banking sector uses tax havens much more than other UK businesses; the Cayman Islands and Switzerland are particularly popular destinations for HSBC, which has more than 556 subsidiaries in tax havens.

Even LloydsTSB, which is controlled by UK tax payers, has 97 companies in the Channel Islands and 203 offshore subsidiaries. It is difficult to imagine what level of financial Armageddon is needed for bankers not to get a bonus or for government to stand up to the banks and make them pay their fair share of taxes. As TUC General Secretary Brendan Barber said: "If the government refuses to challenge these multi-billion pounds rewards for failure, the least tax payers deserve is a bonus tax to help pay for the mess they are creating."

Perverse rewards are everywhere. One of the major challenges our society faces is tackling the obesity explosion. The NHS estimates that there are over a million people in the UK with medical problems due to obesity – principally strokes, diabetes, coronary disease and cancer. All the signs are that this number will increase. In the US, new crematoria have higher powered jets to replace traditional cremators, in order to burn obese and super obese corpses. After years of supersizing your meal at McDonalds, you can supersize your coffin and grave. American coffins and graves are 15% wider than they were 30 years ago. Some US airlines now ask passengers to declare their weight, to avoid flight problems from having too many obese and super obese passengers on board. Others charge super obese passengers for two seats (I wonder if they get two meals), because of the amount of space they take up.

In a survey of customers, Ryan Air found that 69% of their passengers felt that obese and super obese passengers should be charged for two seats. So far they've ruled out a 'fat penalty', but only because it would slow down check-in procedures.

Despite this, the UK's welfare benefits system rewards obesity. Obese claimants receive higher benefits for food and clothing because their costs are higher than those of people with an average BMI. I regularly see super obese people training at my gym under the GP referral programme. I can understand the argument about trying to get these people to lose weight and get fit, to reduce the future costs of their healthcare. However, the fee-paying gym users like myself receive no incentive for exercising regularly, not smoking and eating healthily. Why not give people tax breaks for looking after themselves, or subsidise healthy living by imposing heavy taxes on unhealthy food and drinks, as we do on cigarettes?

People who inflict problems on themselves or others – obesity, smoking, alcoholism, vandalism, anti-social behaviour and so on – should not be rewarded for their actions. Moreover, disproportionate amounts of public expenditure should not be spent on people who wilfully and persistently abuse themselves, the system and others.

Incentivising the right behaviour

My point is that rewards are everywhere and we, as a society, should manage them intelligently. I believe that we should develop more and better rewards, rather than running around removing ones we disapprove of. As a society we need to get our priorities right and recognise the value of people's contribution to the positive development of society. At present, we often get the balance wrong. Wayne Rooney is idolised for earning £200,000 a week, while a south London head teacher, who has turned round a failing school in challenging circumstances, is castigated for earning more than £200,000 a year. Education Secretary Michael Gove then pronounces that there should be a cap on heads' salaries so that none earn more than the Prime Minister – as if that were some useful measure of worth. The PM's annual salary is £142,500, but Will Hutton, who led the independent review into fair pay in the public sector, said this figure should not be used as any kind of benchmark. He pointed out that all the PM's benefits – such as use of Chequers, cars, travel, clothing, food and so on – are worth at least £600,000 a year.

Incentivising and encouraging people to behave positively, understand and exceed their potential and enjoy life, whilst fulfilling their responsibilities to others, is the way forward for British society. As Colin Powell, Four Star General, former US Secretary of State, who was awarded two Purple Hearts and the Soldier's Medal for Heroism, states in his book on leadership: "You have to understand that you can't please everyone and that you have to piss off the right people rather than all the people." In other words, if we want to tackle problems, we must not impose blanket punishments that hit good people, because of the illegal or unacceptable behaviours of a minority.

We must accentuate the positive and eliminate the negative. Admiral Nelson would never talk about defeat or evacuation procedures from his aptly named flagship HMS Victory. Napoleon Bonaparte wanted brave soldiers and therefore he rewarded bravery and great performance. Napoleon always promoted lucky generals, because doubtless he knew that what other people call good luck is rarely a matter of chance. As the famous golfer Gary Player once remarked: "The more I practise the luckier I get." For myself, I find that luck occurs when preparation coincides with opportunity.

Obstacles to fair reward

Our welfare system is a serious obstacle to a fair approach to rewards and incentives. It was designed by Beveridge in the 1940s to be, not a permanent way of life, but a safety net: 60 years on it has become a spider's web, trapping people in dependency and making poverty comfortable.

The welfare benefits system offers few rewards for positive behaviour. It does have an elaborate edifice of penalties, which people learn to avoid. The Work and Pensions Secretary Iain Duncan Smith has, perhaps for the first time ever, introduced the concept of reward into the system with his acknowledgement that work has to pay. He has taken on board the fact that, as benefits advisers have been pointing out for years, an unemployed person who takes up a job loses so many benefits almost straight away, including housing benefit as well as income support, that he or she could actually be financially worse off when they start work. Becoming one of the highest marginal rate taxpayers in the UK, coupled with the extra expense of going to work, is a huge incentive for an unemployed person to stay on the dole!

Duncan Smith is prepared to allow benefits to be withdrawn more gradually so that a person is supported into work. In other words, the system will offer a small reward for taking up work, rather than a swift penalty. Duncan Smith is accepting that the extra cost to the benefits system is worth it in the short term, for the greater goal of having more people in employment in the long run.

We need to think intelligently about these issues, because our society is not comfortable with reward. In particular, we are not comfortable with the idea of reward for the people who access public services – that is, principally, the young, the elderly and the low-income. We are also frequently ambivalent about rewarding those who deliver the services, a large bulk of whom are on very low wages.

Look at the way we reward people who have saved all their lives. If, when they reach retirement age, they need to go into residential care, they have to fund this themselves, using up their assets until their capital drops below £23,250, whereas people who don't own their own home and have no savings have their care costs paid by the state. While there might be sound reasons for this policy, in terms of public finance, it is perceived as bitterly unfair by elderly people and their families. People feel it as a slap in the face at the end of a lifetime of hard work. They feel the rewards are greater for those who haven't put in the hard work. Crazy though it may sound, it is perfectly possible for somebody to be supported financially from birth to death by the state, through the care system, penal system, housing benefit system, welfare benefit system, culminating in their funeral being paid for by taxpayers.

Inequity between different parts of the UK also causes resentment. Scotland and Wales have free prescription charges, free higher education, free residential care and other benefits. In Northern Ireland residents have never paid for their water charges. English taxpayers have to fund all these things themselves, while also subsidising other parts of the UK.

If public services are short on rewards, when it comes to penalties they have a whole armoury at their disposal. Unfortunately, people simply find ways around these. I used to work for a local authority and spent a lot of time chasing rent arrears. One Saturday I was sitting in a pub on an overspill estate, after a football match, and heard two men from the opposing team talking at the next table. One was examining an official-looking letter in a window envelope. Before he had even opened it, the other chap said to him: "That's from the council mate. It's an AL7." His friend had no idea what an AL7 was. "Well," explained his mate, "you're obviously in rent arrears and they have twelve of these letters – AL1, AL2, AL3 and so on. On your twelfth you'll get a notice of seeking possession and that's alright because then it goes to court. That probably won't be for another year or two." So the other guy said, "What should I do with this one?" His mate replied: "Bin it. When you get the AL12, give them a ring, throw £150, £200 at them and it'll go back to stage one." He knew the council's rent recovery system better than most of the people who worked there. Perhaps we should have employed him to collect rent on a percentage basis!

His advice was spot on. That was exactly what the procedures were and that was why we were not efficient and effective rent collectors. I learned those lessons and that is why we've adopted an approach encouraging and rewarding rent payment with incentives, rather than tackling the problem with expensive, and not particularly effective, enforcement, as I explain in Chapter 4.

If you can't change behaviour, remove the opportunity

If people are causing trouble, you can try to punish them – or you can try to change their behaviour, or change the situation that makes their antics possible.

Coming back to tower blocks, why are they the location for so much social tension? Having lived in some, I can tell you why. You live on a floor where there are several flats, and you may or may not strike up good relationships with your neighbours. Tower block entrances are often architecturally brutal, festooned with council notices and very often the lift stinks of urine. You rarely see or know the people who live above or below you. Those above you drive you crazy when they move furniture, flush the toilet in the middle of the night, play music, have the telly on loud and clomp about. Unbeknown to you, the people on the floor below feel the same way about you, though you are oblivious to their feelings because you never see them. People blame other residents and don't understand that the problems are caused by poor insulation and architectural antagonism. Suspicion and mistrust engender feelings of fear, anger and frustration, which can build up and result in unfortunate, but understandable, aggressive outbursts.

Crime is committed, by and large, in places where criminals can get away with it, or think they can get away with it. Badly lit streets or neighbourhoods where people don't know each other, where there are no 'eyes on the street' and no community cohesion, provide perfect havens for criminality. The opposite of this is the kind of sense of place described by the eminent Chinese-American geographer Yi Fu Tuan in his book *Topophilia*, where he advocates the importance of creating places where people feel happy, safe and comfortable.

We had a problem of fear of crime and anti-social behaviour in some of our tower blocks. They should have been nice places to live, offering flats with fantastic views, but they were difficult to let and unpopular with residents.

The lack of community spirit in these unhappy vertical neighbourhoods was ripe for exploitation by local yobs. In the evenings, they came in to sit in the warm, smoke dope on the stairs and urinate in the lift. If seen, they were unchallenged by residents, who felt intimidated, and furthermore had no idea whether the lads lived in the block or not.

The industry standard response to this situation is usually CCTV. Some of my colleagues visited another development kitted out with electronic gates, cameras that follow you as you walk around, a control suite with a big bank of screens and so on. It was a bit like a prison, except that residents were allowed to go in and out. We were invited to spend £450,000 on a security system that would supposedly be the solution to our problems.

I asked myself, how would CCTV help? Intuitively we might believe that CCTV would deter anti-social behaviour. But yobs cover themselves up with hoodies, balaclavas, ski masks and sunglasses. Installation of cameras would not by itself foster happy relationships among residents. Indeed having CCTV cameras on every corner tends to turn a place into a Colditz-style barracks, which stigmatises a building and makes it look dodgy.

What we really needed to do was to install noise insulation between floors, but even more importantly to build a community of people who respected each other and understood the importance of looking out for neighbours. We had to get residents talking to each other, because only then could the community itself prevent youths turning the place into their own anti-social playground.

My first question was, "how were these yobs getting into the building?" We had already installed a £250,000 door entry system: surely this was enough to make the building secure? To find out, on several evenings I hung around the tower blocks for a few hours late at night, observing the shenanigans.

It transpired that these youths either tailgated residents as they were walking into the block or randomly pressed doorbells until a resident got so fed up with the constant ringing that they let the intruder in. I noticed one of them place a small pebble at the bottom of our quarter of a million pound doorframe, which stopped the door clicking shut. With one pebble he had completely bypassed and disabled some of the best security equipment on the planet. Then he settled down with his mates for a nice spliff. Before I got stoned myself through passive inhalation, I phoned the police who responded promptly and effectively.

A few days later, we knocked on doors and spoke to every resident. I discussed the problems we were having, with the wrong sorts of behaviour by the wrong sort of people, and asked for their help in sorting out these problems in an adult way. Worryingly, hardly anybody in the block knew each other. Residents' meetings had attracted only a handful of people and were described to me as boring. Clearly (bearing in mind the reward idea) people needed an incentive to get together. So we organised various community events, including cheese and wine receptions and community singing, and we developed community gardens to bring people together. Importantly, we also had some high profile evictions to make it clear where we stood on people paying the rent and abiding by their tenancy agreements.

Residents in those blocks now know and greet each other much more than ever before. As a temporary measure we employed security guards (usually called concierges); we brought in a graffiti artist to make communal areas look funky and improve the ambiance and sense of place. But primarily it was the residents who changed the culture of their vertical neighbourhood. We know there's an improvement because people tell us. There is now a healthy demand for flats in the blocks: word has got around, people want to be there... vandals don't!

This is an example of how a rewards-based approach produced the results that I'm sure a punitive approach would not have obtained. Investment was needed, but it was social investment not CCTV. A landlord investing in its housing and its communities should be seen as a positive move, not a waste of money. On the other hand, I knew we had to take preventative, rehabilitative and enforcement action. It might sound dictatorial, but on their own the residents would not have come together to take action. They were too busy mistrusting each other and leading isolated lives: the conditions were not right for community spirit. A whole range of improvements, financial and community incentives have had a beneficial effect.

Accentuate the positive, eliminate the negative

As a society, we spend a huge amount of money on the negative and have been doing so for many years. Local authorities spend about £250m a year on CCTV camera systems. You might say this is the price we pay for a secure society, except that we are not secure: fear of crime is still very high. The question is this: at a time of austerity, how can we ensure that every pound we spend of public money produces positive gains for our society and does not reward the behaviours that we seek to eliminate? We need to stop devoting so much time, energy and money to dealing with those members of society whose behaviour is not consistent with a just and honest society.

My argument in this book is that there is another way. We can save money and create happier neighbourhoods and societies by rewarding the good, instead of squandering increasing amounts of time and money on the bad.

We should specify the behaviours we want and encourage people to behave in the ways that produce happy, healthy, well-educated, crime-free people and places. A three pronged approach of prevention, rehabilitation and enforcement works, especially when the greatest emphasis and investment is placed upon prevention. This is not behavioural fascism or some attempt to control people through Pavlovian conditioning. Companies, churches, scouts, the police, the judiciary all insist on behavioural codes of conduct for their members and reward accordingly, so why should we not for society as a whole?

At a time of restraint, cut backs, the future uncertainties of climate change and increasing demands on the UK's coffers, through an ageing population, it is critically important that every penny of public expenditure produces positive outcomes and that we do not spend our hard-earned money rewarding bad behaviours and correcting self-inflicted problems.

We should take a fresh look at how public money is spent. When Jamie Oliver started his school meals campaign in 2005, there was national shock when it was revealed that the country spent more per head on prison meals than school meals – 60p per prison meal, a mere 35p per child meal. I'm not saying prisoners shouldn't have decent food, but why had we thought the nutrition of children (our society's future) was worth less than that of jail birds? Of course, school children are not in a position to complain. If they had, they would not have been taken seriously: school meals have traditionally been terrible and we all have our personal horror stories – mine was the stinky, bony fish pie with sloppy mashed potato served up every Friday. Typically, the only meals worse than school dinners are the hospital meals served to sick people trying to become healthy!

For some reason, as a nation, we thought it was OK for school food to be cheap and low-quality, even though, for some kids, school dinner will be the only cooked meal they have in a day. Despite Jamie Oliver's efforts, there was, and still is, a lot of resistance to the idea that children should have the 'reward' of fresh, tasty, properly cooked food. Yet all the evidence shows that healthy food helps children perform better at school and in many cases improves the behaviour of troubled kids. Putting it another way – if we as a nation had spent more on school dinners over the years, we might be spending less on prison dinners now.

Getting more for less

In these challenging austere times, getting high levels of productivity from every workforce, particularly in the public sector, is essential. Resources are scarce and will get more scarce in the foreseeable future. That should impel us to take action now.

Rewarding decent, law abiding behaviour will engender fulfilment and help reduce anti-social behaviour and human and financial wastage. Encouraging people to take personal responsibility for their health, happiness, education and behaviour is more important now than ever before. We need to start creating workplaces where people want to be and where they give of their best. This is an absolute prerequisite for raising morale, stimulating motivation and ultimately getting important jobs done with a smile on people's faces.

These are the sorts of issues I'm going to explore in this book. I am proposing a meritocratic approach to work, education, health and many other elements of society, in a concerted effort to focus limited resources on achieving the outcomes that create a society we can enjoy and be proud of.

Chapter 2

The Curve

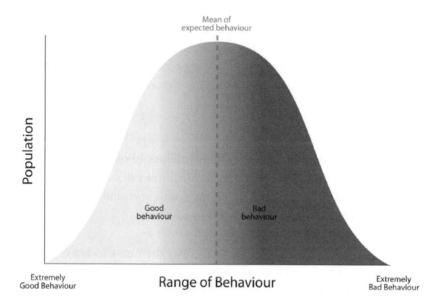

Expected Range of Behaviour

This is the curve. It is an invaluable way of understanding what is going on in society. The diagram above is a kind of generic curve, but you could plot one for pretty much any kind of behaviour or situation. The statisticians call it a normal distribution curve.

If the normal pattern of behaviour within a society (without any outside influence on it) is plotted, we can see that some people would exhibit very good behaviour, some people would exhibit very bad behaviour, but the bulk of the population would be in the middle and the distribution would occur around an average or mean level.

The important point is how the curve can move. If some people behave badly and there is no sanction against them doing so – or indeed they are actually seen to benefit from it – while those who exhibit good behaviour do not receive recognition or reward, there will be a tendency for sections of society to copy the example of the bad behaviour.

Let's imagine this curve represents the number of social housing tenants who pay their rent within certain time parameters (you could do something very similar for, say, householders paying their council tax or businesses paying their VAT). The scale goes from 'paying on time' at the left, to 'not paying' at the right, through various stages of paying a week late, paying after a reminder, paying after several reminders, not paying until there is a court order… and so on.

The vertical scale is the actual number of people. From a statistical point of view it is not surprising that most people are clustered in the middle. But it is where in the middle that is significant.

To the far left are the really reliable, good people who always pay on time and have never thought of doing anything else. Millions of tenants like my Auntie Beryl and Uncle Jim and my mum and dad fall into this category. When my Uncle Jim sadly died and I was helping my auntie sort out their affairs, I discovered he had paid his rent two months in advance.

To the far right are the people who never pay their rent and have no intention of doing so. They consume enormous amounts of other people's time and energy and are usually well known to a multitude of "state industries" like social services, the Department for Work and Pensions, housing benefit offices and the police. I am not talking here about people who can't pay: these are the ones who won't pay, many of whom will be members of David Cameron's 120,000 UK problem families. These won't-payers are a headache for landlords and can be a menace to society. They are not large in number but almost all landlords spend the majority of their time with them. Consequently, most housing officers will know their names and can recount at length their experiences with them, whereas they will rarely know the names of their customers who always pay on time.

Probably about 5 to 10% of the relevant population (here, social housing tenants) fall into each of the 'very good' or 'very bad' categories at either pole on the graph. They are mostly fixed in their ways: it takes a lot to budge them.

What is interesting is the 80% or so in the middle of the curve, because their behaviour does change.

In the 1950s, when many of my family members took up their tenancies, the top of the curve – that is, the greatest number of people – would have been to the left of the halfway point. In other words, the bulk of people paid their rent more or less on time, without fuss. If they were late, it was probably because they were disorganised or had been hit by some domestic crisis. People paid their rent regularly: it was the norm.

In the 60 years since then, more and more people in social housing – that is, council tenants and housing association tenants – have come to be regularly behind with their rent. Some of these debts are small, others very significant, but overall the arrears represent an enormous loss of income for social landlords.

What has happened is that the curve has moved to the right. This graph illustrates what you see when the behaviour of the average person (depicted by the mean) becomes worse, compared to the first graph.

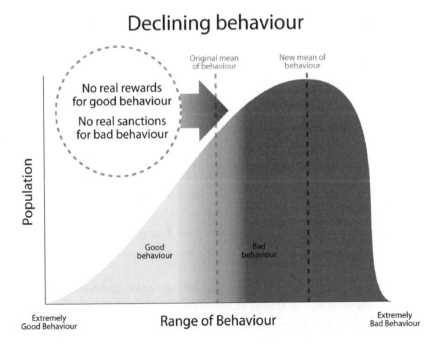

Declining behaviour

Original mean of behaviour

New mean of behaviour

No real rewards for good behaviour

No real sanctions for bad behaviour

Population

Good behaviour

Bad behaviour

Extremely Good Behaviour

Range of Behaviour

Extremely Bad Behaviour

Why has the behaviour of rent payers – in other words their readiness to pay in full and on time – deteriorated? It might be thought the reason is economic: we have higher unemployment than in the 1950s, particularly among social housing tenants, and relatively higher rents. But this cannot be the reason because, in the vast majority of cases, housing benefit is there to cover the rent if the tenant's income is not sufficient. The amount paid out in housing benefit in the UK is huge: more than £22 billion in 2011 paid out to 4.94 million claimants. The number of people receiving housing benefit has been climbing steadily in recent years, so, although there are sometimes delays in an individual getting their benefit through, it is undoubtedly a major support system for tenants on low incomes.

The real reason people get into arrears is essentially to do with culture and behaviour. My family members were products of another era, when behaviour norms were different. They took pride in paying their rent, or indeed any bill, on time. It was part of their value system: their view of what it meant to live a decent and successful life.

That attitude has more or less evaporated. Few people now count 'paying bills on time' as the mark of a successful life. On the contrary, over the past 30 years, having high levels of debt has become the norm for individuals and indeed governments. People are now much more comfortable funding their housing, consumer goods, and even their education, through debt. People in rent arrears will almost certainly have other debts too (some on extortionately high levels of interest) and often they will regard rent arrears as a kind of interest-free loan – a debt that can be run up without immediate cost or consequences.

However, failing to pay your rent is not behaviour that simply has no consequences. The cost is to the social housing provider, in a double whammy because people in rent arrears are usually a landlord's most expensive customers in other ways too. The impact falls on the neighbourhood as a whole, including on those neighbours who do pay their rent. The problem is that the impact is not perceived, and the bad payers see no reason to change their ways.

They have no incentive to change their behaviour because sanctions against them are limited, while in almost every circumstance they receive the same, if not better, services from their landlords as the good payers. Compared with the good payers, non-payers order more repairs (typically three times the average), have the untidiest gardens, and take up more of the housing professionals' time than rent-paying tenants. This is the experience of most housing providers in the UK and is caused by outdated laws and their unintended consequences, as I will come on to explain.

Why does behaviour change?

Behaviour concerns us all. It is people's behaviour – not their beliefs – that determines whether a society is a good one to live in or not. For society to work, which at the very least means for us all to get on with our lives free from threats to our person and property, everyone's behaviour has to be within certain acceptable parameters. If some people do not behave in that way, society has to spend a lot of money on clearing up the consequences, guarding other people against their behaviour and so on. It is expensive. If bad behaviour improved, we as a society would have a lot more resources to spend. It sounds obvious, but it also sounds difficult to address. Nevertheless, in our current straitened economic circumstances we have to address it, if we want our society to improve and not be in a state of constant decline, with inordinate amounts of public money being spent on negative and potentially destructive activities.

Over the past 40 years, those on the front line of dealing with anti-social behaviour have become deeply involved with why people behave the way they do. Is it social conditions? Family history? Educational failures? Deprivation? Financial circumstances? The list goes on.

I'm not denying that all of those, and many more, are factors, but I'm not concerned with those here. I start from the position that anyone over the age of 10 (and certainly any rational adult) can take charge of their own behaviour, and modify it if they want to. Poverty is always a serious issue and should be addressed. But if you're an adult, being poor is not an excuse for being filthy, foul-mouthed or dishonest. Those are behaviour choices. There are always other people on low incomes who have chosen differently. High income earners are not free from bad behaviour either.

The question is, why does behaviour change? My argument is that it changes according to the ways the people at the extreme ends of the graph are treated.

Let's face it, not many people are as reliable and upstanding as my Auntie

Beryl, my Uncle Jim or my mum and dad. But neither do most people want to lead a life of crime. On the whole, they do what they perceive others around them are doing, and if something is a bit questionable, some do what they think they can get away with.

A proven example here is littering. If you catch up with someone who has just chucked their burger carton on the ground and ask them why they did that, their responses will be something like:

a. "What's it got to do with you, ★★★★..."
b. "Er, dunno, didn't think..."
c. "It's not my fault, there are no litter bins round here."
d. "Everyone else throws their litter on the ground."

If you want people to change their behaviour, the first thing is to get them to think and take personal responsibility for their actions. I'll expand on this in the next chapter.

Response c is probably true – local authorities have removed many litter bins, partly for security reasons following the IRA bomb in a bin at Victoria Station, and partly because there are better things for them to spend their money on than emptying litter bins. The message 'take your litter home with you' has been with us for many years now.

Response d is interesting, because it illustrates how people modify their behaviour in accordance with what they perceive other people are doing. The best way to stop people chucking litter is to have a clean environment and public realm, which people respect. Look at Singapore – famous for not only its pristine streets but also the impeccable public behaviour of its residents.

If people see rubbish strewn around them, they get the message that everyone else does it, there are no penalties and nobody cares. The well-known 'zero tolerance' policy pioneered in New York started with clearing litter and graffiti in order to tackle crime. At first, no-one could see the connection, but it became apparent that if people perceived that an environment was respected, and minor anti-social behaviour was not tolerated, it acted as a brake on serious anti-social behaviour, property crime and muggings. In one of our neighbourhoods in Salford our hanging baskets programme not only spruced the place up but residents noticed that the bin men also sharpened up their act in response and the whole environment became more pleasant.

So coming back to rent arrears, how are people at the left and right poles of the graph treated? What happens if you always pay your rent on time? Nothing much. Your landlord takes you for granted. What happens if you don't pay your rent? Again, nothing much. Or at least nothing for quite a while. As I mentioned in chapter 1, the reminder letters will keep dropping through your letterbox. Your landlord will threaten eviction, but you will have noticed that your neighbours have got away with being in rent arrears for years and are still comfortably in their home, with the plasma HD 40 inch telly they've bought with the money they haven't paid in rent.

If, by chance, you fail to cough up a few hundred quid to appease your landlord and you do indeed go to court, there's nothing much to worry about. The judge will look at your arrears and order you to pay them off at a rate of a pound a week, on top of your usual rent. This does nothing to help your landlord's arrears problem, but meanwhile a large amount of public money has gone on the administration, court time and various other costs of bringing you to justice.

The good, the bad – and the . . .

It is a shame that we take the good 10% of customers for granted, because not only do they save public authorities a great deal of unacknowledged money by paying their dues on time, but they are also usually lovely people too. They are the people who are reliable, punctual, honest and happy. They are not resentful and envious: when their neighbours spend the rent money on a holiday in Florida, they might criticise, but they don't start thinking, "perhaps we could do that…?"

They are the people whom, if you're lucky enough to have them as a neighbour or a workmate, you miss when they're away. They're the people who make you smile when they come into the room. In contrast, those people at the other end of the scale are the ones you sarcastically smile about when they leave the room. You can't wait for them to go on holiday (or to prison) and you pray they don't come back.

Sadly, the nation spends most of its energy and resources on the people who are unreliable, feckless and dishonest: the sort of whom people say "they think the world owes them a living." At the extreme is, for example, the ghastly Karen Matthews in Dewsbury, who, not content with an income of £1,600 a month from her various benefits, hatched a plan to raise more money by kidnapping her daughter Shannon and claim a newspaper's £50,000 reward for 'finding' her. Sentencing Matthews in January 2009, the judge commented that the search for Shannon had cost the public purse £3.2m, not to mention all the unpaid hours local volunteers had spent searching and campaigning.

Matthews is an extreme example, but in a sense what she was doing was only an extension of behaviours that have become fairly normal in society: being a single mother with children by various fathers, living on a combination of benefits generated by the fact of being a lone mother, cashing in on the media fascination with the 'victim of crime'. She wasn't clever enough to invent any of these paradigms of behaviour: they were around in society for her to take advantage of.

But here I'm not going after the Karen Matthews of this world. She is part of the cohort of troublesome families who make up 1% of our population, cost us 8 billion quid a year and run health, police and social services ragged. Undoubtedly their behaviour has to be tackled, but I'm interested in the middle 80%. This is the bulk of people in a neighbourhood, and their behaviour determines the culture of that neighbourhood. By neighbourhood I mean a housing estate, a workplace, a football team, school playground or even social media network – anywhere that has its own culture, a place to which people 'belong'. These people in the middle modify their behaviour in accordance with what happens at either pole of the graph.

So if kids at school see their fellow pupils rewarded for full attendance, for handing their essays in on time, for wearing their uniform smartly and so on, they'll think, yes, I'll do that. They can see the point of behaving in the way that the school wants.

If, on the other hand, they see pupils who haven't done their essays on time simply getting an extension, and then perhaps receiving more marks than the ones who met the deadline, they will quickly lose faith in the system. They will conclude there is nothing to be gained through abiding by the rules.

Authorities and policymakers don't always think about the justice implications of what they decide. But ordinary people feel unfairness acutely. It's the justice issue which has an effect on the floating behaviour among that 80%.

If you're left of the middle of the curve you're not likely to go too far to the right of the curve. But if you're to the right of it, because you come from a culture where standards were not high, you think – I'll have a bit of that. The kid who's not doing well at school and spends his day being shouted at by adults sees his peers drop out of school and hang round the streets. His grandma says they'll come to a bad end but, as far as he can see, they don't – instead they are taken up as runners for the drug dealers and soon they have designer clothes and jewellery and girlfriends. What is he going to think?

It's all about reward and justice. The rewards for the drug-gangs' runners are immediate and tangible. They may also be short-lived, dangerous and are definitely illegal, but some kids don't think far enough ahead to worry about that.

The problem is that there's very little else, in today's society, which offers equally attractive, and attainable, rewards for kids with no qualifications. Record levels of youth unemployment, higher education costs and rising consumer expectations, compound the problem. In the 'good old days' of fuller employment, an apprenticeship didn't offer much in terms of monetary reward, but it did offer a young person a challenge, camaraderie, and a recognised place in society. Furthermore, apprentices, like lawyers and medical students, knew they were entering a rewards-based system: if they worked hard and learned the skills, they would get on. Effort put in now would be repaid later. Many of my friends who started as apprentices have gone on to be very successful in business and life.

As a society we have abandoned this model and not put anything in its place. Attempts have been made to re-introduce the apprenticeship idea, but these schemes tend to be small-scale. Unskilled young people are told that the only route for them is to gain qualifications. This is an easy assertion to make, but many kids see qualifications as unattainable and even if they did get them, they only lead into a working life comprising a series of low-paid, short-term jobs... while the young people are often saddled with significant debts built up at university.

As well as society rewarding what it does want (young people in education, training or work), it should also be ensuring that there are no rewards for what it does not want. Unfortunately, not much is done to stop the drug-gang runners getting their reward. They are not a priority for police and the judicial system because they are small fry and their earnings are paltry compared to the bigger drugs players. But what happens to the runners is not insignificant: the kid hanging round on the street corner is having a bigger effect on behaviour in his community than might be apparent at first sight.

So this is the question for policymakers: is society rewarding the values it approves of and penalising the behaviour it dislikes?

Time and again, the answer is no.

Local authorities used to hand out home improvement grants. These normally went to homes that were run-down, which is hardly surprising – except that in practice this meant that if you made the effort to maintain your house, you never got a grant. When councils and housing associations modernise estates, they typically have a 'worst first' policy. They fail to allow for the fact that, on an estate of homes all built at the same time, the homes in worst condition are usually inhabited by the worst people, who have turned the place into a wreck. Meanwhile, their neighbours who have treated their home with respect have to wait years – sometimes indefinitely – for a new kitchen and double glazing.

The big danger is that people on the good side of the curve see laziness and irresponsibility rewarded. This is not what the local authority intended – but in reality it is what happens.

The moving curve

Most people would agree that standards of social behaviour are much worse now than 30 or 40 years ago. That's not just because we look at the past through rose-tinted spectacles: the following graphs show that there has been a very real rise in the annual figures for three social indicators – crime, divorce and alcohol-related deaths.

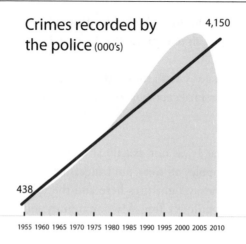

Crimes recorded by the police (000's)

4,150

438

1955 1960 1965 1970 1975 1980 1985 1990 1995 2000 2005 2010

Divorce

119,589

30,870

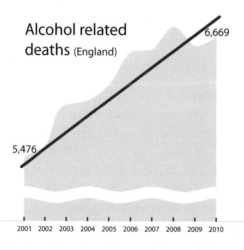

Alcohol related deaths (England)

6,669

5,476

2001 2002 2003 2004 2005 2006 2007 2008 2009 2010

These are just three indicators which show that our perception that things are getting worse is not just an illusion fuelled by nostalgia.

If you let people get away with things, the average standard of behaviour deteriorates and what was unacceptable 10 years ago becomes normal. The curve moves to the right.

I have to confess that I was not exactly an angel when I was a kid. Me and my mates would steal apples off trees, put bangers up car exhausts, knock on old ladies' doors and run away, light fires here and there. We didn't actually hurt anyone, apart from an unlucky frog. My community found my behaviour appalling. If you ask people nowadays what they thought of an area where occasionally a banger went off in someone's exhaust, one frog got blown up, some bottles of milk went missing, some apples off a tree, they'd say it's quite a nice neighbourhood. However, during my time as a bad boy my behaviour completely violated the standards of the working-class culture where I grew up, and I knew that and took the consequences.

Contrast that with what a teenage troublemaker can do in today's society. Recently a favoured target is a mother with young children, loading their shopping into the car in a supermarket car park. A lad gets into the car, holds a syringe filled with red liquid to the child's face and tells the mother they will inject the baby with HIV positive blood unless she drives to the nearest cashpoint and gives him her money.

Who ever thought of such a macabre thing to do? It's actually ketchup in the syringe but no terrified mother is going to take that chance. But that's what 'bad behaviour' can mean now. It makes you yearn for the days of stolen apples and bangers in car exhausts. The kids get away with it if they're picked up by the police, because they are technically not carrying an offensive weapon.

Adapting to the worst

Over the last few years, very many cases have hit the headlines that have made us stop and ask – how barbaric can society get? I am thinking of Fiona Pilkington, who killed herself along with her disabled daughter Francecca in 2007, after 10 years of bullying and harassment by local youths who ruled the street. Only a few months later Gary Newlove was kicked to death outside his house by a gang that terrorised his street in Warrington.

These cases shocked the nation and brought home that anti-social behaviour is not just a nuisance, but can be murderous. Many people's thought was – surely we will all come to our senses and finally put a stop to this kind of violence, because things can't get any worse.

But this is not how it works. The curve keeps skewing to the right. We should never underestimate people's ability to think of worse and worse things until they are threatening a baby with a syringe.

The horrific cases don't make things better; in fact they ultimately make things worse because we get used to the extremes and adapt. The Fiona Pilkington case made people aware that harassment of disabled people is a widespread problem, and no doubt the police are now much more responsive to such complaints. But often, acknowledging an issue means people start managing the problem, not eliminating it. When the Equality and Human Rights Commission Scotland subsequently launched an inquiry into the harassment of disabled people, commissioner Morag Alexander commented: "Disabled people experiencing harassment can become conditioned to hostile treatment, or are sometimes told to ignore it by those around them... They may also go to enormous lengths to avoid putting themselves at risk which can limit their freedom and opportunities."

It should be said that attitudes to disabled people and people with learning difficulties have improved enormously in British society. Fifty years ago, for example, children with Downs Syndrome were sent away to a 'home' out of sight; now, many go to mainstream schools, at least at primary stage. Rights of disabled access are enshrined in law. But if attitudes have improved, behaviour has deteriorated. That behaviour might only be perpetrated by a tiny minority, but it can be lethal.

For society to improve, behaviour needs to change as well as attitudes. Most people would agree Britain is overall a much more racially tolerant and integrated place than it was in the 1960s and 1970s, but knowing that is not much consolation to the Asian family getting bricks thrown at their windows and turds pushed through their letterbox by white youths.

Behaviour in society rarely changes for the better by itself. But a concerted effort to stop certain behaviours can work. Deaths on the roads have dropped significantly since the 1970s, after seat belts were made compulsory and strict drink-driving laws were enforced. At the time, opponents declared wearing seatbelts and not being able to have 'one for the road' were infringements of drivers' freedom; no-one would argue that now.

Teenage knife crime is a clear example of how the curve moves, to everyone's detriment. Even 15 years ago, ordinary schoolchildren would not have dreamed of carrying knives. Then the bad kids started using knives to steal their fellow pupils' money and mobile phones. So other kids began carrying knives for self defence. After a while, knives became acceptable among young people who previously would not have thought of possessing a weapon. The curve shudders relentlessly to the right. Teenagers get into fights, and a fight with a knife is very different from a fight without one. There were terrible cases of tragic deaths, with the victim often being the young person who was simply trying to stop the violence.

This was the case when 16 year old Ben Kinsella was knifed to death in London in 2008. His sister, actress Brooke Kinsella, was commissioned by the government in 2010 to report on anti-knife crime initiatives among young people. Her report notes: "Firstly, young people felt afraid that others were carrying weapons and so claimed they needed to carry knives themselves for self-protection: the 'fear' factor. Secondly, other young people carried knives because it was seen as a fashionable or cool thing to do: the 'fashion' factor. These 'fear and fashion' factors that lead to the decision to carry a knife were evident at every project I visited."

Interestingly, she comments that the young people she talked to, in various parts of the country, usually had very clear ideas as to why a particular anti-knife crime project wasn't working and what would make it work better. The adults involved often had little grasp of what young people valued, respected or feared. This ties in with one of my themes, which I'll come to later in the book when I talk about motivating people: to get the best out of people, you have to treat them as they would like to be treated, not as you would like to be treated. Kinsella also says that at the same time as tackling criminal behaviour, there needs to be more acknowledgement of the fact that the vast majority of young people are decent and law abiding. In other words, there should be more reward and recognition going to good behaviour.

The rise in youth knife crime demonstrates that deterioration in behaviour is a process, a series of events and responses.

I remember going to visit Norah Peyton, an astonishing elderly lady who was a one woman campaigner against crime in her community; she was named Neighbour of the Year in the Pride of Britain Awards 2001 for her work. Her estate in Gorton, Manchester, was horrendous: people openly dealing drugs on the streets; kids screeching cars round corners; tyres on the lampposts, trainers hanging from the telephone wires (who knows why?); packs of feral dogs roaming the neighbourhood like some kind of urban wild boar, apparently living on a staple diet of bin bags.

We sat outside in her impeccable garden, drinking Earl Grey tea, while the madness raged around us. "They'll never steal my sanity," she assured me.

Her presence was a reminder that the estate was not created as bad as it was: it became that way, year by year. At one time it was a respectable and desirable place to live. But as things got worse, the good people moved out. Others moved in who couldn't be housed elsewhere, or had been evicted from other places, and the curve once again moved to the right.

Norah was one of the last decent householders still in her home. To say she refused to be intimidated is an understatement. She was fearless: she would go up to drug dealers, take the drugs off them and throw them down the drain. She put herself in danger by doing so and once was shot at with an air pistol, while she was in her wheelchair.

She died in 2009, in her 80s, a legendary figure. There are examples of other estates which are lucky enough to have a tough old matriarch like her, who will stand up to the violence.

But the solution to dealing with bad estates is not to have a Norah living there. There has to be a much better organised and less risky approach, which pushes the curve as fast as possible to the left, because this will result in dramatic improvements in average behaviours, raising expectations and standards. It can be done, but only with a conscious and concerted effort. It is easier to adjust to the deteriorating situation than to try to improve it. Irwell Valley colleagues routinely wear stab vests when they are out visiting our customers; I wear one myself. It is not so much our residents that we worry about, as we know them personally. But you can never be too careful. When you think about it, this is a depressing step: we are right to protect our colleagues, but all we have done is adapt to the increased threat of violence. We have done nothing to stop that violence.

It is not just on estates that you find a tangible and perceptible deterioration in the way that people behave.

Go to any town centre after 11pm on a Friday or Saturday night – whether it is a northern city or a home counties market town – and there will be groups of screeching, lurching lads and ladettes, peeing in the gutter and falling into fountains. They are not teenagers: most are in their 20s and often in their 30s, certainly old enough to know right from wrong. But as well as making fools of themselves and intimidating passers-by, they often resort to criminal damage too. On Sunday morning there's always a furious retailer boarding up her smashed shop window.

In the main, these will be young people with steady jobs, hence with money to spend on alcohol and recreational drugs. On Monday morning they will be neat and tidy, back behind the building society counter or in front of their computer. Their parents would not have behaved like that in public on a Saturday night, so why do they?

Alcohol is usually blamed, but there is a strong element of acceptability too. People are not embarrassed about making fools of themselves and damaging property: their friends all do it too. Everyone knows it is a laugh. They don't worry that people will think ill of them in any way. Bad behaviour has become the norm and if you don't do it, you're no fun. Raising the price of vodka is not going to solve that problem.

In so many ways we have got used to poorer standards of behaviour. If you complain, you sound like some old fashioned Mary Whitehouse figure, unable to cope with the edgy modern world.

Technology has brought us new ways to behave badly. Look at how people conduct themselves on the internet. I'm not talking about paedophiles cruising for victims, I mean ordinary people who air their opinions. Take a look at the online feedback to an article in one of the broadsheets – *The Daily Telegraph* or

The Guardian – and you'll see the outpouring of bile and bigotry (not to mention bad spelling). Protected by the anonymity of cyberspace, people love to make their comments as hurtful as possible. It's dispiriting.

Purposeful action

In my experience, the curve can be pulled back, but only through purposeful, organised action. Left to their own devices, most people are not going to raise their standards of behaviour, and certainly not because politicians or other authority figures exhort them to do so.

Take the kid who's dropped out of school and is vulnerable to being lured into a gang. There are inspiring stories of young people, from poor, dysfunctional families, who have gone on to great things. But most people are not that focused or determined; most people do not have some exceptional sporting or artistic talent that will lift them clear of the circumstances they were born into. Most young people simply do what their mates do.

So if we want them to do something other than drift into a life of petty crime and drug addiction, we as a society have to act. If we want teenagers and young adults to understand the difference between right and wrong, to be well-educated, optimistic, and have civic pride and social responsibility, we as a society have to work at that all the time.

It is the same as if you were managing a workforce, or a football team, where you want certain values in place in order to achieve success. You have to make sure that the values you want are congruent with the opportunities you've put in place. Equally, you have to make sure that the values you don't want are not being rewarded.

So the kid on the street corner sees crime being rewarded. He will only get a different message if there is a police crackdown making the penalties swiftly obvious.

But also, looking around him, he sees the reward system our liberal society – for all sort of well-meaning reasons – has put in place for him. He sees worklessness, if not exactly richly rewarded, certainly not penalised. He sees sexual irresponsibility rewarded. For young men, fathering a child frequently incurs no responsibility at all, either financial or emotional. For young women, having a child is positively rewarding in countless ways: as a lone parent they gain money and opportunities others do not have. I am not just talking about the stance taken by the authorities here, the benefit rules and so on. Fifty years ago, being the father of a child was taken very seriously; now, it seems, little pressure is put on young men by either the mothers of their children, or their own families, to support their kids in any way. A major shift in attitudes has taken place here, for a complex variety of reasons, but the end result is a situation which is detrimental to children and expensive for the public purse. Furthermore, it is so commonplace that few people comment on it or suggest things could be different.

Do we really think carefully about the messages we are sending to the next generation? My organisation is involved in a number of schemes with young people who have been causing trouble, trying to encourage them to change their ways and stop anti-social behaviour turning into criminal behaviour.

I was once visiting a youth club to talk about this when a kid came up to me and said, "Excuse me mister. Do I have to smash windows to go camping in the Lake District?" I realised that, as far as they can see, we take the bad kids away on holiday while the good kids have to plod along to school.

The negative expenditure burden

The overall deterioration that I'm talking about is costing us a lot of money. Having an under-educated, under-motivated population, with little idea of how to take personal responsibility or contribute to society means billions are wasted. There's a huge negative expenditure burden for society. We know that we already spend £200bn on the welfare state. The Department for Communities and Local Government carried out research in 2011 that pinpointed the waste of money involved in dealing with the most troubled families. They estimate there are around 120,000 of these families who have a toxic cocktail of problems – parents not in work, children missing school, low income, illness and mental health issues and so on. The DCLG estimates £9bn is being spent annually on these families – £75,000 per family per year. But £8bn of this is spent on reacting to the various problems, in particular, taking children into care where necessary and dealing with the crimes committed by parents and children within these families. Only £1bn of the £9bn is spent trying to turn these families' lives around.

Add to these 120,000 families a larger swathe of households whose circumstances are less extreme but who are mired in difficulties – lack of work, debt, children's poor behaviour and so on – and it is clear there is a huge ongoing negative expenditure burden for society.

It is encouraging to note that the government is using a reward programme to help these families and local authorities will get funding to deal with them on a 'payment by results' basis. This rehabilitation is welcome, but we must ask how and why we got here in the first place and ensure that it never happens again. Think of the opportunity cost involved in spending £8bn on people who make up a mere 0.2% of the population.

You could argue that such rehabilitation programmes reward bad behaviour, and indeed they do in the short term. But the long term effect is more important. If as a society we learn from our mistakes and do not allow out of control behaviour to go unpunished, while we reward the behaviours we want to see, then we have a better chance of avoiding this waste of money in future.

It's obvious that criminal behaviour costs society money, but what about personal irresponsibility? How much does it cost councils to clear up dog mess and chewing gum? Why does the health service have to spend so much on treating diseases that people have basically brought on themselves, through smoking and over-eating? Health trusts are having to buy 'bariatric' ambulances, costing up to £90,000 each, which have reinforced lifting gear, wider stretchers and so on, to take larger patients. One manager at a trust told the BBC: "Only 10 years ago your average patient was 12 to 13 stone, now that's probably 17 to 18 stone. And we quite regularly see patients around 30 stone in weight and even bigger than that."

We should be worried about those sorts of figures – a 30% gain in average weight in only 10 years – at a time when no-one can say they don't know about the basics of healthy eating.

We've realised now that as a society we only have limited resources. We should be viewing this, not in terms of whether we should make x% or y% of cuts, but whether we are spending those resources on the right things at all.

We should be looking to spend money in areas where it can move the curve. An example is the NHS campaign to get people to stop smoking. Moving the curve to the left will have benefits in all sorts of areas, not just on the smoker's health but on their children's health, for example. The ban on smoking in public places was derided as an attack on civil liberties, but it has had an effect.

While smoking continues to decline, the health service will be dealing with the consequences of it for many years to come. However, now that fewer people smoke and are seen to smoke, it has become clearer that smoking is a choice. Of course, nicotine is addictive and giving up isn't easy, but most people would acknowledge now that if you smoke, that's your choice and you have no right to inflict your habit on other people. The element of personal responsibility is recognised. That is crucial to changing behaviour.

Chapter 3

Moving the Curve

When the *Big Issue* magazine was launched by John Bird and Gordon Roddick, back in the early 1990s, at first the homeless people who came forward to be vendors were not asked to pay upfront for their copies of the magazine. They simply took copies and were expected to report back with the earnings. Rather a lot of vendors came back empty handed, saying they'd lost the money, been mugged on the way back… and so on.

So the approach switched to making the vendors pay for their copies up front. That way, the cash they earned from sales was theirs to keep. Currently, they buy the magazines for £1 and sell them for £2. There was resistance to this idea, and not just among the vendors. The liberal instinct of some people was to say that was too harsh – you can't expect destitute homeless people to pay cash up front. But it worked: vendors did find the money, and there were very few incidents of the earnings being mysteriously lost.

As a result, the *Big Issue* was able to become a viable, self-financing project that has helped many thousands of homeless people over the years. The previous business model, where it acted more like a charity, with a heavy emphasis on rights rather than responsibilities, giving handouts rather than hand-ups, would have resulted in the project only lasting a couple of months.

The *Big Issue* model treats the vendors as participants in a business transaction, rather than as 'homeless people' incapable of taking responsibility for themselves. When the vendors had to take responsibility for themselves, they did: the ones, who couldn't or didn't want to, did not benefit from the advantages of being a seller.

Many *Big Issue* sellers have testified that becoming a vendor changed their lives. Earning a legitimate income, rather than living on handouts, enabled them to break free of the behaviour that had dragged them down. I am not saying people 'choose' to live on the streets – most had ended up there due to a tragic set of circumstances – but once they are there, various kinds of dependencies keep them there and they abandon personal responsibility for their lives.

Someone who really understands this situation is Bob Armstrong, one of my mentors, who performed a remarkable job as the executive director of the Omaha Housing Authority in Nebraska. Bob is an African American who was very active in the civil rights movement in the 1960s: his mission at Omaha was not just to run a housing authority but to change the lives of its customers, the tenants, forever.

Bob Armstrong has said to me on many occasions: "If you make poverty and homelessness comfortable, people will stay poor and homeless." They will lose any sense of responsibility for their own lives and become victims. The *Big Issue* project doesn't treat homeless people as victims – it treats them as individuals who can take personal responsibility for their actions.

For people to genuinely change their behaviour, they must take personal responsibility: they must see that their actions are their own choice, whatever the surrounding circumstances, and that their behaviour has consequences for themselves and for other people. To quote Bob Armstrong again: "Poverty is born out of circumstance. But if you're filthy, rude or badly behaved those are lifestyle choices which should not be tolerated."

One of the most necessary, but difficult, things about being a parent is teaching children personal responsibility: explaining to the toddler that she is the one who crayoned on the wall ("teddy did it") or to the teenager that he is the one who didn't do his maths homework ("I never had time after football") and that there is a reason why other people don't approve.

Unfortunately, a lot of people reach adulthood without ever getting the hang of personal responsibility. Things are made worse by what seems to be the naturally negative mindset we have here in Britain. They are also made worse by the dependency culture that has grown up since the 1940s, unintentionally fostered by the welfare state.

People who don't understand personal responsibility are always looking for someone else to blame, or someone else to copy and they tend to be easily swayed towards the bad end of the curve. Previous generations seem to have had a better sense of personal responsibility, in my view, perhaps due to the experiences of living through the war and being brought up in a context of stable extended families, strong communities, lower divorce rates and so on. Auntie Beryl and Uncle Jim, along with the vast majority of tenants, understood that they must pay their rent as a matter of priority. The fact that others failed to pay had no influence on their behaviour. Today, the complexity of the modern state means many people do not make the link between what they pay (or do not pay) and the services they receive. Even if you haven't paid your council tax, the bin men still empty your bin every fortnight (and council tax dodgers would be outraged if they didn't).

The cable deal

At Omaha Housing Authority, Bob Armstrong tackled this problem head on. Public housing in the US is very much at the bottom of the pile. Tenants are almost all black and all poor but Bob understands the culture of poverty and invented a variety of programmes to address systemic problems. His approach to rent collection for example was incredibly clever. When he joined Omaha HA, he found rent arrears were running at a colossal 38%. As he said, "I thought this was low rent housing, not no rent housing." In a UK housing association the problem would have had people calling for consultants to be brought in, a working party to be set up and possibly intervention from the regulator, a new computer system, revised procedures and so on and so forth. Bob did not bother with any of this.

He approached the problem intelligently and made an arrangement with the local cable TV company. Tenants could get a 10 dollar a month discount on the cable subscription and the housing authority collected the cable payment along with the rent. This meant that if you didn't pay the rent, when you switched on the telly, a sign came up on the blank screen saying, "no signal received because of rent delinquency."

Rent arrears dropped from 38% to less than 1% within weeks. People couldn't get away with not paying their rent because their kids went ballistic if the cable was pulled and they couldn't watch their basketball, NFU and baseball games.

Tenants were not penalised in order to get them to pay their rent. In fact they gained by having a discount on their cable TV. They also gained further because, out of the 10 dollars, Omaha HA put one dollar aside a month and invested it in a community foundation, used to send tenants' kids to college. Many have gone to university through that scheme, which is pretty much the only educational foundation in the USA funded by poor folks for poor folks. Bob also sought to eliminate negative expenditure and he recycled funds to provide study centres to improve education and work opportunities, in an effort to break the cycle of despair and hopelessness.

He understood the negative mindset his tenants were trapped in. It went along the lines of: "We're poor and there's nothing we can do about it. We're bored so we'll get involved in drugs, crime, nuisance or whatever and, because we're poor, that's okay."

One of his most powerful maxims is: "excuses are reasons for failure". This sounds tough when you think that there are probably a host of reasons why the Omaha tenants were poor and leading unfulfilled lives. But his inventive style of rent collection showed that people who saw themselves as too poor to pay the rent, could find the money when it was in their interests to do so. When they had the incentive, they started behaving with personal responsibility.

Once Bob had tenants who paid their rent, and so had the basic minimum requirement for a functioning housing authority, he took it from a 'failing authority' with 14% voids and $1 million wasted on repairing vandalism every year, to an inspirational authority offering self sufficiency and 'up and out' programmes to its tenants.

His contention, which challenges the fundamental pillars of UK social housing policy, is that poor people don't need public housing. What they need is to be taught to be successful and self-sufficient people and then they will find their own solutions. Clearly in this country we take the view that there should always be a safety net for people, but this should not become a spider's web entrapping people in conditions which stunt their development as human beings.

If public housing tenants and *Big Issue* sellers can take personal responsibility, change their behaviour and be inspired and motivated to succeed, so can everyone else. The starting point for my approach to both customers and colleagues has been the same: we simply ask people to take responsibility for managing their behaviour and their emotions, and to ensure that they understand the contribution they are supposed to make to our community.

As a business we seek to create these conditions in which colleagues and customers can seek enlightenment and fulfilment and unlock their potential as human beings. We do this by reinforcing positive behaviours as part of our meritocratic philosophy. The goal is for all of us to direct our behaviours so that we have successful, happy neighbourhoods and workplaces.

Some people understand that responsibility, others don't. Why do some people not understand it?

"How are you doing?"

So often I travel into work and experience around me the evidence of negative mindsets. I don't just mean litter, vandalism and all the other signs of anti-social behaviour. I mean the way people talk: people at work, out shopping, people with good jobs and nice houses.

Listen to the typical responses to that harmless question – "How are you doing?"

"All right." "Not bad". Hardly enthusiastic, but positively upbeat compared to the other replies: "Can't complain." "Surviving." "Still breathing." "Getting there." (Getting where?). "Soldiering on." "Mustn't grumble." "Ooh I wish it was Friday" (we've got a "Thank God it's Monday" culture in our office). I don't want people moping round the office, whingeing and whining and being miserable, saying, "Ooh this week's dragging". "I've had a grueller of a week." "How are you? Ooh terrible, I live for my weekends and my holidays… "

I was in the bakers buying a wheat free loaf for Lynne and I heard a lady order a steak pie and a custard tart. She must have been a regular because as she left the assistant said, "See you next week Doris." "If God spares me…" Doris sighed. As I walked out Doris became meteorological and grumbled, "Oooh this wind doesn't go round you, it goes through you." Luckily for Doris I have seen her since… God works in mysterious ways his wonders to perform!

It's only language, and maybe here in the north-west we're prone to a bit of gloom, but if you talk everything down like that – nothing is ever good, you're always a victim – you see the world that way. How can you make a positive contribution to your workplace or your community if the best anything can be is 'not bad', 'average' or 'satisfactory'?

We like to pride ourselves on British understatement of course. But sometimes a bit of overstatement would be more cheerful, or even just statement. We make fun of the Americans for being over-enthusiastic and upbeat, but that can be very refreshing. Enthusiasm is contagious, and so is pessimism. It's back to the curve again and how behaviour is changed.

Bob Armstrong took me to a place called Gates Bar-B-Q in Kansas. The building was an unprepossessing shack, but inside it was a theatrical display of ribs and beef burger preparation. Needless to say, it was very friendly and we were greeted with a "Hi Mr Armstrong, fantastic to see you sir, how can I help you?" as soon as we stepped through the door. The people that work there put on an amazing performance, juggling racks of ribs like a circus act (very similar to the Pikes Place Fish Boys in Seattle). We were served by a young man whose badge told us his name was Dave, occupation Flipper. At the end of his performance I said, "How are you today Dave?" and he enthusiastically and spontaneously said, "Sir, I am absolutely fantastic. And you know, I thought I was great *yesterday*! You hurry back and see us real soon Doctor."

When I got back to Irwell Valley after that particular experience, I bumped into one of our managers and asked him how he was. He said, "Ah, not bad. Can't complain, if you do no one listens." He always said that, and I'd never noticed before. Dave in Gates Bar-B-Q probably lived pretty much on tips. My manager had a nice house, company car, pension, a wallet full of credit cards – and things were never better than "not bad". And I realised that his whole team never performed better than "not bad." He set the tone, he set the pace and he also had to leave.

Like everyone else these days, we have some Polish guys working for us. We took them on to help with our grounds maintenance. They were very impressive: turning up prompt at 7 am and working hard all day – too hard for their English colleagues, who tried to get them to slow down. Whenever you asked them how they were, they said, "Fantastic. I love it here!"

We gave them the induction course we do for all our colleagues. They watched some training videos, we laid on food and we also had them doing a bit of communal singing (we're large on singing). I noticed one of the guys was taking photos of it all on his phone. He turned to me and said: "I want to show my friends – I work for this great company, who give me food, a uniform, teach me to sing and also let me watch TV, with pay. Fantastic, unbelievable!"

Months later I saw the same guy again and asked him how he was. "Not bad," he said. I told him, "The negative folks have got you. They've dragged you down to their level."

The thing is, employers haven't been taking on Polish workers for their novelty value. They've proved themselves good workers and skilled at their jobs. It all goes together: positive attitude, enthusiasm, willingness to work hard, pride in the job, fulfilment and an enlightened approach.

We all know what the opposite is: the British worker, with the two hour lunch breaks, indifference to the job and constant moaning, for whom nothing is ever better than "not bad." It's a stereotype, but there's truth in it. Ironically, our generous benefits system also allows people to make lifestyle choices based on mindsets like, "It's not worth my while working… I can't be arsed with all that work palaver."

There's something of a superstitious element in this negative mindset, as if at the back of our minds we fear that if we don't complain, something bad might really happen. If we welcome something warmly, we're tempting fate. But in reality, if we're enthusiastic and positive, there's a much greater chance of further good things happening. At the very least, people will like us more and enjoy our company.

In the words of Paul McCartney: "What's the use of worrying? No use." We know that 99% of what we worry about never happens. Think how much more fulfilled and happier we would be if we switched all the negative energy we expend on worrying, complaining, being frightened of criticism and avoiding risks, into positive energy directed towards fulfilment, self belief and confidence.

Moaning is a great substitute for action. If you're the complainant, you're always in the right. You have every excuse for why you're not more successful. I say to everyone, colleagues as well as customers, if you want to complain, complain to someone who can do something about it. Don't moan to your neighbour or your friends when you're supposed to be socialising and enjoying yourself. You'll frustrate and annoy them and they can never help you solve your problems anyway. Instead, always take it up with someone who has the authority to sort the problem out. Remember 10 two letter words: "if it is to be, it is up to me!"

What does it mean, to take personal responsibility? There was a good description of the kind of thing I'm talking about, expressed by top Spanish footballer Xavi in an interview with *The Guardian*. "When you arrive at Barcelona the first thing they teach you is: think," he said. "Think, think, think… Lift your head up, move, see, think… before you get the pass know what the next move is, and if you're getting this pass look to see if that guy is free."

Personal responsibility is about lifting your head up, looking and thinking before you act. Instead of doing something out of instinct or habit, asking yourself what the consequences will be. If you do this, how will it help others? How can others help you? How can you move things forward? This kind of thinking needs to be explicitly encouraged amongst people.

To take personal responsibility requires a positive attitude, a belief that you can act, and that your actions will achieve something. Some of those actions won't be successful, but you move on and try again. We learn in a variety of ways and learning from our mistakes is one of the most important ways human beings develop.

A lot of people don't think like this. They have a negativity at their core which makes them feel nothing they do will be any good and so it's not even worth trying.

Undoubtedly, if you grow up in difficult circumstances, you lack that sense of possibility. People tend to rise to the level of expectations of others around them. If you're told you're crap or useless often enough, you might come to believe it. If you're from an environment where no-one you know has ever had a job, why would you apply for one yourself? What would make you think that you could ever get one? It is so much easier if you grow up in an environment where you see efforts being rewarded and achievement being within your grasp. Confidence breeds confidence and success breeds success.

But we have to find a way of giving people that sense of possibility if they are ever to move forward and change their behaviour. With a downbeat, gloomy media that likes to focus on personal tragedy, a capricious climate and an astonishing hypocrisy in government and the City, it's not surprising that British people get negative and cynical. If we want that to change we have to take active steps.

Sing when you're winning

At Irwell Valley we are very keen on creating the conditions in which people want to come to work and which trigger motivation. Singing is something that we use as a great team and confidence builder and is a wonderfully liberating experience for everyone. Singing cannot help but cheer you up and energise you – if you don't believe me, ask Gareth Malone! If you know what you're doing and can overcome the trepidation, so that you are confident, relaxed, knowing how to breath and project, then you have acquired not only important skills for singing, but also attributes which will have a hugely beneficial impact throughout your life. All our managers have regular sessions with a performance coach – not to get them on to *The Voice* (unless they really want to) but to give them the skills they need to provide confident leadership and to help them communicate with our colleagues.

We offer singing classes in the office, but often people are reluctant to join in. "I can't sing," they say. "I wish I could." We ask, " Have you ever tried, have you ever been taught?" Usually the answer is no. They've learned to do a lot of things in their lives, for instance learned to swim and to drive, but they assume singing isn't something that can be learned: you either have it or you don't.

On the contrary, singing is something everyone enjoys and can be learned. You only have to look at children singing in the playground to see what a natural, positive experience it is. One of the reasons we hold singing classes and other challenging events, such as learning how to break wood with your fists, is to demonstrate to people how important it is to break down the artificial barriers we erect which obstruct all areas of lives. We try to change mindsets and coax people to actively seek positivity and fulfilment. It's all part of our effort to create a 'can do' culture.

Many years ago, singing used to be something that everyone did, in church, in the pub or around the piano at home. Now it has become a specialised skill: something that people on the telly do, something you have to be 'good' at. So people don't like to try, for fear of looking stupid. However, the urge to sing is usually still there, underneath. If you go to a karaoke bar at weekends you'll see an array of alter-egos strutting their stuff, fantasising about being Mick Jagger or Beyoncé.

At the heart of many people's lack of fulfilment is a fear of failure and criticism. It starts round about the age of 11 or 12. As Luther Vandross says: "Life removes innocence from a child." Most children up to that age have confidence and an appetite for life; they are mimics, actors, dancers and acrobats. But when they go to secondary school, they become self-conscious and sometimes that relaxed sparkle disappears. I remember at that age being told to stop showing off, to grow up, be sensible, realistic and so on.

The playground is an important neighbourhood. Certain strong characters will lead behaviour – the curve follows them. It's not the nice kids who run the playground, or the academic ones, or even the best looking ones. It's the ones who command respect, for whatever reason, and they rarely use their power in a benign way. They target anyone who is different, and the other kids follow them. So if you're a girl who goes to football training, or a boy who brings a violin into school, you find yourself the target of insults and you have to be tough to stick it out. Many don't: they drop the violin lessons, leaving their mother saying, "I don't understand it. He always loved music…"

Physical bullying doesn't have to be involved. Name-calling and gossip is enough to destroy confidence. The saying goes: 'sticks and stones will break my bones but words will never hurt me'. Nothing could be further from the truth. Names undermine you for years. Meanwhile the playground leaders have discovered that the most powerful weapon at their disposal is their mouth and that it's remarkably easy to destroy someone's confidence and ambition and stifle their ability to achieve. A lot of people enjoy that power trip. We can all think of teachers we've had and managers we've worked for who relished their ability to humiliate and crush with a word. Usually it's an approach taken to preserve their position, a controlling style adopted to hold back emerging talent.

Constant criticism kills. It doesn't produce results: it just paralyses. I used to play football with a team whose manager lambasted us for the slightest mistake.

We never played well, in fact we never really played at all; we just kept our heads down and tried not to be the one who did anything wrong. I left.

Understanding your personal power

Sadly, a lot of human beings have long since been defeated by criticism. The lesson they have taken from setbacks and failures is not, "well that didn't work. I'm going to do it differently next time," but, "well that didn't work. I'm not going to try again."

Admittedly it takes courage to say to yourself: "I feel brilliant, wonderful. This is going to be a great day for me. I'm going to try some new skills and at the end of the day I'm going to evaluate where I am. I might make a fool of myself but I don't mind, because in order to swim you've got to sink a bit and swallow a mouthful of water."

To be brave enough to say that, with conviction, you have to understand that you have the personal power to affect the way things go and affect people around you. We emphasise frequently that everyone is in a team, one way or another, and anything anyone does affects us all. We are not all equal but we're all as important as each other. All individuals have a power over each other, and therefore the responsibility to use that power well. But many people don't realise that they've got it.

Of course circumstances rule our actions too: our environment, other people and so on. But often people use those external things as an excuse for not performing well. They become a kind of comfort blanket. Technology is a favourite one. I can't count the number of times people have assured me their team will perform much better when they've all got email/the intranet/ document imaging/ data warehousing. I think of the fantastic reservoir system the Victorians put in to supply Manchester with fresh water – seven reservoirs coming down from the Peak District, all designed without the aid of a computer and built with picks and shovels.

We've become very reliant on gadgets, as if equipment were a substitute for action. I heard a business woman talking on the train, assuring someone that the project she was working on would be delivered on time. "I'll complete it as soon as I get my phone upgrade," she said. If you look around any town, you see a lot of overweight people walking around in tracksuits and trainers. They don't appear to do the exercise, but they feel good wearing the gear. It's a kind of vicarious fitness.

I gave a motivational talk to a rugby club: its teams were not performing as well as they might and the club was struggling financially because members were not paying their subscriptions. The players had all sorts of reasons why they were not winning games. But I asked them, "What resources do you really need? You've got your fitness – most important – your kit, pitches, coaches, balls, training sessions. Are there any more resources you need? No. So what you need now is to be resourceful – you need to actually use the resources you've got."

I also asked them whether they paid their subs. They didn't like to admit it, but I knew the best players were the worst payers. They thought they could get away with not paying because the club wouldn't get rid of them. I told them that on the contrary – they were the players others looked up to, so they should set an example by paying their subs.

These young men had not understood their personal responsibility: a responsibility to play to the best of their ability and play as a team, but also to support the club which made their rugby possible.

So if you want to change behaviour within a certain group, neighbourhood, workforce and so on, the starting point is to say to people: you all have personal responsibility for your own actions. We want you to behave well and we expect that you will. If the resources are in place for you, there is no excuse for not meeting expectations.

Then, to reinforce the message and ensure that we get the behaviour we want, at Irwell Valley we have instigated systems of reward, as I'll explain in the next chapter. Essentially, we are rewarding the behaviours we want, in order to eliminate the behaviours we don't want.

Some people understand the message of personal responsibility straight away, others never get it.

Our organisation has twice given jobs to serving prisoners. It is part of the rehabilitation scheme for prisoners, allowing people approaching the end of their sentence to get work experience, so that they are better able to rebuild their lives on leaving jail.

Our first convict had been sentenced to seven years for drug trafficking. But he had the chance for parole after three years, if he completed a programme of work within the community. So he had every incentive to make a success of his stint with us.

We gave him work as a Neighbourhood Manager and he started off well. Then after about four weeks his colleagues reported that he was never around. Investigation revealed that he had managed to hire a car (which he was not allowed to do) and had got himself a girlfriend and a stall on Bury market, where he was spending most of his time.

I brought him in and explained that this was not good. We both wanted to make his placement work. For myself, I believe strongly that rehabilitation is vital, if we are to avoid the situation whereby half of prisoners end up back in jail, often because they have not been able to get a job or a home. I felt we were the kind of employer that could help by having a prisoner placement programme.

He had the chance to avoid going back inside, and it all rested on the weekly phone call I made to the prison. If I told them he was not complying with requirements, he would be back behind bars on Monday morning and not coming out for three and a half years.

Of course he was contrite and promised to behave – which he did for about a month. But then he was up to his old tricks again, so, very reluctantly, I made that phone call.

After that, my colleagues were not keen to have another prisoner. They felt we'd 'done' prisoners and it hadn't worked. But I felt we'd had the wrong guy.

We did take another convict and his placement was a success. He gained his parole and left. He probably didn't enjoy working for us, because we knew his background.

We were a transition for him, and he moved on to another job, where he could start afresh as a free man.

So you can offer people the opportunities and the resources and some aren't capable of responding. Never mind – try again with people who are.

For both of these prisoners, there was a very clear reward on offer if they modified their behaviour. Our second convict understood this and he stuck with the placement, even though it was difficult for him. I don't know why our first guy didn't understand. I suppose he thought he was cleverer than us and could get away with it. He was wrong.

At Irwell Valley we have set out to make a very clear connection between the way people behave – customers and colleagues – and the rewards they receive. This is the essence of our meritocratic philosophy called Gold Service.

Chapter 4

The Gold Mine

Back in 1998, we asked a simple, radical and important question: why do we treat all our customers the same? Why were we giving our best customers, those who paid their rent on time and looked after their homes, the same service as our worst customers? Ironically, our best customers were probably getting a worse service, because we paid little attention to them. They requested fewer repairs and took up little of our time, while our difficult customers demanded more of our attention and used up more of our resources – all the time causing problems that affected our good customers' lives.

Our big question challenged a lot of the assumptions on which the UK's social housing system is built. In challenging those assumptions, we started to unpack some of the issues that were creating unhappy customers in our neighbourhoods.

Up until 1998, we operated in the same way as virtually all other housing providers. We made no distinction between those tenants who paid their rent, looked after their homes, got on well with their neighbours and planted roses in their front gardens, and those in rent arrears, many of whom were anti-social, who neglected and damaged their homes and whose gardens often had bedroom furniture and a mouldy fridge scattered around them. Crazily, we knew the names of our worst customers, but not our best customers, simply because we saw more of the troublemakers.

In principle social housing is a service. Our customers get a home and the management and repairs service provided by us. They pay for all this through rent (even if in around 50% of cases their rent is paid by the state through housing benefit).

Social landlords are businesses. But unlike mainstream businesses, consumption is not linked to payment and defaulters are entitled legally to demand services even if they break all the rules and don't pay their rent. The ultimate sanction is eviction.

So in practice, social housing is not a 'service' or 'business' as anyone in the commercial world would understand it. There are good reasons for this. Landlord and tenant legislation has tried to strike a balance between the rights and responsibilities of landlords and of tenants. In the 1960s legislation was introduced to protect tenants from the nefarious practices of bad private-sector landlords, most notably Peter Rachman and his modern day equivalent Nicholas van Hoogstraten. Clearly tenants need protection from dodgy practices. However the legislation has back-fired, big time. Although most housing providers may not publicly admit this, they all know that in many cases the same laws now protect bad tenants from good landlords.

Housing services cannot be withdrawn just because the consumer does not pay. Until they are evicted, tenants can continue to heavily consume housing services at their leisure. Getting an eviction is a cumbersome, drawn out process. Many people who get a social housing tenancy can hang on to it as long as they like, while playing ducks and drakes with their landlord, harassing their neighbours and taking more than their fair share of other state benefits.

The fact that people who don't pay and break the rules are entitled to the same, if not more, services as those who pay and behave is wrong. It can also have the undesirable effect of encouraging more people to join in. I believe that this paradox has fuelled the wider spread of anti-social behaviour, and also fuelled other people's disillusionment that problems will never be dealt with.

For a number of well-intentioned but ill thought-out reasons, the state has come to treat low income households as a unique species. In trying to be fair and not discriminate, legislators have left the social housing sector operating under a framework which treats everybody the same, irrespective of how they behave. No other service on the planet is provided on this basis and it bewilders tenants and anyone outside the social housing world when you try to explain it.

Wherever else they go, be it the supermarket, the petrol station or the cinema, tenants are treated as consumers with both rights and responsibilities. In all of these transactions tenants pay for their consumables at the point of purchase. Sadly many have got used to the idea that they don't have to pay their rent, but will still get their housing and related services anyway.

Our landlord and tenant laws, drawn up to protect good tenants from bad landlords, have not been modified to take account of the fact that tenancies are no longer with grasping slum landlords but with highly regulated bodies like ourselves. Democratically accountable social landlords are subject to all sorts of checks and balances to ensure they are operating to the highest standards. So why are they treated in the courts as if they were the likes of Peter Rachman?

The law is protecting bad tenants from good landlords. Under the present legislation, it is extremely difficult (and costly) to evict tenants who refuse to meet their responsibilities to pay rent and look after their property. If a social landlord has the right to start a tenancy, I believe it should also have the right to end it. Both parties to a tenancy must fulfil their obligations. The law should be changed so that social landlords can end a tenancy quickly, and without going to court, when tenants are not meeting their obligations. My organisation would be prepared to finance any appeal made by a tenant we had evicted, and compensate them appropriately if we were found to have acted unfairly or unreasonably.

In the absence of any other sanctions, giving regulated landlords the power to evict without going to court would significantly help us to protect good tenants from their anti-social neighbours and bring an almost immediate halt to rent arrears. It goes back to the curve: we need to push it to the left by taking significant action against the defaulters, while simultaneously rewarding those who pay and look after their homes. This would encourage the behaviours that we want.

Living with the neighbours from hell is no joke. I've experienced it myself and I've had people say to me, "I love my house. I just wish I could pick it up and move it somewhere else."

But they can't. Instead, many have to watch while the landlord installs a new kitchen or bathroom or fixes a front door that's been kicked in at the homes of those neighbours who are making their lives a misery – because landlords treat their customers equally.

How would you feel if you were out shopping and saw other people piling their trolleys high and wheeling them out of the store without paying? And when you reported this to the supermarket management, they just said, "There's

nothing we can do about it. We'll have to chase them up for payment later."
Then on top of that, the shoplifters brought a few goods back and demanded
to exchange them for better ones...

Rights without responsibilities

A fundamental problem is that people have come to see social housing as a
right, not a service. Furthermore, they regard it as a right that doesn't carry with
it significant responsibilities. The link between paying rent and receiving the
facilities was broken 50 years ago and it has never been mended.

The housing benefit system has encouraged this warped mindset. It is very
difficult to explain to anyone in the commercial sector how things work for
housing providers, where our only income is rent and we have virtually no control over payment.

I tried to explain it to Julian Richer, when he chaired our Gold Service Eval-
uation and Development Panel. Our conversation went something like this.

"So, Tom, how do your customers pay for their homes?

"Well, imagine the government passes a law allocating hi-fis on the basis of
need rather than ability to pay. A customer enters your shop, picks a hi-fi and
your colleagues help them complete a hi-fi benefit application. The customer
takes the hi-fi home and waits for their benefit to arrive.

"And when do I get paid Tom?"

"The legal position is that a local authority should process your customer's
hi-fi benefit within 14 days. Actually it ranges from 6 to 26 weeks and only 5%
of claims are dealt with on time."

*"So they take the hi-fi home, without paying, and use it while I'm waiting for the coun-
cil to pay out my money?"*

"You are also legally responsible to fully repair the hi-fi from day one."

"You cannot be serious!"

"If the hi-fi blows up, maims or kills your customer you're looking at compensation, referral to the Hi-Fi Ombudsman and potentially corporate manslaughter."

"What? My hi-fi is in their home, they've paid nothing, I have to fix it even if they've trashed it themselves, and if it blows up I go to prison! Where's my payment?"

"The hi-fi benefit is paid to your customer. They decide whether or not to pay you. After three months you can apply for direct benefit payments, serve a notice seeking hi-fi possession and repossess through the court which, if the household has children, takes between six and 12 months."

"So, you're telling me that they can wreck my hi-fi and I have to repair it, but I might not get paid until a year later, and only then if a judge awards in my favour?"

"That's it Julian. Welcome to the wonderful world of social housing."

The balance of rights and responsibilities between social landlord and tenant is very skewed. Quite properly tenants have many rights, but oddly they have few enforceable responsibilities. It's ridiculous that under the current rules it is easier to rent a social housing property than it is to rent a DVD. A social landlord is letting out a property worth, say, £150,000, but is not allowed to demand any deposit from the tenants, to inquire into their previous housing history or take references. If you go to Blockbusters you have to give full information, including your bank account details, before you can rent a £10 DVD. The more challenging the neighbourhood, the keener businesses are to protect their interests, not surprisingly. If you go to Naz's video shop in Salford, they will take names and addresses of six of your friends, plus your national insurance number and mobile phone number, before you can walk out of the door with your box set of *Shameless*.

Social landlords have no control, to a large extent, over whom they house, because access to social housing is determined by need. Furthermore, there's little to stop people taking on tenancies they can't afford. In order to get housing benefit you need to have a tenancy. Once you've got the tenancy, that's a legal arrangement with the landlord. If you are not awarded housing benefit, you still have the legal arrangement and there's little the landlord can do to make you pay. If you are awarded housing benefit, you can still decide not to spend the money on rent and instead blow it on something more exciting, like a holiday.

Back in the late 1990s, like most social housing providers, Irwell Valley found itself facing a range of problems: on the one hand, social and environmental issues on our estates were growing; on the other hand it was increasingly difficult to collect the rent that would provide the income to tackle these issues. In 1997–98 our rent arrears were running at nearly 9%, higher than the average for regional housing associations, which was 6.4% at the time. Traditional methods of delivering housing services were leading to diminishing returns.

When we examined our statistics closely, it was striking how much the bad customers were costing us. Basically, across all of our properties, around 80% of our spending was going on only 20% of our tenants – and those 20% were the worst customers.

We had a typical profile for a housing association: only 40% of our tenants were paying their rent regularly, so 60% were in arrears to some extent. The people who didn't pay their rent ordered three times as many repairs as those who did and we estimated it was costing us around £3 million a year in colleague time spent on dealing with negativity such as rent arrears, empty properties and vandalism. This was money *not* being spent on actually improving people's homes and environments.

What could we do? We could devote more money and effort to pursuing more eviction notices and clamping down on nuisance tenants. Or we could take a totally different approach. Our radical idea was to tackle the problem of bad customers by rewarding our best customers. We called it Gold Service.

Recognising loyalty

The idea was simple: we wanted to recognise the loyalty of our good customers, by giving them rewards. We also wanted to change the behaviour of others by giving them incentives to pay their rent and abide by the terms of their tenancy agreement. At the same time as rewarding our best customers we decided to take tough rehabilitative and enforcement action against our worst customers, with the overall aim to shift the behavioural curve of our customers to the left and develop new norms of great behaviour.

Our regulator kindly financed probably the most radical survey ever to be carried out in social housing – one which many housing professionals did not want to take place for fear of validating what everybody in housing knew, deep down. I actively encouraged the genie out of the bottle.

One chief executive was so incensed by our approach that she wrote an article in a professional housing journal, accusing me of being a "quack doctor – snake oil salesman" and our company of introducing "authoritarian state terrorism". My response to this was, let's see how our customers truly feel.

We engaged a professional research company which asked customers some simple questions such as, do you think there should be some sort of reward for paying your rent on time? More than 75% said yes. Interestingly the 25% who said no were mainly people who paid their rent regularly, because they thought that was the right thing to do and believed it was odd to reward someone for behaving normally. Our survey also included tenants in arrears, who thought that rent-paying tenants should receive a better service than them, which illustrates that rent defaulters do have a sense of justice.

Logically, we then asked the question: what should we do to people who don't pay their rent, or wreck their neighbourhood and/or breach their tenancy conditions? Here, 80% said take action against them.

Now it began to get very serious, we asked the million dollar question, what action should we take against these bad tenants? Many called for a reduction in the services they received, but by far the most favoured action was to evict them as fast as possible. I suspect that eviction was the most popular option selected because we didn't offer hanging, stoning or crucifixion!

Our customers' opinions gave us a massive wake-up call, and a responsibility to do something about it. Uniquely, our survey picked up and gave voice to the core gripes that many people experience in their neighbourhoods. People are bewildered by the audacity and cockiness of troublemakers and often ask, "Why are these people allowed to get away with what they're up to? Why can't the housing officers stop it? Why do their homes get modernised before mine and why do they have a new front door fitted when everybody knows that they kicked it in last Saturday night?"

Our Gold Service philosophy was swiftly accepted in our neighbourhoods because it addresses a fundamental question of fairness. People liked it because it redressed the injustices that characterise our society. As landlords we were incredibly frustrated by the behaviours of a significant minority. It was grossly unfair that people who didn't pay their rent when it was due, and disrespected their homes and neighbourhoods, could largely continue their behaviour unchallenged.

We also had to consider our actions as a landlord: were we giving a first class service? And how did our customers feel about us? Were we treating people fairly, as consumers who expect a certain level of service in return for their money?

Furthermore, does society act fairly towards people living in social housing? The answer is frequently no: rented social housing is often portrayed as a 'loser' form of housing. It is stigmatised and residents on estates with a poor reputation – a bad postcode – are discriminated against in countless ways such as being unable to get house insurance.

Are the social problems experienced in neighbourhoods, at some level, a response to the unfairness residents saw all around them? I would argue that the success of Gold Service shows that they are, and that by tackling unfairness, we have made lasting, practical gains.

Our approach may shed some light on the motivation of the 2011 summer rioters. The analysis of the summer riots by the Home Office and Ministry of Justice shows that a large majority of those rioters arrested lived in our country's most deprived homes, in poor neighbourhoods and were people who struggled at school. It reveals that most looters were entangled in the spider's web of deprivation, unemployment, and criminality. Almost two thirds of the young rioters lived in the poorest districts in England and 42% of them were on free school meals.

David Cameron stated on 11 August 2011: "At the heart of all the violence sits the issue of street gangs who co-ordinated attacks on police and looted." But Mr Cameron, supported by Ed Miliband, Theresa May and Iain Duncan Smith, could not have got it more wrong. Only 13% of those arrested were gang members, rising to 19% in London.

Of course being a victim of so-called systemic societal problems does not justify the actions and behaviours of the summer rioters. Equally, knowing that poverty was a big contributing factor to the rioting is of cold comfort to the business community whose livelihoods were threatened – and in some instances destroyed, such as the owner of the baby wear shop in Ealing who found her stock had been taken out into the street and set on fire. Julian Richer's discreet philanthropy and generosity obviously counted for nothing when four of his shops were looted, at a cost of over half a million pounds. In addition to the financial impact, anybody who has been burgled will empathise with the feelings of violation experienced by the communities affected.

As was apparent at the time, much of the rioting was blatantly about looting and material gain. More than half of crimes perpetrated in the four days in August were against businesses, with electrical and clothing stores the top targets; only 19% were against vehicles and 13% were muggings.

As cases went to court, it emerged that 66% of the rioters were classified as having special educational needs (that is 300% higher than the national average), over a third had been expelled from school and only one in 10 had achieved the five A*-C GCSE grades.

The summer riots are another example of the reaction of people who do not feel a part of a rewarding society. There appears to be a growing alienation and disillusionment throughout our society, particularly among young people. Do such extreme events as the riots have to occur before we start learning lessons? Perhaps we should note that the majority of prisoners in the American penal system cannot read and write and that the US government can predict with a fair degree of accuracy the percentage of high school kids who will end up in prison, simply by looking at levels of illiteracy and innumeracy.

Our Gold Service philosophy addressed the injustices felt by the vast majority of law-abiding people who quietly contribute to communities, and whose citizenship often goes unnoticed. We designed it to try to restore pride and sense of justice into communities and to reward positive behaviour.

It has always been about changing behaviour. We changed our behaviour as a landlord and offered tenants a new deal. We invited them to change their behaviour and take responsibilities in exchange for privileges and extra services.

We asked ourselves, what might happen if we had high expectations of our customers and planned our service on that basis, offering customers a modern contract that matched the arrangements they have with every other supplier of goods and services that they deal with? What would happen if we treated our tenants with dignity and respect? Could we motivate people to improve their behaviour without threatening to take away their home?

How Gold Service works

Gold Service was set up as a voluntary scheme. Residents had to apply for membership by completing a simple form. They then had to satisfy the membership criteria, which were very straightforward:

- They must pay their rent on time for at least six weeks;
- They must pay their rent, plus any arrangement to repay arrears, for a period of at least 12 weeks;
- They must not break any other terms of their tenancy agreement.

If they fall short of these criteria after joining, they have their membership status suspended. We can do that in a minute – we don't mess about and we don't have to go to court.

We tried to make Gold Service simple to join, and simple to rejoin if membership is suspended. This does happen, usually because the resident has got into arrears, but as long as there are no other problems, membership is reinstated provided they abide by agreements.

At the same time, non-members of Gold Service were not penalised. They continued to receive the same level of service that any other housing provider in the UK delivers. The hope was that they would want more and would aim to join Gold Service by changing their behaviour. For the vast majority of residents, this is how it has worked out.

At its introduction, only 40% of Irwell Valley's customers qualified for Gold Service. By 2012, 92% were either members or had applied to become members. In itself that statistic is an indicator of a major shift in behaviour and attitude among our residents.

When we started, tenants ineligible for Gold Service reported significantly more repairs than Gold Service members. In other words, the bad customers were more demanding, and expensive, than the good customers. As the number of Gold Service members increased, this shifted to an even split between members and non-members and now most of our repairs are reported by Gold Service members, taking advantage of the fast service guaranteed by Gold Service membership. Because we get the work done promptly and efficiently, the average cost of repair is falling while customer satisfaction is rising.

After more than 12 years of steady success with Gold Service, we took a long, hard look at the scheme to ensure it would continue to provide the incentives we want. So in April 2012 we radically overhauled Gold Service and introduced a two tier scheme: Diamond Service and Standard Service. Standard customers are those who are not receiving anything extra – the people who are refusing to pay rent and persisting in wrecking their neighbourhoods. However, they continue to receive the statutory service.

For Diamond Service, we have a range of benefits, building on those offered by Gold Service.

In designing Gold Service, we bore in mind that the rewards for members had to be achievable and attractive enough to act as a real incentive and affect behavioural change. We have regularly reviewed and improved the benefits over the years. Lessons from the commercial sector show that to retain their effect, incentives have to keep moving and offer new things, so that people don't take them for granted. If you're going to have a rewards-based system, you can't stand still: you have to make sure the rewards are always attractive. Julian Richer emphasises this in his book *The Richer Way*: "What seems like a wonderful perk one year is taken for granted the next. It is only human nature to want more…Management's job is to keep the excitement going and this is the hardest part of motivation."

We have a range of benefits, offering gains for both individual households and the community as a whole. The basis of Gold Service was a cashback scheme. For each week a member qualified for Gold Service, they received £1. They had a personalised membership card, doubling up as a debit card on to which the Gold Service points were uploaded in November. This meant members got up to £52 just in time for Christmas. A long list of retailers accepted the card: not only local shops but large Manchester stores like Debenhams, House of Fraser, Selfridges and Argos.

Members could also choose what to do with their Gold Service cashback points. Instead of being taken as cash, they could be credited to the member's own home improvement account, or, for example, paid into a credit union account.

For Diamond Service, we have abolished the weekly voucher, as customers told us they found it less attractive, and customers are now entered into a draw for £3,000 each week. We hope this will be a powerful incentive for people to become, and remain, part of the scheme.

A key feature of Gold Service is the faster repairs service. We promised that we would provide a service to Gold Service members which would be better than the normal social housing sector standards. So for Gold Service members we undertook to complete emergency repairs in three hours, urgent repairs in three days and routine repairs in 14 calendar days.

Other benefits have included access to education and training grants and our multi million pound Golden Foundation. We brought in ways to use Gold Service monies in the community: our Community Gold encouraged residents to club together and obtain something of benefit for them all. When they pooled their points, we doubled the value. Examples of this are where elderly residents in sheltered housing bought musical equipment and large TVs for their communal lounges, while others invested in garden plants, bulbs and fountains.

A rewards system has to keep pushing forwards. A few years into Gold Service, we realised we wanted to reward our most loyal customers better, so all Gold Service members who maintained consistent membership over a two year period were automatically upgraded to Solid Gold membership. This gave them privileged customer service, extra money, regular prize draws, together with unlimited choices when it comes to upgrading their bathrooms, kitchens or front doors. They can even go to B & Q and other major suppliers, pick a kitchen of their choice which will be delivered to their home and fitted by us!

Results of Gold Service

Within three years of its introduction, Gold Service had produced measurable improvements. Rent arrears, which stood at 8.94% of rent due in 1998, dropped dramatically and are now less than 3%. Our target is zero arrears. We now collect over 100% of the rent due, which means we are collecting old arrears as well as current payments. Now, two thirds of our residents have no arrears at all and almost all of the rest are paying their rent and their debts. We have successfully created the payment culture we were seeking by rewarding the behaviours and outcomes which are good for our business and our customers.

As Gold Service became established and arrears dropped, evictions also dropped from 51 to 16 in 2010-11 and to their lowest ever level of 11 in 2011-12, which included only five customers who had not paid their rent in 2011. Our spending on security and tackling vandalism went down by a third.

What this meant was that we were getting better results, but spending more time and money rewarding people and less time and money penalising them. We had pushed the curve to the left.

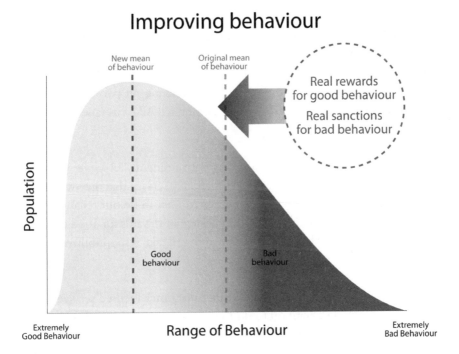

The return on Gold Service

At the beginning we calculated the true costs of dealing with all the trouble-some residents, rent arrears, anti-social behaviour and so on. We called this the negative expenditure budget – that is, all the areas of expenditure that were not adding value to our business. Three years after Gold Service was brought in, we calculated that the operational costs of Gold Service – which included the cashback, rewards and running costs – were £390,000. The savings in negative expenditure totalled £710,000. In effect, for every £1 spent on Gold Service, we received £2 back in savings.

In 2011 we spent around £363,000 a year on Gold Service, £260,000 of which went into residents' pockets as cashback. The savings have always continued, because we no longer have to spend the sums on chasing rents, processing evictions and so on that we were paying out back in the 1990s. This has freed up money to be spent on improving our services and the deal we offer our customers.

Gold Service was never just about savings, nor only about changing residents' behaviour. We effectively have reinvented ourselves as a housing business.

We all, landlords and customers, needed to get out of the rut of declining performance and declining expectations – the 'not bad' mindset. We stopped tolerating people who didn't pay their rent or respected their neighbourhood. Our residents stopped tolerating the repairs team turning up two weeks after the problem was reported. We all sharpened up our act. All of us raised our expectations and performance.

We set out to change our relationships with residents. First, we wanted our customers to have a high quality, value-for-money service that they would value and be keen not to lose. We wanted people to *want* to be our tenants and nobody else's. Gold Service then offered a package of rewards for good customers, to motivate people to change their behaviour and take responsibility for fulfilling their side of the tenancy agreement.

This required us to deliver a high quality, customer focused service. We had to change our whole operation to do this, with a new structure based on integrated specialist teams, and a radical new approach to our workforce. We set out to recruit and retain dedicated and enthusiastic people. We also had to get rid of dead wood, jobsworths and the thank-God-it's-Friday brigade.

We concentrated on trying to create the conditions in which people love coming to work, on unlocking potential and providing motivational opportunities with good pay and benefits, and ensuring everybody who works for us enjoys themselves. No business can deliver its vision unless it has fantastic people who believe in it.   Finally, we have tried to keep the whole thing simple, so that everyone understands what our business is all about.

Gold Service is not some exclusive club with arcane rules. It is a straightforward, easy-to-access service. We've got tenants on Gold Service who have Alzheimers, tenants who live in supported housing, and those who live in a hostel for troubled teenagers. We offer great deals, which tenants value and know that, if they don't meet the terms, they will lose. The challenge we set ourselves was to motivate people, inspire them and incentivise them. By doing that you create demand and we want people to demand our homes above any others on the planet.

A vision and a philosophy

Gold Service is not new or unique. Nineteenth century industrial philanthropists such as Lord Leverhulme, Robert Owen, Titus Salt and Lord Cadbury pioneered attempts to provide, not only good quality homes but a strong social environment too. In the 1990s, Bob Armstrong's Omaha Housing Authority showed what could be done in terms of self-sufficiency and motivational programmes for low income households.

Philanthropists are considered paternalistic these days. Their 'top down' approach to providing housing for their workforce or for low income households is out of tune with the ideas of market provision and freedom of choice. However, they undeniably provided work, homes and environments that people really aspired to. Spend time at any of the philanthropic villages, modelled on the Garden City principles of Ebenezer Howard, and the high quality environment and facilities provided through a combination of enlightenment, religion and social concerns are strikingly apparent.

It is interesting that the philanthropists, and the Omaha Housing Authority, saw their job as landlords as being about much more than the provision of roofs over people's heads. They put measures and facilities in place to allow people to develop themselves, make a success of their lives, learn entrepreneurial skills and ultimately, perhaps, become economically strong enough to decide whether they wanted to remain as tenants or not. Bob Armstrong never made any secret of the fact that he wanted residents to move up and out: a measure of success was how many people were able to move out of public housing, he believed.

The assumption these days is that social housing has no function except as a place to put people who can't afford to live anywhere better. The idea of social housing estates as good communities which have a particular strength of their own is usually misunderstood by owner-occupiers. Yet elsewhere in Europe, particularly Holland and Scandinavia, social housing is seen as a much more desirable option than in the UK.

Many social housing communities are fantastic places to live and people actively choose to live there, as they provide ideal neighbourhoods in which to bring up their families.

I know this from experience. I was brought up by my parents on a Garden City estate, built by the steel company John Summers and Sons to house workers and managers. We lived next door to two police houses. There were no voids, no graffiti, no vandalism, no anti-social behaviour and no rent arrears.

It was a marvellous place to live and grow up in. I never felt stigmatised or second class. With my mates I went to a good school and there were plenty of opportunities for us to get involved in football, tennis, youth clubs, scouts, sea and air cadets and so on. As I've admitted, I was a bit of a rebel, but I didn't go badly off the rails. Values were instilled into us from the start. If we messed about on our estate, not only would neighbours confront us, but my dad would also be informed at work.

Everyone kept their rent payments up-to-date, partly as a matter of personal pride but also because we didn't want to lose the home we valued. In other words, we all had something at stake. I have tried to build the same philosophy into Gold Service.

With Gold Service, we are trying to create a situation in which there is something at stake for our residents. It is now the case that people who pay their rent, look after their homes and do not infringe the rights of their neighbours, receive a greatly enhanced service from that offered to tenants who breach their contractual responsibilities. Gold Service cannot change the legislative framework. But by bringing in discretionary services and products people like, and want, we get back into a healthier balance of rights and responsibilities, saving money, restoring pride and encouraging success and fulfillment.

We have transformed the traditional relationship between landlord and tenant. Gold Service demonstrates that customer loyalty is as relevant to our business as it is to any other market sector. Our approach has worked because it is based on justice, fairness, toughness and is rooted in the psychology of human behaviour. That approach will continue with Diamond Service.

Tough but fair

With Gold Service, we provided an incentive for our customers to fulfill their responsibilities. We back that up with firm and swift action when people break the rules. Rewards only mean anything if the penalties mean something too.

Our previous approach to rent collection and arrears was very traditional and suffered from diminished returns. Standard letters were sent out and the process was long, drawn out and ineffective.

Now, we act quickly and decisively and at all stages of contact, Gold Service principles are applied. Tenants are made aware of their debt within a week, by letter or phone call. If they are Gold Service members, they receive a notice informing them that they are about to be suspended from Gold Service immediately because of rent default.

We do not make any empty threats. If a tenant doesn't pay (won't pay is different than can't pay), they are removed from Gold Service immediately. Breach your responsibilities and you no longer qualify – it's like reaching the limit on your credit card!

At that point, most take steps to get out of arrears, but their Gold Service membership is suspended until they do.

For others, we instigate legal proceedings promptly. Notices of Intention to Seek Possession are issued within three weeks and court proceedings begin at the earliest possible opportunity to obtain a Suspended Possession Order. This process is undertaken without fail.

Every possible opportunity is taken to talk to people, encourage them to pay and remind them of their rights and responsibilities and the benefits of Gold Service. I and other senior colleagues often visit tenants with high arrears to explain what is going to happen.

Everyone who reports a repair has his or her rent account checked by call centre operators. Good payers are thanked and their repairs ordered immediately. Bad payers are immediately referred to legal services to discuss the debt. Tough but fair action is taken.

This does not prevent us recognising genuine hardship. Every effort is made to maximise people's incomes. Skilled legal services and debt prevention officers deal sensitively with people's problems and have the power to help alleviate financial hardship. It is important to distinguish between people who need help (i.e. a hand up) and wilful, persistent debtors (with an insatiable thirst for hand outs).

A tough approach doesn't necessarily mean more evictions, as our performance confirms. In our experience evictions have reduced, because more people have paid, changed their behaviour and worked with us to get out of a cycle of debt and despair. Our philosophy had a big impact, as did early contact, firm but fair dealings and an emphasis on debt prevention and rehabilitation rather than enforcement. Letting people get deeper and deeper into debt does not do them any favours.

Reinforcing the message

One of our most contentious areas has been our policy of improvements for Gold Service members only.

When we embark on an improvement package – for example new windows or kitchens – this is available only to Gold Service members. In other words, non-members are not included unless the work is absolutely necessary, statutory or of a health and safety nature. Our maxim for non-members is to fix wherever possible, but not improve.

Is this unfair? For membership of Gold Service to mean anything, members have to see that they are getting something better than non-members.

Before any programme of improvement work is started, our colleagues visit residents, explain the nature of the programme and inform those in arrears that, unless a payment arrangement is made with the legal services team, they will not be getting the improvements. This has proved to be an extremely effective negotiating tool.

In one of our neighbourhoods, for example, new windows and doors were being installed. Three non-members were told they were ineligible for improvements until they agreed to repay their rent arrears. Two did pay up, became Gold Service members and had their homes modernised at the same time as everyone else; both tenants remain Gold Service members. The other resident abandoned the property.

Improving people's homes is an important part of any housing provider's job. However, it has to be done in the full knowledge that very often providers improve their worse customers' homes before their best customers' homes. This is usually because the worst customers' homes are in the worst state and therefore go to the top of the queue. But effectively it means the worst customers get preferential treatment. This psychology needs to be reversed. One of the main arguments that run through this book is that society should encourage and positively reward the values and behaviours that it wants people to aspire to. The corollary of this is that it should, wherever possible, and as sympathetically as possible, not reinforce the behaviours and values that it does not want.

Investing substantial amounts of money in the homes of those customers who are already in rent default, who very often order large numbers of repairs and make little contribution to their community, sends out all the wrong messages. Not only does it reinforce bad behaviour but it also causes frustration and bewilderment in the hearts and minds of good residents.

The same goes for the way in which day to day repairs are carried out. This transaction is an opportunity for any provider to link the importance of rent payments to the consumption of services. I believe that we are one of the few organisations in the country which checks every customer's rent account and discusses this with a customer every time they order a repair.

Our Gold and Solid Gold members get their repairs done extremely fast. Standard members receive the national standard of service (within one day for emergencies and five days for non-urgent repairs) but are also reminded of their rent paying obligations and informed of all of the benefits that they are missing out on.

Reinforcing relationships which emphasise the rights as well as the responsibilities of customers and providers is at the heart of everything we do. By continually linking payment to consumption we have managed to remind people of the benefits of paying their rent which together with other incentives and enforcement action has helped to create a payment, rather than an arrears, culture amongst our customers.

Since Easter 2010 I have had face to face encounters with more than 3,000 of our customers at evening social events, where we ask them questions about the way we operate and the values upon which our services are based. At every event, 100% of customers have stated they believe that paying rent on time is very important.

The results of our government funded consultation in 1998 have not changed. Residents still believe that people who pay their rent on time should get a more enhanced service than rent defaulters; and that rent defaulters should be evicted if they wilfully and persistently refuse to pay. This may seem a no-brainer to people outside the social housing sector, yet within it, it still causes consternation amongst housing professionals up and down the country, because in my opinion they don't understand the simplicity and importance of the business we are in.

The lessons from Gold Service

Gold Service is not really about the prize draw or the many other rewards. It is really about how we have reinvented ourselves and the relationship with our customers.

It is a value-based philosophy which we aim to live and breathe; we put it into practice in every action we do. It underpins our meritocratic remuneration and benefits package and our service delivery.

For many years we, like everyone else, spent the bulk of our time and money on our worst and most difficult residents. They received most of our attention, consumed most of our resources and drove many of our colleagues bonkers. We reset that position by rewarding the behaviours that our business relies on and which are morally just, benefiting the neighbourhoods and communities.

Perhaps it seems odd that we pay people to behave. Why should we pay people to pay their rent, when they are contractually obliged to do so, in theory? Well yes, in theory, but in practice some people do pay and some people don't. As a result of our reinvention we now run a highly successful efficient business which our customers value and our colleagues enjoy and respect. We have achieved this simply by clarifying what is important, what is right, and getting on with it.

We now spend most of our time with our good customers, raising the quality of the services we provide and their expectations. We continually look for new and more efficient and effective ways of ensuring that our best customers live in our best homes and enjoy our best services.

Paradoxically, new customers often get treated better than existing customers. You see this often in business: look how banks frequently offer their best rates exclusively to new savers. When landlords want to relet a property, they will paint it, renovate the kitchen and bathroom and so on. So new tenants move into a freshly done-up home, while their neighbours, who have been diligently paying their rent for 20 years, may be stuck with an old kitchen and bathroom. We don't think that is acceptable, so the principle we have applied since 2010 is that our best customers, who have usually been with us for many years, have preferential access to our best homes.

Because our Gold Service philosophy has worked, we spend far less money and time on the negatives and instead invest in enhancements to people's lives and neighbourhoods. The list of benefits we provide includes education grants, youth workers, swimming and exercise classes, school sponsorship, band stands, fruit trees, fountains, Christmas trees, carol concerts, rock and roll social events, variety shows and yes... hot tubs, which are very popular amongst our elderly customers. For my colleagues and I, having this relationship with our customers is much more fun than sweeping rubbish, picking up dog shit, mopping out urine drenched lifts and harassing low income people to pay their rent.

No society or business should do anything which reinforces or rewards bad behaviour, waste, negativity and disillusionment. We need to give people ambition, hope and the skills to be successful and self sufficient, whilst recognising people's capabilities.

A housing service should be so good that you don't even notice it – you just get on with your life. Regulators and consultants should stop continually inventing more complicated ways of doing simple things and insisting on actions that customers don't want and that don't add value. Simplification, business knowledge, customer focus and understanding the psychology of human behaviour and taking a leaf out of the tremendous works achieved by utopian philanthropists and the Garden City movement – these are lessons that we should all heed.

Chapter 5

Public services: time for a revolution

Can we improve the UK's public services? Is it even thinkable to talk about improving public services when, at a time of deep budget cuts, job losses and enormous pressure on the public purse, the highest aspiration might seem to be just to 'maintain' them?

I believe it is time for a radical revolution in public services. I actually think it would be mad to try to maintain them in their current state which, quite frankly, is not good.

It is noticeable that in 2011 people rallied around library services, which they genuinely value, but were not visibly rushing to the defence of other local authority services under threat of cuts. There has hardly been some mass consumer uprising in defence of five star quality public services, because the services just aren't that good.

More profoundly, the occupations and anti-capitalism demonstrations in London, Madrid, New York and elsewhere are indicators of a dissatisfaction that will only grow, unless confidence is restored in democracy and citizens begin to believe that they get a fair deal. Most public services are necessary for the functioning of a decent and ordered society, so why do they have such a bad reputation with both the public and central governments? And is it inevitable that they offer poor value for money?

These are questions we need to address if we are to tackle the problems in society as a whole. Good public services have a big role to play in dealing with those problems, and preventing them; bad services add to the problems or even, unwittingly, cause some in the first place. Public services should provide a platform upon which our society can achieve greatness and our economy can thrive. Germany and the Netherlands are great examples of this.

Ask anyone in Britain what they think of their local public services, and they will usually have a good word for teachers and nurses and, very often, their bin men, because rubbish collection is a very visible service and people appreciate it if it's done well. All the others, from the housing benefit to the architects' department, are seen vaguely by most people as 'pen-pushing bureaucrats' with gold-plated pensions. People have little idea what they do and therefore regard them as a waste of money.

This may be unfair, but really the hostile and intractable nature of public bureaucracy is to blame. Advancements in customer service have been made, but most people still dread having to deal with officialdom. Trying to claim any sort of benefit, talking to HM Revenues and Customs, ordering a new wheelie bin, re-registering your car with DVLC, or getting a new passport (with your photo rejected three times because you appear to be smiling or your nose is 1mm too far to the left of the picture) – they're all nightmare scenarios. If you think these are bad, ask anybody who's been pursued like a criminal fugitive by the Child Support Agency!

Public service staff appear trained to expect the worst from their customers: they assume you're going to be difficult. We, in turn, have become conditioned to expect, at best, an indifferent service from them. In many local authorities inefficiency is built into the system and they know their customers are in no position to complain – you certainly cannot withhold your council tax if you feel you have had a poor or inefficient service. I find it bizarre that councils have the option of jailing their customers who may have expressed their concerns about value for money.

Our organisation receives just over 50% of its income from housing benefit, which is paid to us from nine local authorities. Housing benefit payment delays are a perennial problem: we have had cases where customers waited almost a year for payment to come through. It is frequently paid four weeks in arrears and is an incredibly complicated and cumbersome form of housing subsidy, costing our nation £20bn or more per year. Imagine if local authorities processed their staff payroll along the same lines as housing benefit, paying staff up to 26 weeks in arrears because of 'incomplete payroll information'. Would their workforce accept that?

Of course, public sector services are nearly always monopoly industries. There is very little commercial imperative for them to improve because the people who use them can rarely, if ever, exercise customer choice. People can't vote with their feet or even with their money and say, "Salford's building control services were hopeless last time, so next time I'm going to Oldham's". Equally you can't recommend your local authority services to a friend who lives in a neighbouring area.

According to a 2007 report from the Department for Communities and Local Government, only 54% of people said they were satisfied with their council's services overall. Interestingly, in that same survey, around 75% of people said their area was a good place to live, where people got along well together. So there is strong community spirit and loyalty in the country, which public services are failing to tap into.

The penalty/reward balance

One of the problems is that public services have the penalty/reward balance all wrong. Local authorities routinely talk these days of their 'customers' but the word doesn't mean to them what it means to the commercial sector, partly because their customers can't shop around for a better service, and partly because, for public service providers, the customer is always wrong. Everyone has their horror story. I was taken aback to be faced with a sign in Stretford swimming baths which firmly proclaimed that nobody with diarrhoea was allowed to swim. I have no idea how they planned to monitor that... In the name of efficiency, doctors' surgeries introduce rules whereby you can only book an appointment by phone between 8am and 8.45am – you're not allowed to book one in person at the surgery. A friend of mine turned up at her surgery to be told she could only book an appointment by phone. She therefore dialled the receptionist from her mobile whilst standing in the waiting room and was given an appointment for later that morning.

Take recycling, an important issue which has been colossally badly handled by councils up and down the country. To get households to carry out recycling – a process which required people to change their habits and which therefore was never going to be easy – most councils instantly started off with threats and penalties. They made no effort to get residents' co-operation with the recycling task. Instead, people who barely understood what was going on were fined for not putting their greens in the brown bin and putting their yellow pages in the blue box and so on. A new bogey-person was created – the bin police... who seem to be mentored by East German Stasi.

There is another way. The Royal Borough of Windsor and Maidenhead chose to use the reward approach: residents can sign up to the RecycleBank scheme and earn points according to how much they recycle. The points get them discounts at local shops and services (including big names like Marks and Spencer and Legoland) or can be donated to schools or charities. When the borough ran this as a pilot scheme in 2009, participants' recycling went up by 35% and since then the scheme has been rolled out to more than 60,000 households.

Through this scheme, Windsor and Maidenhead will gain, not only increased recycling levels, but also greater goodwill from their residents. Sorting your rubbish out is never going to be a fun pastime, but a little bit of incentive makes it more pleasurable. The balance is shifted from resentment at a duty, to buy-in to a scheme that benefits the environment. Councils need to remember people are not all eco-maniacs who enjoy having their kitchens cluttered with various bins for food, tins, bottles, papers, plastic and so on, or who enjoy the streetscape that the wheelie bin furniture provides.

Another contentious issue in many areas is parking charges. Penalty-based parking charges in hospital and council car parks are deeply resented, in contrast to pay-on-exit charges which are generally viewed as fair. People hate having to pay a £50 penalty for being five minutes over their parking time and usually regard the whole thing as a cynical money-making exercise. Local authorities and health trusts don't seem to have realised how much these schemes have cost them in terms of public goodwill. Equally, devolving the responsibility to nefarious private-sector parking bandits who rapidly escalate a £30 fine to £250 does not absolve local authorities and health trusts of their responsibilities. Pick up any local paper and it will be full of complaints about unfair parking fines. It may be trivial but these are the issues which make people feel the public sector is an unjust and unfeeling machine.

Public authorities tend to take a legalistic approach that does not seem capable of dealing with individual cases. I have a regular monthly standing order to pay my council tax. One year I forgot to increase it and I received a huge document from the council, with dire threats in red ink, warning me that if I didn't pay the outstanding amount (£70) immediately, I would be taken to court and then presumably put in chains and thrown into a dungeon. Another year my standing order, which was due to run for 10 months actually ran for 12. Very kindly, the council said that they would make an adjustment and I therefore did not pay my council tax for the first two months of the new year. Again this produced threats of summonses.

When I rang up the council tax department, they were most pleasant and helpful and sorted things out straight away. But I was still smarting from the heavy duty threats, which were disproportionate to my 'offence'. The bureaucracy assumed I was a defaulter: no-one had taken the trouble to look at my file and say, this man has paid regularly for years, he has probably made a mistake, or maybe we have.

In other words, I was a good customer who was being treated like a bad customer and I resented that. The public sector is absolutely Olympian in its ability to antagonise people.

Product core and product surround

Why is this? One of the reasons is that public services have a poor grasp of the concept of product core/product surround.

Product core/product surround is something that marketing people take very seriously and we've devoted a lot of thought to it at Irwell Valley. To take a car as an example, its product core is the engine, the electronics, chassis and so on: everything that makes a car go. Around 80% of the cost of manufacture goes on the product core. Yet most drivers these days take little notice of the product core, unless it goes wrong.

The product surround only accounts for 20% of the cost of production, yet firms spend billions on developing the product surround of their vehicles, because that is what sells the car. Colour, styling and all the gadgets and gimmicks down to heated seating and nifty drinks holders – these are the things that people notice and on which they base their decision to buy.

With housing, the product core is really location location location. But people tend to choose a house on the product surround – whether they like the kitchen units and so on. Of course, kitchen units can be changed, while the location cannot – but most people are not that logical when they make their decision.

The product core/product surround concept tells us a lot about why people are dissatisfied with public services, when the services themselves feel they are doing a good job. To some extent they are right: often the product core is sound. When you get your new passport, you can be sure it is secure and fit for purpose. Unfortunately, what people remember is the product surround and the headache of having their photos rejected, the staff attitude, bureaucracy, queues at the Post Office and having to pay extra for a speedier service.

If you are homeless, the product core is quite good: when you approach the authorities you can be off the streets and have a roof over your head within hours. But the product surround – all the forms you have to fill in, the way you are talked to – is stressful and probably leaves you angry and resentful.

Product core/product surround is particularly relevant to the health service. The product core – the medical treatment – is a specialised service which few unqualified people understand. So most health consumers base their opinion of the service on the product surround, which can be dreadful.

Undoubtedly the health product core in the UK is good: we have highly trained people who are skilled at their jobs and have the technology to carry out advanced procedures.

But while hospitals are increasingly good at saving lives, they are increasingly bad at caring for people. Recent surveys have reported this, but anyone who has been in hospital as either a visitor or a patient already knows. From the overpriced car park to the overheated wards, the waiting rooms with their three-legged chairs, the wheelchairs with buckled wheels mouldering in a corner and the toilets with sticky floors, the whole environment makes you depressed, irritated and uncomfortable. The organisation is usually chaotic, with the patient or their companion typically having to relate their case history to a succession of nurses and junior doctors, each of whom then disappears, never to be seen again, so that you have to go through the same procedure with the next person. And I'm not even going to start on the awful food. Why is hospital food so bad? It's much worse than prison food. I presume this is because, once again, the consumer has no choice, but it is baffling why hospitals cannot see that diet is an important part of people's care and recuperation.

Underneath these visible annoyances are more serious problems. The failure to maintain basic cleanliness has meant people who have gone into hospital for routine procedures have come out crippled, through MRSA. One of our local hospitals is nicknamed Septicaemia General and most people, the elderly in particular, dread going there.

Everyone knows these problems. Every health trust has promised to tackle them, but somehow nothing really improves. Yet people always compliment the nurses and doctors – they do feel that there are people in the health service doing their best.

The failure of personal responsibility

At the heart of these public services is a fundamental inability to actually give a good service. Why? It is not to do with money: it is to do with people. A good nurse earns the same as a bad nurse. The difference is down to personal responsibility. With the health service, when you are ill and at your most vulnerable, you find yourself in an environment which is structured so that you feel no-one takes personal responsibility for you.

I visited a friend in hospital once. For the three days he was in there, there was a sign above his bed saying: 'your personal nurse is…' A name was written in. This nurse never appeared. We asked for her one evening, when my friend was in distress. None of the other nurses were sure who she was.

Contrast a hospital with a hospice. You would think that a hospice, where all the patients are terminally ill, would be a far worse place to be. In fact the opposite is true: the ones I've seen have been happy, peaceful places, where people receive a very high standard of care. The paid staff and the volunteers who work there treat the patients as equals, as human beings who deserve to be treated with dignity and honesty.

Because they are charities, relying largely on volunteers, hospices don't have a public sector mentality. The people who work there quite naturally take personal responsibility for the care of the patients; they wouldn't think of doing otherwise. At Nightingale House in Wrexham, where my mother Josie died, the care was of an incredibly high nature. They offered a la carte menus, Sky TV, beautiful gardens and a drinks trolley. Was this because residents were terminally ill or because of the personal responsibility taken by staff and volunteers to provide people with a dignified and respectful experience?

Most public services are structured to suit the professional, legal or bureau-cratic requirements of the organisation. They are not structured to suit the needs of the people receiving the service. Indeed, the customer is often re-garded as a nuisance or an interruption who prevents staff from getting on with their job.

It is noticeable that our worse problems in public services are to do with the delivery of care, in some form or other. The greatest failures, some tragic and shameful, have been in social services, hospitals, old people's homes, youth of-fenders institutions and children's homes. In all these places, staff have to pro-vide care to people who are vulnerable, but also frequently difficult, demanding, unco-operative and exploitative. Giving care in these circumstances is extremely hard work – but this is not acknowledged by organisations. Providing care should be the product core of these services, yet over the years it has been pushed to the side, with the product core now regarded as compliance with regulations, form-filling, reporting to inspectors and keeping within budget (al-though many health trusts are struggling with their finances).

This failure of care can be seen throughout society and reflects our deep-down unwillingness to engage with other people as individuals. Society's pri-orities can be seen clearly in old people's homes and nursing homes, which operate in the marketplace. The administrative staff will always be paid more than the care staff. In fact care worker jobs are pretty much at minimum wage, and, in terms of social cachet, rank barely higher than a cleaning job.

So is it surprising that our public services are poor when the people dealing with that irrational, unpredictable thing, the customer, are nearly always the most junior, at the bottom of the hierarchy, over-stretched and under-valued?

What I'm talking about here, once again, is behaviour. Care is behaviour. Ad-ministering medication correctly is essential in a hospital ward or nursing home, but it isn't care: care is responding to the patient or resident as an individual, with particular needs.

The fascinating thing is that staff behaviour doesn't cost anything. It's a non-cost item for people to say good morning with a smile, to be upbeat, to gen-uinely listen to what the customer/patient/resident is saying. Once you have those things, you can begin to transform the product surround. Maybe the paint will still be peeling and the chairs slashed, but people will have a much better experience of the service.

It's a well known saying that it's people who make the place. If we want customers to have a better experience of public services, we need to change the behaviour of people delivering those services, particularly the ones who provide the product surround. That has to be done through excellent management and courageous leadership, creating inspirational environments which encourage motivation.

Welcome to Planet Housing Officer

At the same time, we have to look at our public services staff and ask, what are they being asked to do? Are we asking teachers to teach, or provide a stream of detailed lesson plans, or impose discipline on troubled children who have chaotic home lives? These are three different kinds of jobs, calling for different skills: which do we want them to do? Do we want social workers at all? And if we want them, do we want them to spend their time at the computer, or to be out there face to face with their clients? Are welfare benefits officers supposed to enable people to claim benefits, or to motivate people to find and fulfil their potential and thereby minimise the number of people claiming?

The chances are frontline staff will spend most of their time dealing with the worst customers – the aggressive, the dishonest, the disruptive, the 20% who take up 80% of their time. Is it their job to deal with people who are drugged up, drunk or have mental health problems? In some cases, yes it will be, but we need to be clear about what we are asking them to do, or else we should not be surprised if their performance suffers because they are caught up with problems that they have responsibility for, but no authority to solve. Nobody should be asked to take responsibility for anything that they don't have the authority to solve.

When Irwell Valley was facing some of its toughest challenges, I used to walk around some neighbourhoods and think, "Welcome to Planet Housing Officer."

Planet Housing Officer was a grim place, populated by hostile troublemakers and low-life, its environment filled with graffiti, dumped rubbish and wrecked buildings. Its daily life was often dominated by evictions, vandalism, voids, nuisance, arrears, white dog muck, tyres over lamp-posts, trainers hanging off telephone lines, lots of people smoking, hoodies, drinkers, bookies and ASBOs.

We have many neighbourhoods that are fantastic. They are calm, friendly and a pleasure to live in. In the past our housing officers never visited those places because 80% of their time was spent on Planet Housing Officer. That was what their job had come to be all about, and no-one had suggested any different. They had no time, nor any reason, to meet the nice tenants, the Auntie Beryls, who would give them a cup of tea and a smile.

So how could we expect them to step out of that morass of despair, helplessness and hopelessness and become an upbeat, motivated, customer service expert, taking pride in their achievements and in the opportunity they have to work closely with our customers?

It is much easier to give fantastic customer service in the housing sector if you avoid Planet Housing Officer. Call centre staff are largely insulated from the negativity and they do a good job, often sorting out people's problems over the phone with patience and cheerfulness. Equally IT, finance and back-office staff rarely find themselves on Planet Housing Officer. But front line housing repairs and maintenance colleagues were plodding around for most of their working week in this quagmire of misery, complaints and everything else that inevitably would make them deeply cynical.

The people who caused this scenario might only have been a very small proportion of the client base, but they were the ones whose names and homes our officers knew. It is ironic that in every housing organisation I visit, staff know the names of the worst customers and not the best ones, because they never meet their best customers. Through our philosophy of Gold Service, leadership, careful recruitment and coaching we have managed to turn this round so that we engage with our best customers for most of the time, and develop active relationships with them.

Cultural change

Transforming a public sector organisation into one with an up-beat, can-do mentality, where people treat each other with dignity and respect, enjoy their rights, fulfil their responsibilities, and are eager to find and fulfil their potential, needs fundamental cultural change. To make Gold Service work we had to restructure the organisation radically, and I'll say more about this in the next chapter.

Restructuring is nothing new to the public sector or to housing associations, in fact some public services live with constant restructuring, but we didn't do the textbook management change exhorted by consultants. We simplified and flattened the management and board structures, directed far more resources towards the front line, and put motivation and inspiration at the core of our ethos.

You cannot expect downtrodden, mistrusted and mistreated people to give legendary customer service. Unfortunately, creating the conditions in which public sector workers can generally enjoy high levels of motivation is an uphill struggle, given the way public services are usually run. Most of them operate in a culture of low expectation and conflicting messages, where staff are told one thing, but expected to do something else.

When our organisation took over the Sale estate from Manchester City Council, in a stock transfer deal, five housing officers also transferred to us from the city council. Between them, they had nearly 100 years of service in local government. They had a traditional approach to their work, were very subdued and had low self esteem. This is probably not surprising, given that Sale tenants had delivered a massive vote of no confidence in them, 93% of the tenants voting in favour of the estate leaving the city council and being taken on by Irwell Valley. The ex-council employees amazed us by insisting on clocking on and off. We were quite happy for them to put their hours on the timesheet like everyone else, but they were highly resistant to change. They transferred, as is usual in these cases, with TUPE (transferred under protected employment) rights. This is a deal designed to protect public sector workers if their jobs are privatised. I didn't realise until we inherited our TUPE staff, that they are more protected than Minke whales. We wanted to get them off TUPE so that we could increase their pay It took us three years to persuade them to relinquish TUPE, but being solid old stagers they continued to be the only people in the organisation who clocked on and off four times a day, five days a week until they retired.

Maybe it's not surprising that they weren't the most dynamic and go-ahead of people, but their attitudes did encapsulate all that I found wearisome when working for local authorities and which we all combat at Irwell Valley. It's the 'not bad' attitude again.

One of the things we try to do is to break the public sector mindset by reminding people what a fantastic opportunity we have to make a huge difference to people's lives whilst developing our own personal and professional skills. We should celebrate that, by saying, not, "I wish it was Friday", but, "thank God it's Monday."

Michelangelo epitomised the need for ambition when he stated: "The greatest danger for most of us is not that we set ourselves targets that are too high and then miss them, but that we set them too low and hit them."

I once visited the Sistine Chapel in the Vatican and imagined how the ceiling would look if a public sector maintenance team won the contract to paint it. Of course it would be magnolia. You can imagine the painters happily slapping it on to the cherubs and cherubims, walloping it into the corners, maybe adding a bit of artex here and there, with the main ambition being to get off the job as soon as possible and definitely no later than 4pm.

Being an ambitious, high achieving organisation does not sit well with the way public services operate. Traditional public sector work ethics and methods are a big part of the problem. Local authorities may have stripped out layers of management in recent years, but they are still dominated by hierarchies and bureaucracies. Politics is ever present, of course, but cannot be discussed openly. In local government you frequently have an incongruence between the stated values of the organisation and those of the people who run it. Certainly in housing I found that as an employee you struggled with this alien concept of customer care, which often conflicted with the other messages you were getting – the leader wants this, the executive member for housing wants that, the trade unions will not have that and we can't do this because of health and safety... A lot of very intelligent, altruistic and committed people work in councils, health trusts and government departments and agencies, but they find it very difficult to do the job they really want to do or, more importantly, the job that they know they should do.

Challenging the received wisdom

I have made every effort to employ a wide range of people from a variety of different backgrounds, who have the right mentality, are flexible and who want to succeed. We employed people from estate agents to take over our lettings because, although the people who ran our lettings sections were good, they were locked into the lethargic public sector mindset.

The social housing business has many assumptions, which I regularly challenge. One of these is: empty properties must be immediately sheeted up – that is, have steel sheets nailed over the doors and windows. No-one does this in the owner-occupied sector, but everyone does it in the social housing sector, so a perfectly good home looks intimidating, unwanted and vandalised, and in fact pollutes the entire street.

Years ago, one of our housing officers took a tenant to see a property. She undid the steel door and told the tenant to go into this murky little dungeon. "You nip in and I'll stay out here to make sure my car's alright," she said. The prospective tenant didn't exactly get a huge signal that this was a desirable place for her and her family to live, and we realised that the housing officer's future with us could be calculated in minutes.

Our ex-estate agent lettings colleagues brought a refreshing attitude to the job, challenging received public sector wisdom. They asked questions like, why can't we let properties on the same day they become empty, and why is there difficulty letting end of terrace properties, when these are at a premium in the private sector? It became clear that the standard answers to these questions were really no more than fatuous excuses: we can't let properties on the same day because sometimes people abandon their homes without warning and we haven't got another tenant lined up to move in. People feel vulnerable in end of terraces because they think they will be more at risk of burglary. In contrast, as former estate agents, our new colleagues worked from the premise that these were desirable properties, because being end of terrace means you live in a semi-detached property, with one less neighbour to worry about. With this positive attitude towards these properties, they were very successful in letting them.

They came up with strategies for letting good properties in bad neighbourhoods, for sheltered accommodation, young person's accommodation and hostel and family homes. They worked their socks off to eliminate down-time, along the lines that Easy Jet and Ryan Air use (without the hidden small print penalties) – so much so that we let almost 40% of our properties on the same day they become vacant and all the rest within an average of five days, compared to the north west average of 44 days! We are vigorously working towards letting every property on the same day it becomes vacant.

They were willing to go out to properties at night, and were happy to open up show houses or meet prospective tenants at the weekend, as that was what they had been used to in the private sector. They arranged their way of working around what customers wanted, not around their personal lives.

Our leadership coaches helped them understand the importance of rent to our business, (it being our only source of income) and schooled them in the regulatory framework, which did mean they had to tone down some of their private sector estate agent enthusiasm. We made it clear that you need to be straight with prospective tenants and it's no good telling people that a two-up, two-down in the highest crime division in Salford is a nice little fisherman's cottage. We hope to have a long-term relationship with our tenants, so it has to be based on truth from the outset. We also told them we don't want our properties filled with headbangers who are going to take up all legal services' time trying to evict them. They needed to find people who both understand the rules and also qualify for the property because they're in need, and they also had to be mindful of our equal opportunities programmes which sit at the centre of all of our policies.

Public services are nearly always based on assumptions that are set in concrete and often are a serious obstacle to excellent service delivery. This is true in social housing and I'll bet it is the same for any service you care to mention. It takes strong leadership to challenge these assumptions, but that is the only way to obtain the efficiency gains that are so necessary, sought after and so difficult to achieve in public services.

In the owner-occupied sector, for example, when you move house, it is almost always the case that the previous owner moves out and the new owner moves in on the same day, usually around 12 noon. It makes for a rather fraught few hours, but people's enthusiasm carries them through. They badger their estate agents and solicitors, cajole the removal men, organise the gas and electric readings, open the door and shout "we're in!"

In the social housing sector, things are nothing like that. The average is 44 working days to let a property – which means a two month rent loss. If you multiply this by the number of lettings an organisation makes every year (between 12 and 15% of their properties) you're talking huge sums of money.

The assumption, for years, has been that this is how lettings have to operate. When we were taking 21 days to get a property occupied, our performance looked pretty good against the national average. As mentioned, we're down to five days and 40% let on the day they become empty. Five working days is great, except that it still means the place is standing empty for a week, losing valuable rent.

So you have to take an axe to the assumptions. Why does it take 44 days to let a property? The typical social housing response is, oh well it's because of health and safety, we have to carry out checks on the gas appliances and so on.

Of course this is necessary, but it doesn't take 44 days to do. It could easily be done in the days before the previous tenant moves out. Again, there may be work needed to the kitchen and bathroom, but this work should be done when the new tenant moves in, and to their requirements, just as happens when you buy a house. The new tenant will move in to a place that has a less than perfect kitchen and bathroom, but the upside is that they know these will be refurbished or refitted in exactly the way they want them, and we can promise to prioritise that work whilst we're receiving rent.

Our principle is that our best customers should get first pick of our properties. Typically we have 500 relets a year and our best customers are entitled to move into one of these homes if they so choose. We work with them so that they get the fixtures and fittings they want, not what we think they want. We also organise it so that someone moves in to their former house the day they move out.

With people's co-operation, we can achieve back-to-back lettings: one in one out, which means no rent loss, no sheeting-up or neighbourhood blight, no vandalism or damage to the property, reduced administration, happy customers and millions of pounds saved every year. This approach could easily be applied nationally and would yield massive savings.

You have to obsessively challenge assumptions. For example, one of the excuses offered to prop up excessive relet times was that we couldn't possibly let our properties on the same day they became empty, because customers had abandoned their homes without prior warning. Very often housing professionals accepted this excuse without question. But we believe that excuses are reasons for failure.

People don't abandon the roof over their head on the spur of the moment: there is always a chain of events leading up to that, a history of debt and so on. We expect our managers to know their customers well enough to hear the alarm bells ringing when there is a risk of abandonment and take action to avert it. We have now got abandonments down to less than 1% of our relets – that is, only two per year.

All of the assumptions within the social housing sector, that rent arrears, empty properties and bad debts are inevitable, must equally be challenged and serious concentrated thought applied to solving these issues, which I believe only occur because we allow them to through our professional conditioning. These three issues cost housing associations in England and Wales alone three quarters of a billion pounds a year. Over the lifetime of a Parliament, if housing associations collected their rent and let all their properties on the day they become empty, they would save just under £4 billion. I'm sure even Michelangelo would acknowledge that that is worth aiming for.

Our experience demonstrates that it is perfectly possible to tackle seemingly intractable problems, if you are ambitious, motivated and believe that you can succeed. If human beings can fly to the moon, replace people's hearts and lungs and invent submarines that can navigate under the polar ice caps, then surely we can collect rent!

Target zero

Housing associations have three main areas of expenditure. First there is the loan debt on our properties: that is a given cost every year, which we can't change. The other two areas, over which we do have discretion, are staff costs and repair and maintenance costs.

Maintenance is the cost which is most flexible – you can easily choose to do more of it or less of it, depending on your budget. But whether you do more or less affects the service to your customers. Organisations say, this is the number of staff we've got, this is the debt we've got, so this is what we have left over to spend on the quality of our properties.

In contrast, our priorities are different. We take our debt costs, then say – what do we want to do for our customers? The sum left over is for staff. You can also raise the enumerator i.e., collect more rent!

We lose in two ways through rent arrears: firstly by not getting the income, and secondly by spending time and money chasing the debt. If we are getting the rent collected (and don't forget it has already come out of the public purse in the form of housing benefit), we have many more choices. We can spend more on colleagues, improve the service to customers, or repay our loans more quickly.

Since 2010 we've had five zero targets, one of which is zero rent arrears. In his book *On Leadership*, Allan Leighton says we will never achieve ambitious targets unless we set ambitious ones. Despite having a low level of arrears, thanks to Gold Service, we have committed ourselves to driving forwards even faster towards a complete payment culture, rather than an arrears culture.

To most social landlords, having such a target will seem crazy. But we as a company, in partnership with our customers, have decided that we will not tolerate rent arrears. Nobody said it would be easy, but the harder you try you luckier you get, and there are neighbourhoods where we've already achieved our goal.

Back in December 2008, just after the market crash, we bought properties on a privately built estate, in what was effectively a fire sale. At the time, property prices were falling but nobody knew what the market floor was, so taking the decision to buy was something of a gamble. However it was a successful move, and we gained 32 properties including four-bedroomed, detached houses with double garage, pepperpotted throughout a desirable development.

We were determined that this venture should make a profit from day one. We also knew that our operations would require sensitive management. Our properties were surrounded by others on the estate which had been had bought at the height of the market for over a quarter of a million pounds and were now being sold at an average price of £70,000. We recognised that the owners would be sceptical about a housing association (with all the usual connotations and stereotypes about our customers) moving in, fearing that we would dump undesirables in there, drag house values down and wreck the place.

I'm proud to say that it is one of the best acquisitions we have ever made. Tenants have displayed almost perfect behaviour and run up not a single pound in rent arrears. It is impossible to tell our properties from the owner-occupied houses. I've had only two letters from our customers, one family asking if they could install a wrought iron gate and the other requesting permission to put up a satellite dish. There have been no complaints from owner-occupiers. Only two properties have become available in the three years we've owned them and they were let on the same day they became vacant. There is no dog muck, graffiti or vandalism. There are beautiful flower beds, clean and well maintained gardens and people are happily getting on with their lives.

Yes, we were careful about whom we housed on that estate, but we didn't cherry pick. Some of the tenants are in work, others are not. We used six month probationary tenancies in case we had to weed out any troublemakers (with a probationary tenancy you can evict without going to court if the customers fail to meet the requirements of their tenancy agreement) but we didn't have to take any action. I believe that people there pay their rent because they value their homes and the services we provide and because they have been told from the outset that non-payment of rent is not an option. Most of them probably still can't believe their luck, living in such nice homes.

Rent arrears are usually nothing to do with lack of money. If people are suffering genuine hardship, there are ways to help them, but our most difficult debtors are not usually suffering hardship at all. A couple of years ago we evicted a household who were real neighbours from hell, complete with brace of rottweilers. They were heavily in arrears but the man rang me up and offered to pay £500 off the debt so they wouldn't be evicted.

I said no, they'd had their chance to pay many times. "OK, a grand," he said. No, I said. He said, "Come on Tom, fifteen hundred quid." Again I said no. He insisted: "Look Tom, what if I give you two grand?"

I don't know where he was going to get the money from, but he seemed in no doubt that he could deliver. Nevertheless, I said no. Because I knew that even if they coughed up the money this time, they'd go straight back to not paying and make their neighbours' lives a misery. We did offer to rehouse them in our family intervention project, which is specifically designed to teach families how to behave, but it in the end they abandoned the property, leaving abusive graffiti sprayed all over the walls. Although we couldn't re-let this property on the same day it was abandoned, we did nevertheless manage to re-let it in nine days. We don't miss having them as tenants, but it was interesting that they could find the money if they wanted to.

We need to be clear what our role is. We are landlords, and I don't regard it as our job to continue to provide accommodation for people who flagrantly, wilfully and repeatedly break the rules. We always aim to provide an excellent service and in doing so have to be strong enough to take a tough line with people who abuse our colleagues and our customers, wasting our time and money.

This can be difficult: it is not easy to stand up to bullies but there is no way round this. It is worth noting that recent social services failures, such as the terrible Baby P or Khyra Ishaq cases, came about largely because a succession of people – social workers, health workers, even the police – were not strong enough (or felt they did not have enough support from their superiors) to stand up to bullying abusers. It was easier for them not to take personal responsibility, and their managers and leaders allowed that to happen.

Dealing with tough situations requires bottle, strong motivation, a clear grasp of what your job is and where your authority and support come from. It is the leader's job to create the conditions to generate positivity and enthuse people. The leader must provide a simple, compelling vision of the future, engendering confidence in everyone. Having the courage of your convictions and continually being prepared to challene the status quo and demand advancement should be taken as normal – and should be applauded.

Chapter 6

Managing and motivating

So how can you create the kind of organisation and society which not only delivers public services, but also enhances and improves people's lives – efficiently and effectively, without wasting money?

We had to ask ourselves this big question, because it was no good promising Gold Service to our customers if our organisation wasn't up to the task of delivering it, in terms of both its structure and the willingness and ability of our people. We've developed a business and service delivery model here which works, and which can be applied to other business and public services. I also believe that our philosophy has broader applicability throughout society.

In the last few years, I've learned a lot from Julian Richer. His hi-fi and TV retail chain, Richer Sounds, is famous for its top-class customer care, and his guiding principle has always been clear and strong. As he puts it in his book *The Richer Way*: "Respect for people has to be at the heart of your organisation. Only then will you have a well motivated and productive workforce. Only then will that flow into good customer service and only then will your business prosper."

The strength of Julian's approach is that he has a clearly thought-out and structured approach to motivating his staff. He recognises that pay is only one of the things motivating people, and that work has to be fun as well as disciplined. This is not some cuddly feel-good thinking, but an approach that produces results in the highly competitive world of electronics retailing.

His arguments are just as relevant to public services as to the commercial sector – perhaps even more relevant, given the low state of morale and performance in the public sector, now exacerbated by the coalition government's public expenditure cuts. "The important thing is to develop a systematic and effective approach to motivating staff," Julian Richer says in his book. "Anyone can do this. You do not have to have charismatic managers or be in a glamorous industry to have well motivated staff. There is no excuse for not getting the best out of your workforce."

New Mutualism

We've coined the phrase 'New Mutualism' to describe our approach. Our organisation is non-profit making: we aim to make a surplus each year, to be invested back into the business. Everyone who works here is an employee, including myself. We're saying: our purpose as an organisation is to benefit the customers, but we, as employees, are also beneficiaries of the work we do here. Working together, we gain a mutual benefit, and also have a mutual responsibility to ensure the organisation is effective and strong. Our maxim is, treat people with dignity and respect. Furthermore, treat people as *they* would like to be treated, not as you would like to be treated.

An organisation is at its best when the people who work there believe in it, understand it and have a stake in it. They have to know that it is in their interests for the business to be successful. In the commercial sector, for example, John Lewis does this directly by making all its employees shareholders in the company. At Irwell Valley, our customers are our shareholders and we have the advantage that what we do is of benefit to the community. We attract committed colleagues who want to make a difference to other people's lives. I see this as a massive strength which, potentially, all business and public services have. We continually try to capitalise on our ethics and make sure that we maintain and build on our colleagues' commitment, instead of letting it dribble away in bureaucracy and ineffectual pettiness.

The leadership of the organisation needs to make sure every person in the workforce understands the mutual benefit and the mutual responsibility that binds everyone together.

This responsibility is very much put to the test during austere times. When we are faced with public spending cuts, everyone has to pull together to ensure that the organisation continues to deliver a good service. So in 2010 we froze pay and no-one took bonuses. This applied across the board, because one of the things that really undermines an organisation is an 'us and them' situation. We are always conscious of that. None of the managers, including myself as chief executive, has any benefits that others don't have. Pay, of course, varies throughout the organisation, but the benefits – private health care and so on – are universal. I don't have a private office or a personal car parking space or any of the other things managers use to distance themselves from their employees. As I've said, I'm an employee: my employer is the Irwell Valley board. I belong to a union, as I always have done. I can look colleagues in the eye and know there's no perk I have that they haven't got, because that would destroy the whole ethos.

This is crucial, because if you want to claim you're an egalitarian organisation and say that every job is vitally and equally important, you must have practices which are congruent with the message and reinforce it honestly. It is no good trying to motivate people by saying, "We all count, we're all in this together" and then having a hierarchical structure that conveys exactly the opposite message. People are very quick to spot hypocrisy and will have no trust in managers who say "We've all got to make sacrifices" but cling on to their own perks and preside over cultural incongruence .

The curve in the workplace

What we continually strive for with our meritocratic approach is corporate excellence through tough rights and tough responsibilities. The behaviour curve applies just as much to a workplace as any other situation. You have your best employees – keen, organised, effective – on one side of the graph and your worst – lazy, incompetent, chaotic – on the other. Most people are in the middle, but you very much want them to be on the keen and effective side. Hoewever, needless to say, if they see colleagues get away with turning up late for work, taking every Monday off sick, being rude to customers and so on, their own behaviour will start to deteriorate. Workplaces are quite small communities and no-one's behaviour goes unnoticed within a team. Behaviour and morale are linked together and there is, in fact, no satisfaction to be gained from giving a bad service to disgruntled customers, so morale will quickly deteriorate too.

Oganisations need to prevent or arrest this downward spiral. Instead, they must create a situation in which excellent behaviour (in other words, excellent performance at work) is recognised, respected and rewarded. People will aspire to the rewards, improve their performance and an upward spiral will develop, creating an active, motivated workforce with high aspirations and expectations.

Behavioural science has demonstrated that reward is an extremely powerful tool for changing behaviour.

Professor Cary Cooper, Distinguished Professor of Organisational Psychology and Health at Lancaster University Management School, says it has been shown that the key to changing behaviour is to reinforce the behaviour you want, by using praise and reward.

He explains: "In many workplaces, people are managed by negative feedback and fault finding. Managers only tell them about the things they have done wrong. Rarely are people managed by praise and reward. But the most effective way is a balance of both, with regular positive feedback, and negative feedback used in a constructive way."

Numerous studies have shown that in changing and managing other people's behaviour, praise and reward is the most effective management style, Professor Cooper says. "So when people have done well, the manager reinforces that by praising them for doing a good job. There can be a system of reward, financial or through promotion, but day to day the most important factor is the psychological reinforcement through praise and recognition.

"However, it has to be linked to something specific the person has done, or it becomes meaningless. You can't just have a general "you're all great." That has little effect."

When people do get it wrong at work, the manager has to say so and give negative feedback. "But the way you give it is important," Professor Cooper says. "You can be aggressive, focusing on blame, but if you just shout at people, they'll resent it, and they'll lose confidence and feel negative about themselves. It's better to give constructive feedback, saying for instance, "That's a good effort but next time could you do it this way…"

"It's even more effective if you get the person to suggest ways they could have done that job better. It's important to engage people by making them think about what they should be doing, so that they have ownership of the solution. The more you can get people to think of the solution to a problem themselves, the more likely they are to change their behaviour."

Professor Cooper's findings link back to what I've said about personal responsibility – acknowledging mistakes and coming up with solutions.

All we ask of our colleagues is, to use the cliché, a fair day's work for a fair day's pay. We provide the fair day's pay (and more); what we are trying to do is motivate people to deliver that fair day's work. We are only asking for seven hours work each day – but we want seven hours of committed, intelligent and effective work. We don't want people working long hours. I've watched people be present in an office all day and do nothing. I've seen other people come in to a situation for half an hour and revolutionise it.

Happy and unhappy neighbourhoods

Looking at the health of an organisation, you have to remember that a work-place – accounts office, local housing office, call centre – is a neighbourhood of people, and like any other neighbourhood it can be either happy or unhappy, either pulling together, or riddled with cynicism and anti-social behaviour.

I've noticed that a key indicator of an organisation in terminal decline is the state of its tea fund. If you want an example of how human beings can tear each other to bits, while their bosses wonder, oblivious, why performance is so poor, just look at your average office tea fund.

I once did some consultancy work at a local authority. The director wanted advice on how to 'empower' staff. Empower them to do what, I wondered? I presumed she didn't mean empower them to be rude to customers and go home early. Well, to be a bit more positive and work better as a team, the director thought.

The staff didn't have many benefits, apart from flexitime. I asked: "What values do you have here? How do you convey those values to staff? How do you tap into their belief systems?" She said they had a staff conference once a year. I know what staff conferences are like: the bosses stand up in front of everyone, tell them how great they all are but difficult times lie ahead etc. Then for the rest of the year staff are pretty much ignored.

"Do you do anything special as a team?" I asked. "Er, we go for a drink at Christmas," she suggested. And do they get free coffee and tea in the office? She said: "No. We have a tea fund, well we used to have a tea fund. But now everybody in the office brews up individually…"

I knew why. An office with a tea fund is an office with serious issues. Think about it. The most junior member of staff is usually put in charge of collecting the money and buying the drinks, milk and biscuits. He stocks up on Nescafe, a box of PG Tips, a few pints of semi-skimmed and a packet of custard creams. Immediately, people aren't happy. Some want Earl Grey, one only drinks Lapsang Souchong, several demand decaffeinated coffee. The slimmers want skimmed milk, the non-slimmers are grumbling that there aren't any Hobnobs.

Then there's the jar of money into which people are supposed to pay. Some people pay in every week, others don't. Some people say, "Hang on, she drinks twice as much as me, why isn't she paying double?" and so it goes on. The money jar usually has three or four IOUs in it so when the milkman comes, there isn't enough to pay him and people complain there's no milk. A junior member of staff is doing one of the most complex pieces of organisational activity in existence and people are just giving him grief all the time, when after all he's not being paid to buy bourbon biscuits, he's being paid to calculate housing benefit or whatever. It usually ends up with an argument in the kitchen. The person in charge of the tea fund punches the person who has put in all the IOUs; he then gets disciplined and refuses to do the tea fund any more.

Meanwhile, the bosses, of course, have free tea and coffee.

Something like this had clearly happened in this local authority office. I opened the fridge and there were about 20 bottles of milk in there, including one with a label on it saying, "this is Steve's milk don't drink it I've pissed in it". I told the director she had a long, long way to go if she aspired to the self-actualisation of her colleagues…

I once went to an architects' office in Manchester where half the staff had clubbed together to buy a toaster. When you went into the open plan office every morning there was a delicious smell of toast, but if you worked in the wrong half of the office you couldn't have any, because you hadn't contributed to the toaster.

Unless you take action, the workplace neighbourhood will start to be riven with splits in this way, as people carve out territory and set up demarcation lines. Once that is happening, you no longer have a team.

What does 'a team' mean? What does it do? Of course it means people working together with a common goal, but it also means people doing different jobs, fulfilling different roles, but each taking personal responsibility for fulfilling their role and contributing towards the success of the team. Creating a team means understanding failure, managing talent and dealing with belligerent conscientious objectors and spectator critics.

An organisation of leaders

If you have a team where each member is ready to take personal responsibility, you can deliver efficient and effective services. What you don't want is people who are not taking personal responsibility, who are just filling in the hours, passing work on to others, avoiding taking action or – at worst – not turning up for work at all but taking yet another day off sick. This is the situation that too often afflicts businesses. It means that not only is public money being wasted, but customers are not receiving the service they want and need.

To get people to do things, you can try to frighten or repress them into doing it, but the best way is to get them to buy into the job, to understand why it's important and how they contribute to the overall goals. If you have a belief system, such that people believe the work they do is important, you can create the conditions in which they become motivated. If this sounds easy… it's not – it requires a remorseless, minute by minute daily effort.

How to do this? It is about courageous leadership, but it's also about seeking to create an organisation full of leaders, where people believe that they lead in their own right. I don't mean everyone's the boss, I mean they feel they are in charge of their own job and are influential and valued. There's no point in my being under the delusion that I can head an organisation of 170 people and lead all the time on every issue. I do show leadership: I steer our strategic approach and think hard about what we should be doing in the light of social, economic and political conditions. But the big job of a leader is to create conditions in which people can find and fulfil their potential, and understand the responsibilities of their job. This has to take account of people's professional and personal responsibilities. True leaders, dare I say, seek enlightenment and fulfilment for themselves and their colleagues. They spend their time on creating the future, keeping things moving and strengthening the culture.

I get paid to take ultimate responsibility for the performance of my company. But I'm also trying to ensure that everyone else understands what they need to contribute, and feels their contribution is recognised and applauded by us. If you can get that, then people will embrace their responsibility and feel proud of the opportunity that they have been given. It is important to remember that people's performance at work is heavily influenced by their personal development and what happens in their lives. Whilst employers can't be responsible for everything that happens to our colleagues, we need to build trusting and reciprocal relationships which encourage people to be honest about issues that may affect their work, so that appropriate support, help and direction can be offered.

Very successful organisations, leaders and managers have this knack of instilling pride in the workforce. I like the story of the cleaner at Cape Kennedy, back in the heyday of the space programme. When someone asked him what he did, he said, "I help put people on the moon!" There's a similar story about Liverpool Football Club. When Bill Shankly joined the club as its manager in 1959 one of his first actions was to visit the laundry and speak to Ronnie the kit man. Shankly asked him, "What do you do son?" Ronnie replied, "I just wash the kit Mr Shankly." Shanks said, "No you don't son – you help us win the League." True to form, four years later Shanks took Liverpool to his first League Championship trophy.

Bill Shankly showed there what empathetic leadership is. He not only understood that the behind-the-scenes people have a key contribution to make, he also never lost sight of what everyone was working for – in this case, winning the League Championship. Incidentally, the legend goes that after Mr Shankly's visit Ronnie washed and ironed the kit as he'd never washed or ironed before.

Treat people as they'd like to be treated
Leaders set the tone and the pace of every organsation. The best leadership is where the leader creates the conditions in which people fulfil themselves and feel that they are doing it for themselves and their colleagues.

I don't give people the phony "we're all equal" stuff, because it's obvious that some people in the organisation are paid more than others and some are managers while others are not. But I do say, "we're all as important as each other." We all support and challenge each other, we must all respect each other, but we have different responsibilities and we get paid in accordance with that.

In order to get the best out of a person, you must treat them as they would like to be treated – not as *you* would like to be treated, but as *they* would like to be treated. There's a massive difference. One approach is patronising, the other treats each person as a special individual. This is especially important when dealing with equal opportunities and diversity issues. To motivate people, a manager needs to find out what floats each person's boat and what triggers them to contribute to the business to the full. You must try to engender the feelings and commitment that are often displayed by volunteers in hospices, animal rescue centres and other caring organisations, who work for free and make a huge contribution because they believe passionately in the cause.

We expect every person who works for us will buy into the organisation and be hungry to contribute towards our success. But there has to be a reason why they should do that – there has to be something in it for them. We know we have to be loyal to our colleagues in the first instance, if we want colleagues to be loyal to us. Empowering colleagues to work within bounded freedoms is one of the key challenges for every business.

It is no good treating everyone the same because there is a wide range of people, cultures and motivations in every organisation. People work for very different reasons, with different personal goals and aspirations.

So we have accountants who care about getting the figures in order; we've got people working with the financial markets because, after all, we're a business with a £130 million loan portfolio. We have people with expertise in property and building. Many join us because they want to work with people. Others want to work for a not-for-profit, community organisation, because of their personal religious or political beliefs.

Of course, as I said, the various offices or teams are neighbourhoods, with their own cultures. I've always noticed, at the Christmas office party, how rarely people mix (though this changed when we embarked on our residential two day 'Think-a-Thons' of which more later…). You tend to find the finance department sits together, legal services sit together. They feel most comfortable in their own neighbourhood and there is no point in trying to shake that up too much. You have to remember to treat people as they would like to be treated and accommodate the differences.

However it is important to tear down artificial barriers in order to derive the benefits that a critical mass of people who are focused and organised can produce. If you can do that, you've got a great opportunity to liberate, enjoy and profit from the impact of this massive group force. We have a varied community of people, from logical accountants to extrovert social workers, who wouldn't normally rub shoulders. We're a kind of laboratory for initiatives, and ideas swirl around and bump into each another. Inevitably, there's conflict sometimes when the different interests – finance, people, bricks and mortar – pull in different directions. But we actively encourage creative challenge, as long as we are all working towards a common purpose. There's a great chance to have a group of people really putting their energy into the organisation. The potential exists for all organisations to be like that.

Dealing with absenteeism

Absenteeism is one of the major problems affecting all businesses, and a severe drain on resources.

The CBI's regular survey of workplace absenteeism makes the problem clear. It found that in 2011, an average of 8.1 days were lost in sickness leave for every employee in the public sector. This compares with an average 5.9 days lost for every employee in the private sector (quite a high figure in itself).

The highest absence rate was among public sector manual workers, at an average 9.1 days. But non-manual workers also took 50% more sick leave than their counterparts in the private sector.

The CBI survey also looked at the cost to the organisation of each employee's absence, taking into account such things as temporary cover, colleagues' overtime and so on. Public sector bodies reported a median cost per absent employee of £1,040 – a significant burden at a time of intense pressure on public spending.

The CBI has calculated that if public sector absenteeism rates could be brought down to the private sector average, more than £5bn could be saved over the next five years. I would say that if public sector absenteeism rates came down to my organisation's level then savings of £17.5bn would be generated. This is achievable.

Why do such high rates of absenteeism occur? The first point to make is that it is mostly nothing to do with genuine sickness. Of course people will be ill from time to time, some more than others, but that is an issue which can be addressed according to the individual.

Absenteeism on this large scale is more a symptom that something is wrong with the organisation. It normally occurs where there is poor management, bad working conditions, and where there's a lack of respect for the organisation. Some workplaces in the public sector have a culture of absenteeism: people regard it as their right to take a sickie, for example on a Friday and a Monday to give themselves a long weekend. I've worked in places where I've seen people book their sickness in advance.

Leaders must respond to those who take advantage like this, and respond in a consistent and comprehensible way. Absenteeism causes stress among other colleagues, costs the company money and is totally unacceptable.

If nothing is done, it's easy to see the curve moving to the right. If you see your colleagues taking sickies with impunity, when you know they've got nothing more than a hangover, or just want to do a day's shopping, you might begin to think, why don't I do that? You take a couple of days off; nobody says anything. People begin to see it as a right. If, even worse, you see some colleagues getting paid for being at home for six months, with 'a bad back', not only do you lose all faith in your organisation but you may well be tempted to try something similar yourself.

Every time someone throws a sickie, when they are not actually ill, they are imposing a cost on the organisation and their colleagues and doing their customers a disservice. Either the other members of their team have to work harder to cover their absence, or their employer has to pay for temporary cover, or work simply doesn't get done. There is a loss of skills and continuity; customers get annoyed when they find the service is being delivered by people who don't really know the job or are ignorant of the case history. It all adds up to poor services, frustration, resentment and waste.

On the other hand, if there is high sickness absence but no noticeable difference to the team's performance, then management should be aware of that too. Either the absent individuals were not pulling their weight, or the organisation is over staffed and people are effectively being paid to do the equivalent of digging holes and filling them in again.

Our offer to the workforce is: we want you to be a loyal, well turned out, well behaved member of our community. We want you to turn up for work and fulfil your role. This includes understanding that you must take personal responsibility for any absence from work. In return, we will look after you and help you stay healthy, including supporting you through difficult and stressful times in your work, home and social life.

Some organisations tackle sickness absence levels with the punishment approach, imposing the humiliating return to work interview. The idea is that people will avoid going off sick, just so that they don't have to undergo the interview when they get back in the office.

Interviews are invariably conducted by unqualified, ill-equipped managers (like myself), who at best can only have a superficial discussion about why someone has been absent.

What this means is that the conscientious, but genuinely sick, people often drag themselves into work even if they are ill and have something contagious. The liars and cheats will just bluff their way through the interview anyway and if they've got a sick note (liberally dispensed by some GPs at the end of a ten minute assessment) there's nothing you can do about it anyway.

I've heard people say things like, "I'm gonna ask the doctor for a two week sick note." Accommodating GPs often ask, "How long would you like off?" It's crazy.

We've taken the approach of rewarding and encouraging good health and attendance. There is a role for the return to work interview, not to humiliate people, but to ensure their health needs are being met. It's incumbent on an employer to create the conditions to develop a healthy, happy, motivated, inspired and punctual workforce. If you take this approach, it puts you in a much better position to have an honest discussion with someone, instead of starting off with, "Why were you off sick? Has your doctor just written you a phoney note? Why do you always seem to be off on Mondays and Fridays?"

Well, yes, sometimes people have been at a big, monster party all weekend and can't face work on a Monday. We would rather they were honest about it than pretend to be ill and lie to us. But if they really are ill, we want to know about it. If they have an infectious illness, like a cold, we certainly want them to stay at home and, if possible, work from home. We don't want them sneezing all over customers or passing germs round an entire workforce.

We want our frontline staff, especially, to be healthy. Their jobs are the most demanding and, unlike those in the higher echelons of the organisation, they can't work from home if they're feeling off colour.

After we started our meritocracy, we managed to bring sickness absence levels down steadily with a combination of health awareness, anti-smoking policies, motivational programmes, annual medical checks, eye tests, fitness and relaxation packages and so on. That brought us to a position where we could say: if you're ill, we can fix you quickly; if you want to prevent illness, there's all these measures to get you fit and well.

So we have invested in providing private healthcare, dental and eye care for everyone. Our colleagues organise lunchtime classes in things like fitness, guitar, dance, singing, yoga and massage, to keep people relaxed, fit and alert. We have two gyms available for people to use 24/7 and most of the activities on offer are run by colleagues for colleagues, which again is great for connecting people and fostering teamwork.

Furthermore, we recognise that people will go through bad times, so we have flexi time, bereavement leave and professional counselling.

Our approach is generous, but we feel it is justified, as long as the results can be seen in lower absenteeism. For several years this was clearly the case: once we had implemented these measures, we went from around a 5% sickness absence rate, to 3.4%, which by industry standards was better than most.

Priority: zero sickness

Then in 2009 our absentee rate started creeping up. We had to ask ourselves, why? Our Board questioned whether the benefits we offered were cost effective. Why was sickness going up when we had put so much in place to prevent it? Had we genuinely had a bad couple of years, with problems like swine flu going around? Or, human nature being what it is, were people now taking all our benefits for granted and pushing the boundaries by taking more sickness leave?

It did appear that the same people who had swine flu also had 'bird flu', 'man flu', and were no doubt preparing themselves for 'giraffe flu' – symptoms include walking awkwardly with a stiff long neck – and 'ham flu' which is a bit like swine flu but easier to cure!

We looked at the data. Managers were supposed to record the reasons for their people being off sick and to take action where necessary. It turned out the most common reason recorded for a person being off sick was 'other' (39% of all responses), which meant the manager either didn't want to or couldn't be bothered to ask exactly what the reason was. This was no help at all. How could we begin to understand workplace absenteeism if we had no knowledge about two fifths of the incidents of sick leave?

In 2010 we set ourselves five zero priorities, to clarify in people's minds what our business is about. One of these is zero sickness levels. To achieve that, we have to take a three-pronged approach: prevention, rehabilitation and enforcement. Prevention occurs through all the care and activities we offer to keep people healthy. Rehabilitation involves a work-health assessment, with diagnosis and prognosis and a programme of care agreed with qualified health specialists. Enforcement involves taking decisive action against persistent and willful lead-swingers, which can mean withdrawal of sick pay and ultimately dismissal.

One of the key changes we made was that anyone who is ill has to ring our absence line, between 8am and 9am. That call is taken by myself, Angela the deputy chief executive or Neil the assistant chief executive. We talk to them about what is wrong, and whether they can work from home. If they can, we will send their papers and a laptop round to their home.

People often tell us they can't work from home because they can't log on. But there's more to work than being connected to the system. A day at home could be an invaluable opportunity to think about your job, how to do it better, how to improve communication, eradicate waste and improve customer service, all while your in-growing toenail heals.

When they come back to work, they have the benefit of the work-health assessment (WHAR). This is a meeting with myself (or whoever took the initial call), their line manager, one of our coaching academy people, and our own consultant physician, Dr Godfrey. He is an extremely experienced and eminent doctor, so if you are ill, you will want to see Dr Godfrey because he can help you. He will give you a lot more time and thought than your GP, who is under pressure to maintain productivity targets by having you out of the surgery within 10 minutes. On the other hand, if you're not ill, you will not want to be quizzed by Dr Godfrey, because he will suss you out.

Important things can come out of these meetings. Dr Godfrey has sent people home because they shouldn't be in work and helped us understand complex health issues and their impact on colleagues and the workplace. For example, if the employee reveals they have diabetes, Dr Godfrey tells us the implications of that and how it can be managed. This is much better than judgments being made by a manager who has no medical knowledge whatsoever, which is what happens in most companies.

This approach quickly brought our absenteeism rate down to below 0.5% per year, which is a world record as far as I'm aware. In itself it saved us £154,000 in the first year. We no longer have to use temporary staff to do the work of people who were off sick, and the pressure has been taken off colleagues who were covering for their absent co-workers and getting stressed. Importantly, ensuring that all sickness is genuine has stopped the resentment and title tattle that flies round the office when so-and-so is seen to be taking yet another sick day. Sadly but inevitably we will see less and less of Dr Godfrey because our absenteeism is rapidly approaching zero!

It also helped us preserve and maintain our generous benefit package because we can demonstrate its beneficial impact on the bottom line.

The prevention strand is important, for people's mental and emotional health as well as physical. We have counsellors available and we encourage people to see them before problems become unmanageable. Inevitably people have difficulties in their life. If someone is worried about their kid being in trouble at school, their elderly father getting forgetful, and on top of that their car has broken down, it is foolish to think they can leave all that at the door when they come to work. Anxiety will affect their performance, and we think it is better for people to seek help, advice and support, sooner rather than later.

Although I have said a lot here about reducing absenteeism, it is vital that companies support people when they experience genuine issues. Problems strike at random, without warning – bereavement, cancer, car accidents – and people will judge their employer depending on the way they are treated at times of real need. If you want the respect and trust of your workforce, your actions need to be congruent with your stated values. A friend of mine had a stroke, was in hospital for four months and struggled through the rehabilitation process in order to get back to work. His employers were supportive for six months, but then cut his pay and reorganised his job so when he got back to work he found himself in a difficult situation in every way. The organisation's excuse was that their insurance cover on him had run out. They let him down completely. It's this sort of situation which tests how sincere a company is and people watch how its value system translates into action.

For how long, how often and at what cost the company's safety net stays in place is an important judgement call. Looking after people doesn't mean mollycoddling them. But it does mean creating the conditions in which people want to come to work, respect and enjoy the opportunities and seek enlightenment and fulfilment for themselves and their colleagues.

I've said a lot about absenteeism here because it is a problem that afflicts public services – but one that I know from experience can be cured. At present, cuts are being made in service delivery. Some of those services could be preserved if organisations turned their attention instead to tackling the persistent problems that have come to be taken for granted as an inherent part of the public sector, such as low productivity and high sickness absence rates.

These persistent problems are not inevitable: they are a symptom of low motivation, lacklustre management and negative cultures. So how do you raise motivation and create a workplace that people want to come into on a Monday morning? We have used a rewards-based approach, to engender and propagate our meritocracy.

Chapter 7

Diamond Service: the works

Having spent considerable time thinking through our meritocracy philosophy culture and service delivery, the challenge quickly moved on from 'how do we get residents on Gold Service?' to 'how do we get colleagues fired up?'. We had to ensure, both that the structure of the organisation enabled us to deliver the service we promised, and also that our workforce was motivated to do this. We aimed to create a meritocratic organisation, which used a structured system of reward in order to get the best out of people – a Diamond Service for our highest performing colleagues.

To begin with, I knew our customers weren't getting a fantastic service. The organisation was performing reasonably well, for its sector, but it wasn't outstanding or something to be proud of. I was very clear that the reasons for this lay in management, leadership, culture and mindsets.

I knew that we had developed a compelling vision for the future and that I needed enthusiastic and energetic managers who would drive me and our organisation into new territories. Managers everywhere (public and private sector) can come up with a hundred reasons to explain why their organisation is failing when the real reasons are usually weak leadership, hypocritical management, and the uncontrolled growth of subcultures. Managers frequently underestimate the skills and competence of people they work with, apply one rule for their staff but another for themselves and too often don't know how to get the best out of people, and when to do this. They need to build a meritocratic culture with maximum buy-in from motivated, focused, enthusiastic colleagues.

To manage any business well, you need to have a tight grip on the basics – your costs, income and expenditure. The rest of it is nothing to do with the size of the organisation, its location or history. It is down to how you get people to do what you ask them to do. Good leaders need many qualities, including an understanding of how to motivate people. You need to know a lot about the psychology of human behaviour and to be a just, honest and determined person, unafraid of criticism and unaffected by the 'nay sayers' who would tell you why things cannot change. You also need to understand how cultures grow in an organisation and how to control, cultivate and nurture positive ones.

Everybody is affected by their background and experiences in life. I learned a lot in my life from my parents, family, friends, school, church and the street. Being brought up in a solid family with high moral values and a heavy emphasis on the work ethic, combined with my working in heavy industry, performing in bands and playing in football teams have shaped my thinking and helped me enormously.

Experiencing camaraderie, winning, losing, being applauded and booed, being on strike with the miners in 1984, being a bouncer for four years in Liverpool, a trade union negotiator, a front bench advisor in the House of Commons, disciplining and being disciplined, getting divorced and gaining custody of my children have all proven to be invaluable experiences to me, probably more than my academic qualifications.

Powerful positions come with a huge responsibility and opportunity. The person at the top influences people's lives minute by minute, not just those of customers but colleagues too – all those people looking to you to take the lead and offer direction. Many of my management role models are people who have managed me badly in the past. Frequently when I have a problem, I think what they would do and then do the opposite, because what they did, very professionally, was to demotivate and demoralise their people.

It is very important to have practices that are congruent with your stated values. You must avoid saying things that you do not believe in or that do not resonate with the culture and you must never introduce policies or practices that are not going to be used or cannot be explained.

If you say that colleagues are your greatest asset, then every person is entitled to feel that and see it demonstrated in practice. If you say you will treat people with dignity and respect, everyone in the organisation is perfectly entitled to expect to feel treated with dignity and respect. Very often high level statements from the top become progressively meaningless as they filter down the hierarchy. In the end they serve only to undermine an organisation if the culture does not align with the executive speak.

The challenge is to get consistency throughout, irrespective of a company's size, and to be crystal clear about what we call TNTs – the tiny noticeable things that people will pick up on, the contradictions between what you say and what you do as a manager, the systems you set up and your stated objectives and missions and what happens in the dramatic theatre of the office.

Cultivating a culture

The culture of a business is created by the way it is led, how it is managed, what it does and every single thing that the people who work for it do. You need to be sure that you have the culture you want, because a culture effectively defines an organisation. Colleagues, customers and everybody who interacts with it, personally or professionally, experience and digest the culture. What you don't want are subcultures that sabotage your overall goals and progressively corrode values and, ultimately, beliefs and actions.

I once worked for a large company which had eight local offices. If you went from one office to another you'd think you were in a different organisation. Eight separate entities had developed, each with their own subculture, under the broad umbrella of customer services. In addition there was a head office culture which bore little resemblance to the decentralised offices. Whilst it's good for offices to have their own character and individuality, the core values, beliefs and actions need to be broadly consistent throughout an organisation. If your firm states that customers and colleagues must be treated with dignity and respect and as they would like to be treated, then every action the organisation performs should fit neatly into that mandate. Even the difficult tasks – evicting a resident, disciplining or making colleagues redundant – must be done in a way that demonstrates respect and allows the person their dignity. There has to be consistency in the way that various departments or offices do these things. The way to achieve this is to have a leaderful company with bright, enthusiastic managers who naturally express the company's virtues.

Business like McDonald's are past masters at this: you might not love McDonald's but you are in no doubt where you are, what you can eat and what to expect when you visit their restaurants. Having had a Big Mac in Beijing, I can testify to this. It is not surprising therefore that they're one of the few companies in the world which has grown year on year for the last 10 years and will continue to do so.

Our organisation works exclusively in the Greater Manchester area. When we hire people we expect them to join our culture, which is active, enthusiastic, performance driven, based on knowledge and enjoyment. We reward good behaviour more than we punish bad behaviour. We create places where people want to come and enjoy their experiences. Team-building activities are run every day and we try to make sure that all our people work in stimulating environments where there is a strong sense of place, strong learning and strong work ethics – a bit like a university campus with a business and social purpose.

Creating loyalty and setting boundaries

Loyalty is invaluable for an organisation. You can't buy it: you have to build it and earn it. A long term, vibrant relationship with colleagues and customers means you can deliver great service, drawing on experience and tailored to individual needs whilst cutting costs and eliminating waste. Public services, of course, mostly do have long term relationships with their customers – they know exactly who they are and where they live. This is an advantage that is there to be used.

But if you want your colleagues and customers to be loyal, then responsibility for that starts with you, not them. You have to be loyal to them first and display trust in them.

Our own culture is open and honest, and we want people be open and honest with us. Once a level of trust has been built, you can feel confident that colleagues are not going to take advantage of your openness. There might be the occasional person who consciously abuses your trust, but they will be the exception. Unfortunately, in most organisations, command and control structures are solely geared to stopping that one person, not liberating and unlocking the potential of the rest.

Collective punishment, as I recall from school, does not really work. You are better off following General Colin Powell's advice to "piss off the right people."

Office behaviours tend to be quirky: many people respond to new ideas with 'we must have a procedure manual' 'a policy statement' 'a working group' 'a task and finish group' 'KPIs (key performance indicators)' and so on, as if nobody can be trusted to act sensibly – they all have to have it spelled out to them.

For colleagues dealing with problems in neighbourhoods, there clearly have to be boundaries. You can't just allow them to get on horseback and round up the villains and the outlaws (though that might be quite popular). So we have no shortage of rule books, procedure manuals, policy statements, disaster recoveries, health and safety edicts. We've even got a stab vest policy and procedure, which goes: pull the vest over your head, attach it to your chest and hope you get stabbed not shot. But, if someone thinks they know how to handle a situation, we would be quite confident that, in almost every circumstance, they will behave sensibly without recourse to the rule book.

One Christmas, one of our housing colleagues phoned me about a Solid Gold service resident who'd had a flood that had wrecked the house, filled the electrical sockets and ruined all the Christmas presents. Her statutory entitlement was to be placed in a hostel with her children – for Christmas. Bah humbug! Instead, our colleague got her into a nice hotel for five days while we refitted her house, which I believed was a fantastic response. Some people would mutter, "Isn't that just inviting people to flood their homes so they get to go to a hotel for Christmas?" Well no, I'm happy to say no-one has taken such drastic measures.

Doing more with less

Shaking up a company structure is one of the most difficult things anybody can do. But it is a necessity when you want to effect radical change. Removing dead wood from a company is very important, as Jack Walsh, the CEO of America's General Electric Company would demonstrate annually by culling the least performing 10% of his workforce.

When we need to remove dead wood we do, and replace it with happy, motivated enthusiasts. But we also needed a flatter, much more front-loaded structure, because in housing, like many other businesses, the game is won and lost on the front-line. You can have the most brilliant people dreaming up fantastic levels of service, new products, sexy deals and so on. But if the people on the front-line are not highly motivated, and emotionally and intuitively committed to excellence in customer service, then all the ideas and best intentions go nowhere.

At the top of the organisation, you think you're sending very strong messages down to front line people, but by the time they get down to the street sweeper on an estate, they're watered down to the point that they're little droplets. If he's lucky, a few molecules might land on your street sweeper's head. Yet his attitude to the job is absolutely critical to your performance.

At the top you have directors doing strategy, resource allocation and monitoring. Then you have what we call the CDPC – the corporate damp proof course that is middle management. Again, this is where the game can be won or lost. Middle managers often feel like the meat in the sandwich, being bitten to death from above and below. You can have powerful statements, glossy publications, big AGMs and important board meetings, but if middle managers don't 'get' and champion a cause, then you're not penetrating the damp proof course and front line people have no chance of understanding the message you've sent out from on high. We counteract this by what I call our monthly Gdansk Shipyard meetings (inspired by the open style of Poland's Solidarity movement) where myself and other colleagues inform and energise each other. Even so managers can set the wrong tone and the wrong pace, if they have the wrong mindset.

Our unconditional service guarantee for residents is a good example. Unconditional service guarantees are widespread in America: companies like the Sheridan Hotel, pizza delivery companies and restaurants all offer USGs because they are extremely confident in their services and know customers will enjoy what they provide, respect the offer and not take advantage. USGs keep everyone on their toes and truly empower customers. Sadly many organisation see them as a complainer's charter, despite the fact that those who take advantage and abuse the privilege are tiny minority who can be easily identified.

Under our USG, any resident who is not happy with a repair or improvement we have made to their home can instruct an independent technical surveyor to come and assess it. If the expert agrees that the repair has been done poorly, the resident can commission the same or a different contractor to come back to fix it as soon as possible. The original contractor suffers a triple whammy: not getting paid for the first job, paying for the job to be done properly and then compensating the customer with the full value of the repair.

We expect our residents to be totally happy with everything we do and we want any complaints to be sorted out on the doorstep, not left to linger and fester, destroying confidence in the service relationship and ultimately appearing on the Ombudsman's desk. We expect our colleagues and service deliverers to operate as if nothing is too much trouble. It is interesting that since we've introduced our unconditional service guarantee for residents in June 2010, it has never been invoked and that customer satisfaction has risen to 92% (an increase of 5% over this period) compared with the sector average of 82%.

Middle management response to our USG varied: some were enthusiastic, some were cynical, some actively sought to undermine it, because of fear or disbelief. I overhead one manager (who has subsequently moved on to pastures new) present it as follows: "Senior managers have said they're going to introduce this unconditional service guarantee thing. I've never heard anything like it in my life, but I've got to tell you about it or I'll get in trouble." Managerial assassins like this deserve a second chance, but certainly not a third. Managers need to champion and be evangelical about new policies and services – they should never cover their backside and send out inconsistent or contradictory messages.

The CDPC was where the first wave of redundancies hit. Whilst I'm not proud of this, we had to lose some people and posts which had become a bit jaded, cynical and outmoded. Every year since 2002, we've tried to make savings by removing 'chiefs' and recruiting more 'Indians', slenderising the structure and eliminating unnecessary posts. We've reduced our payroll over the past five years by 25%, most of which has taken place in the highest echelons, thereby reducing our costs dramatically. Interestingly, year on year we have outperformed the budget and our performance has never been better. Indeed our regulator recently awarded us the highest possible grading for governance and financial management and performance. You can do more with less, if you've got the right people, in the right place with the right attitude, supported by the right culture and great leaders.

The savings we have made have been channelled into more improvements and frontline colleagues. Skewing resources to the front end is an ongoing process. I try to make sure I have direct contact with our front-line people and personally meet every new colleague for one hour and meet their manager after three months for an assessment. If the first points of contact aren't strong, then the whole organisation is built on shaky foundations and will never be world class.

Another thing we take very seriously is getting colleagues to understand how even their smallest actions affect everything about us, which means answering the phone in a positive way, saying hello, please, thank you, not barging into the lift when people are trying to get out of it, being relaxed, smiling, remembering to breath from the diaphragm, greeting people, saying good morning, good night, and generally being polite, courteous and upbeat.

We make an effort to get them to appreciate the value of our investments and encourage them to be cost conscious and eliminate waste. The American military used an interesting way of informing their GIs about the cost of military equipment. Instead of letting them fire off bullets all day in training, ride their tanks about, smashing into each other, and fly helicopters into the side of the Grand Canyon, they were given credit cards and statements which itemised the cost of the equipment they used. The thinking behind this was that the next time they sat in the back of a their Willis jeep shooting at eagles, perhaps they would consider the cost of the bullets they were using and what they were using them for. Not surprisingly, expenditure plummeted when GIs and pilots started to appreciate the costs of bullets and helicopters.

We've explained to our colleagues the importance of eliminating discrete costs such as sickness, which in 2010 cost us £154,000 in temporary staff cover. Now, we no longer employ temporary staff as our sickness has been dramatically slashed from 3.5% to 0.4%.

If our colleagues don't understand what really counts in our business and are not dedicated to those critical areas, then we may as well pack up and go home. Our priorities are very clear because we only have five of them, which we term our five zeros:

Zero rent arrears
Zero customer dissatisfaction
Zero relet times
Zero unnecessary repairs
Zero sickness

Everybody's performance is assessed on their contribution to our five zeros, which is reinforced by monthly Five Time chats and six monthly coaching checks.

Every Monday, our top team meets in a hotel lobby and discusses how the business performed the previous week, how we expect to perform this week, any key events and how our five priorities look. It can be a tedious grind, but it means we know exactly where we're at. Keeping on top of things weekly allows us to anticipate and deal with emerging problems.

If anything is going wrong with our budgets, we are usually in a great position to plan, adjust and adapt and make sure this is brought to the attention of directors and managers each Monday.

Getting the message across

Every organisation on the planet can improve communication. So how do you make sure everyone in your company knows what's going on? Traditional methods include staff conferences, regular briefings, staff meetings, newsletters, videos and so on. These formal, well-used techniques are usually very dull, and it's difficult to tell how effective they are.

People communicate when it's important to them. The grapevine is usually the most powerful communication network in any organisation and payroll is every organisation's most efficient process. Both are fantastic examples of how effectively people communicate and make things happen when it's in their interest to do so.

A couple of years ago our interest rate rose and we worked out we had to find an extra £100,000 to cover our additional costs. I sent out an email explaining this to our colleagues, asking for any suggestions as to how we might save this money. I received only two replies. I'm sure I would have received many more replies if I had asked colleagues to respond to something that they felt passionate about.

Think-a-Thons

We don't have annual conferences for our colleagues. I think they're a waste of time. Instead we try ways of getting messages to them without their realising it.

Since 2010, all our colleagues have attended a three day residential 'Think-a-Thon' once a year. They spend two nights away at a cottage in Powys, along with people from different departments. They usually visit a housing development on their way to Powys, to help them consider the issues we face. At the venue they have to cook their own food, wash up, keep the place ship shape and abide by company rules – it is work, not a holiday! They are given a budget for food and refreshments and some people have even risen to the challenge with 'Come dine with me' experiences, dressing up in evening wear for the occasion.

Each group is given a set of tasks, based on our five zeros, which they have to think about over the three days. How they do this is entirely up to them. Some have sat out in the grounds with a glass of wine, others got round a dinner table and brainstormed until tea time and then partied until dawn.

The results have been nothing short of staggering. Altogether 12 groups so far have gone on the Think-a-Thon, bringing back more than 800 suggestions for driving onwards with our five priorities. This whole exercise costs a fraction of what a staff conference would cost and the benefits of interpersonal connections, team work and communication have boosted us forward much faster that we could have believed. This great value for money exercise has proved to be one of the most important things we've ever done and will continue in the foreseeable future.

We noticed, however, that about 200 of the suggestions were for things we were already doing (which presumably people weren't aware of) and this pointed to the need to improve communication. Our response has been to focus directly on how we communicate rather than trying to improve things by osmosis or through technical fixes such as intranet and internet.

Communication is the life blood of any company, but too often people forget the verbal and non-verbal basics. Companies tend to rely on the formal mechanics of communications and everybody nowadays has a communications strategy – which I guess only a fraction of employees ever read. We concentrate on the simple human methods: being pleasant, enthusiastic, listening, talking clearly and simply without jargon.

We have re-inductions, because when companies only induct new colleagues, the newcomers often have more up-to-date information than existing ones. So people who've been with us for two years are invited to join re-induction courses.

Every one of our colleagues attends an annual 'presenting with impact' course run by myself with an experienced broadcaster and a camera man. We work with our colleagues on breathing, nerve management, overcoming fear, tone, pronunciation, vowel washing, and particularly how to connect with people verbally and non-verbally. Our course is based on research into audience reactions and ratings of speeches and presentations. According to this, the speaker's words constitute just 9% of the impact of a presentation, tone accounts for 27% and personality 64%.

When you see a person you know address an audience, they often appear like someone you've never met before. They hide their personality, they play safe, they read their notes – or worse still, read their slides – and they don't smile! We encourage people to prepare how they say things. We teach them to use inner self-management techniques and to abandon the traditional cumbersome tools, props and crutches that people cling to and hide behind. 'Be yourself' is our maxim. Your personality is what audiences rate as most important, so why not respond appropriately?

Senior colleagues set the tone and pace of any company. How they behave fundamentally affects communication and other people's behaviours. In addition to our multi-cultural policies I will not tolerate any manager who talks down to people, hides behind their position, is sarcastic, rude, authoritarian or indeed behaves in any way which compromises or contravenes our values and beliefs. We regularly discuss our roles and reactions and spend time thinking about how to achieve consistency and congruence between values, behaviours and what we do and say. All our senior managers attend a weekly presentation and awareness programme for an hour, to help improve their confidence and communication, enhance their awareness, and acknowledge and respect the qualities and attributes of their peers.

Very often senior teams are infested with rivalry and Machiavellian plots and subterfuges. Sadly, people expend tons of negative energy on fighting their corner, blaming each other and trotting out excuses. Issues become massively time consuming because senior managers make them inordinately complicated. Managers will hide behind technical issues and regulations and spout jargon to avoid dealing with what is often a simple matter, like attendance.

These mad behaviours severely limit the time for senior people to solve big problems, to innovate and take risks. They also undermine trust. Working with people you trust and respect is essential. If you don't believe this, try working with people you don't trust and see how much work you get done and how you feel when you put your head on the pillow at night. Building up trust is crucial but high risk: for it to work, people have to build up their confidence in each other and sometimes this means making themselves vulnerable. Professional intimacy is a bit like falling and being in love. It's fantastic, if scary, when it's working, but when it falls apart feelings of anger, hatred and revenge can quickly replace the heady high oxygen intimacy once previously enjoyed by a management team. Don't get me wrong – I'm not suggesting naked meetings in hot tubs or covering each other in baby oil, but you do have to like and enjoy the company of the people you work with, if you want to get the best out of yourself, your colleagues and your company.

Communicating with customers

As part of my 'keeping in touch' programme, I regularly knock on customers' doors and ask them what they think of us. I visit estates and properties at weekends and late at night to check out what's happening.

Over the past two years we have reinvented how we connect with our customers. Colleagues from all our departments join in our monthly resident involvement events and our Christmas programme. Up to 200 residents attend our monthly evening entertainment evenings, which comprise a hotpot supper, one free drink, a raffle, and some live entertainment including crooning, soul and rock and roll. During the evening, residents are asked for their views on key service areas such as rent collection, rewards for good tenancy management, improvement programmes and how they think we should deal with rent defaulters and head bangers in our neighbourhoods.

At Christmas 2011 we held 18 Christmas carol concerts, planted and decorated more than 30 Christmas trees throughout Manchester and offered mulled wine and mince pies to our residents. All colleagues are expected to attend on a rota basis, which brings back-office colleagues from finance, IT and admin into direct contact with customers.

In January 2012 we kicked off our events programme with a talent contest for our residents, which was an unbelievable evening and extremely successful. We had six acts, by residents ranging from nine to 48 years old. Our winner was Kate, a talented young lady who had been homeless and is now being rehabilitated in one of our hostels. When she sang 'Somewhere over the Rainbow' there really was not a dry eye in the house. All the contestants have been given an hour in a studio as a prize and Kate's rendition of her song will be used as music for when people contact us by phone.

You need to have all sorts of channels of communication open, to give people the opportunity to say what they think. We have what we call a bottom-up strategy, designed to draw out views from colleagues and customers. We've moved away from traditional communication methods and utilise social media such as Facebook and Twitter; we also have our own TV station (IVTV) where customers can access services from the comfort of their living room. Facebook and Twitter offer a free service which we use to communicate with customers, posting notices and photos – for example we posted news of our talent show winner the day after the show. We currently have over 600 followers which includes customers, local and national businesses and MPs. Through intensive contact with residents we discovered that a very high proportion of our customers had free access to digital channels and IVTV, which has helped us with our digital inclusion agenda. IVTV is accessed regularly by customers seeking information, reporting repairs and making applications for Gold Service.

Of course if you invite communication, you have to then listen to what people tell you and make sure they know they've been heard. You must be prepared to hear things which challenge you and, most importantly, you must act in response to the views of customers and colleagues. But you also have to be absolutely clear that there are boundaries because, without these, you're going to raise people's expectations pointlessly. Not every suggestion is a good one, not every complaint is justified. Customers may dislike you because you have to say no to their unreasonable request. Leadership is not about trying to make everybody happy – in fact if you try to make everybody happy it's the one sure way of failing.

People in the social housing sector are fond of saying they want to 'empower' colleagues and tenants. For me it's a meaningless term. How far do they want to empower residents? And how will they respond when 'empowered' residents tell them what they really want: "Why can't you evict the family at number 23? Why does it take you so long – can't you just get them out of here?" "I want you to clean this place up and stop those teenagers causing havoc."

I always feel sorry for housing officers who have to respond to issues such as these when they do not have the authority to solve the problems. I'm sure both residents and housing officers are sick to death of tired excuses and housing workers often resort to tenant consultation to try to overcome problems they find intractable. They respond to tenants' concerns by saying things like: "We'd like you to come along to a focus group and tell us about the allocations policy. Should we allocate our properties on points, date order or merit basis?" Tenants generally don't care about allocations policies until they produce the wrong outcomes. At that point they will eloquently tell us that they don't want any more idiots moved into the area.

Preaching about 'empowering' colleagues can be equally meaningless. Many leaders think they can do this by having an away day. They'll get some external guru in to give a little chat about how far we've come since Octavia Hill, followed by a motivational speaker and a bit of meditation. They'll have a nice lunch, show a video in the afternoon, round off with a feedback session and then everyone will go home and will magically have transformed into a fully empowered team at the bleeding edge of modern business practices the next day.

The main benefit from an away day is meeting people. The biggest waste of time will be the chief executive's talk. I've sat through plenty and given a few too and I expect people listening to me have the same experience of disconnection from reality. They're thinking, "So what? You've signed a deal with Banque Euroloot for £15 million. I'm not interested. What I want to know is, is my job safe? Am I getting more money? And why can't I do anything about this tenant who keeps firing pellet guns at me and scratching my car every time I go on the estate?" Real empowerment means treating people with dignity and respect and treating them as they would like to be treated, in a meritocratic business environment.

The challenge of change

Change is a huge issue. Never ever underestimate how massively difficult it is to bring about change in the workplace. When I give talks I tell people, if you want to get an angle on how difficult change is, tonight tell your partner that you're going to sleep on *their* side of the bed. I invite people to ring me and tell me what happened when they demanded to sleep somewhere they've never slept before. Many people do tell me they have tried this and found it helped them change their attitude on life.

We are very much creatures of habit. We like to park in the same space every morning and get annoyed when someone's sitting in 'our' seat at lunchtime. So once you get into a change management programme – whether you're changing the office reception area or the entire welfare state – DO NOT underestimate the power of people's resistance. Remember that the only creatures who truly embrace and love change are babies with dirty nappies.

To get people up for it and to understand it, first make sure you never ask anyone to do anything unreasonable or require them to solve problems that they haven't got the authority to do. Equally don't tell them it won't be difficult, because it will. The first rule of nursing is: don't tell the patient it won't hurt if it will. But we say to everyone, we're not asking you to do anything life threatening. Remember that almost everyone in the social housing sector earns more than squaddies in Iraq and Afghanistan. We expect our people to understand the importance of their role and responsibilities and to be flexible, enthusiastic and willing to find and fulfil their potential. I stress to everybody the importance of understanding our business and the common purpose which runs through all of our jobs. We try to develop the concept of mutualism and stress the importance of reciprocity in working relationships. If at any time a person feels that they are asked to do something unreasonable or have been given responsibility for anything that they don't have authority for, we urge them to speak out.

It is also important to recognise the interaction between personal and professional life. Things can go wrong in both spheres and each affects the other. If you're having a bad time at work you're likely to have a bad time at home and vice versa. It is not easy to isolate either experience. We provide a confidential and independent counselling service which colleagues can access if they feel the need to do so, although we actively encourage people to be open and honest with their coaches, mentors and managers.

Actions speak louder than words

An essential principle of management is: don't say you'll do something if you're not going to do it. If you say to colleagues, "I'm committed to your personal development and unlocking your potential," then follow it up with, "Right, here's the procedure manual. Follow that or you're sacked," you've blown a hole in your case from the start.

I believe that actions speak louder than words, and strive to align our values with behaviours. It is very important to understand and eliminate anything that really winds people up. Animal Farm-type managerial hypocrisy is forbidden. People don't like having a pep talk from a boss who says, "We really need you to work hard with us, in partnership, because at the end of the day, we're all in this together," shortly followed by the boss being seen swanning off to an expensive restaurant for a big expense account meal while colleagues are stuck with a curly sandwich from Netto. Equally, seeing the boss being waited on hand and foot with his cappuccino and biscotti amaretti whilst you're being asked for your £2.00 by the tea fund manager (the poor bastard who has the most difficult and explosive job in any company) doesn't make you feel great and want to self-actualise.

Whose responsibility is it to make colleagues happy, healthy, motivated and inspired? I believe it's a joint responsibility. If I want our 170 employees to go out and treat other people with dignity and respect and be motivated and inspired, then responsibility for most of that starts with me, our board and our executive team. I tell people: "We are a caring organisation. Our colleagues are definitely our greatest asset and I need each and every one of them to be happy, healthy and motivated, punctual and up for it every day. We want company loyalists who are confident, focused on our priorities, great team players who share our values and translate them into reality." But I can't just tell people that I want all those qualities and expect it to just happen. I have to commit everything I can to make our culture a reality, embracing everybody.

This means taking action on a number of different fronts.

The office environment

The dynamics, ergonomics and general atmosphere of where people work has a powerful effect on their performance. Our offices are funky, upbeat, functional and interesting places. We've got fish tanks, bespoke street art graffiti, chill-out zones, a performance and coaching studio, two gyms, showers and iconic, inspirational wall art. Despite this, our costs are half the average for the housing sector. We try to create a sense of place in the office, making it interesting, not opulent or ostentatious and not about the directors.

I don't have my own office, I have the same as everyone else – a desk, a computer and a phone. I am in the office for around four or five hours a day and I spend the rest of the time out and about looking at our neighbourhoods, listening to residents and colleagues, thinking and experiencing other business practices. If I have any complex problems to deal with I will think about them directly after a one mile swim, which I complete religiously every day. I only believe in being in the office for catching up with people and for essential business decision making.

We have an urban lounge, a glass office, a red room and rainbow room. I encourage people not to have meetings at all, and if they must, to keep them no longer than 40 minutes. Meetings should be exciting, important, decision making opportunities. We have an hour glass which sits on the table to remind people how precious time is. I like stand up meetings, where people focus on making decisions and say yes or no rather than prevaricate. I encourage people to behave on a daily basis as they would if they were going on holiday for two weeks the next day. When people are demob happy they have extremely short meetings, work fast and take lots of decisions quickly. In my experience it is rare that any decisions taken under the pressure of going on holiday are any worse than those that people have deliberated and agonised about, or simply dodged.

We provide a wide range of refreshments free of charge and people are encouraged to interact and work together, rather than engage in professional backstabbing, scoring points off each other, abusing their position or playing power politics. Running a £30m business is complicated enough without people indulging in stupid, petty games.

Wages are obviously important in job satisfaction, but equally we humans enjoy reward, respect and recognition. We try to create a dynamic environment that enables this.

Recruiting and retaining colleagues

We've recently transformed our human resources group into a performance and coaching academy (PCA). Human resources can be an unrewarding job in many organisations. Sadly HR teams spend almost all of their time dealing with numpties! Their most positive experiences usually involve maternity matters. As a result of their continuous exposure to employee problems, HR staff are in danger of becoming cynical and end up disliking people – this is why we have reinvented our team.

We are very careful about whom we recruit and how we relate to people when they work for us. Our PCA colleagues' main job is to provide people with the knowledge and skills that will enable them to unlock their potential. They also work very closely with me and my fellow colleagues on dealing with absenteeism, probation, colleague benefits and all of our health, happiness and wellbeing programmes.

We carefully scrutinise every job vacancy to see if it is critically important or an anachronistic vestige of the past. We offer voluntary redundancy every couple of years because we don't want people working for us who don't want to be here (very often the ones who take up the offer are people who are getting a bit jaded and tired, although some very good people have freed up their futures). Our PCA colleagues are professional recruiters. They are unafraid to reject satisfactory or adequate candidates, even after a couple of days interviewing. They know that getting the wrong people on board will inevitably lead to problems in the future. We are all hostages to zany European employment laws, which have created a procedural mine-field, a complainants' charter and a safety net for losers. PCA colleagues work very closely with our 'talent pool' of up and coming enthusiastic, committed, no nonsense colleagues who want to set the place on fire (not literally – I'm not suggesting employing arsonists).

With managers, I'm not interested in their technical skills; I assume we can take their technical competence for granted. What I want to know is how they are going to unlock their own potential and that of everybody else. I expect my managers to inspire and motivate people on a minute by minute basis, to coach and mentor people and to be fantastic role models.

Many of us were promoted into management positions because we excelled at our previous job. Often that past experience does not prepare you for the hugely demanding task of leadership, which is the second most difficult thing I've ever done in my life (bringing up three daughters being the first).

Managers who want to be liked will fail, because the surest way to fail is to try and make everyone happy. You might as well get used to it. Managing people is a lonely trade: it can be upsetting, rewarding, challenging, frightening and often frustrating. It's a bit like being a mum or a dad, in that nothing can prepare you for it. Most people have been managed well and badly and when they get the opportunity to manage and be responsible for others, their good and bad experiences, plus their family background, beliefs and schooling, will heavily influence their style.

Managers need to have the confidence to promote great behaviour and tackle unacceptable behaviour. Doing nothing is not an option.

Pride in your job

The lowest paid people in an organisation often have laborious routines, dare I say boring tasks to perform. I never tell people that we're all equal but I do say we're all as important as each other. Instilling a sense of pride in doing whatever job you do is essential, but great care and attention needs to be paid to people at the lower end of the pay scale. These positions tend to be frontline jobs, the ones on which people will judge your entire company. Frontline colleagues are the first people that your customers see or talk to and are the ones the public see day in day out. Maintaining the environment, answering the phone, photo-copying, doing the post, stuffing envelopes, picking up litter, removing graffiti – these may not be jobs necessitating a vast range of skills or difficult decision making so they will always be on relatively low pay, but the attitude these people have to their work is critical to customer service and company morale.

I regularly remind people that work consumes around 60% of their time and many people spend more time with work colleagues than their family members. Getting to and from work, thinking or worrying about it, all consume large chunks of our lives. If people aren't happy at work they are frittering away their precious time on earth and will look back in years to come and ask themselves where all the time went. I remind people that work is voluntary: we're not in prison and unlike Randle P. MacMurphy in the film "One Flew Over the Cuckoo's Nest", no-one is forced to stay in the work institution. In that film, even the Native American 'Chief' Bromed, who chose not to speak for years, was a voluntary member at the sanatorium.

You should view all your colleagues as special individuals: spend time finding out what motivational triggers they possess and what might unlock their potential. It is important to know what they like, but what might be even better is something they've never tried – that they don't yet know they like.

Forget psychometric testing and profiling. In my view having Russell Grant do their astrology chart would be just as accurate. Some of the most appalling people would do well from psychometric testing, like Dr Harold Shipman, who murdered so many of his elderly patients in Greater Manchester. He was GP to one of our lettings staff and she thought he was fantastic – as did most of his younger patients (the ones that were still alive, that is).

Once you have found the triggers and conditions in which you can motivate and unlock potential it's time to decide what sort of incentives you should offer your people and what is the business case for doing so.

If you ask people what would motivate them, very often they will say more pay, more holidays, and shorter working weeks. Unfortunately, for their employer this is a recipe for bankruptcy. You have to find better ways of motivating people. We pay good salaries and have our people work in funky surroundings, our productivity is high and we've achieved significantly improved results with fewer employees year on year, by focusing on key business requirements, supported by coaching methods and first class IT.

Many of the benefits we offer help to protect the health of our workforce, improve wellbeing and stimulate motivation.

These are some of the main benefits we offer:
- Performance related pay and benefits
- Monthly motivational and inspirational coaching sessions
- Health and wellbeing programmes, including access to advice from our in-house doctor
- Enhanced company illness pay
- Permanent Health Insurance
- Counselling services
- Swimming passes for colleagues and customers
- Massage
- Life Alignment
- Gyms available to all qualifying colleagues where they can train on their own or attend daily classes run by colleagues (pattering, body blitz, running club, kick boxing)
- A £300 incentive to give up smoking
- Christmas party
- Colleagues' birthdays celebrated with a cake and the day off

- Childcare vouchers for colleagues with children under school age.
- Child's first day at school holiday, for parents
- When colleagues become grandparents they can have the day off when they hear the good news
- A free DVD club with all the latest releases available to take home for the night or the weekend
- A stakeholder pension plan
- Up to 32 days holiday per year
- Free private healthcare
- Dental care
- Optical care
- Super flexitime to help with work/life balance
- Interest free loans for bus, tram and train season tickets
- A very low interest car loan scheme
- Interest free colleague support loans
- Career breaks.

The cost of our benefits and other opportunities are relatively low and are paid for annually out of efficiency savings, for example through our reductions in sickness absence and re-let times. Almost every benefit we offer has come from discussions with colleagues and is carefully examined and appraised to ensure that it meets with and supports our goals for a happy, healthy workforce. Yes, we do get outrageous and impractical suggestions and yes, we knock them on the head.

First and foremost you need to know why you are doing things. Simply dispensing largesse is easy. Focused and targeted investment in our workforce has to have a business case, but often it is not easy to accurately measure impacts and outcomes. I'm sure for example that having so few smokers at Irwell Valley is making an important contribution to our almost zero sickness, but this programme has been in operation for over a decade.

Work-based daily classes are not compulsory but they are an acknowledged part of our day. More than 50% of our workforces are currently actively involved in them. If people don't want to or can't attend classes they can chill out in one of our quiet rooms or libraries. The odd one or two inevitably take advantage but we deal with them in a direct, no nonsense way.

If you are generous with benefits, there is always a risk that your generosity will be abused. Christmas parties are a particularly high risk activity, but they are also high worth, because people value them, look forward to them and take the Christmas party seriously. At Christmas parties, the barriers come down: many colleagues are unrecognisable from their day to day image and very often offer forthright views on all aspects of the business in a newly-found confident manner, usually assisted by a few beers. We generally have at least one incident at every party that requires disciplinary action.

There could be a temptation to ban the Christmas party because it is too much trouble, but we think it is better to operate our 'piss off the right people' policy. There's no point in pissing off the wrong people – the majority who were just enjoying themselves – when you can simply take decisive action against the ones who overstepped the mark.

Many businesses have banned Christmas and office parties, because they are worried about health and safety and litigation implications. But making a decision based upon the bad behaviour of a tiny minority is a sure way of creating resentment and anger amongst the rest of the workforce. We all remember how it felt at school when the whole class got detention because of what one person had done and wouldn't own up. The unfairness rankles.

Happy Birthday to you!

Every time you set up a benefit, you also set up issues about fairness and you have to be prepared to handle these firmly. Any discretion needs to be open to challenge and transparent. Our birthday cake policy is a fantastic example of how a simple motivational gesture can cause mayhem.

In my first professional job, when it was my birthday, I was told I had to buy cakes for the whole office. I know that's the tradition in many offices, but it seemed rediculous to me, so I refused. (Years later I empirically tested this with my youngest daughter in an effort to prepare her for work: not surprisingly she was most indignant when I explained to her that she should buy cakes for me and the rest of the family on her birthday). Having failed the birthday cake test, I was then sent to cake Coventry for the rest of my three years in that office. When it was other people's birthdays, they bought cakes for everyone except me. At least I didn't put weight on!

I think it was in reaction to this kind of nonsense that, in an effort to reward good attendance, I introduced our birthday policy. This says that all Diamond colleagues, that is, our top performers, can have the day off on their birthday and also have a cake provided for them.

I thought this was fairly straightforward, but it turned out to be one of the most complicated and controversial things we ever introduced. There was always disagreement over what constitutes good attendance. Managers also struggled to manage in this uncertain environment! One of our colleagues became terminally ill with pancreatic cancer, but managed to turn up for work throughout most of her chemotherapy. She got a cake on her birthday but, being the honorable person she was, felt that her attendance didn't deserve it. No doubt some jobsworth manager might have refused her a cake because she'd had some days off at the Christie Hospital!

Managers still have trouble with our birthday cake programme because it requires them to make judgments about their colleagues' attendance and they don't like having to make such decisions. I think it's very simple: if you've had good, not necessarily perfect attendance, then you qualify. I have had several conversations with groups of colleagues about our birthday policy. The first question I ask them is how many of them have had a birthday in the last 12 months. Sometimes people don't put their hands up – that's very worrying. I then ask how many had the day off and a birthday cake and usually about 75% put their hands up. The plethora of reasons given by the other 25% range included comments like "I had an injury at work so my manager disqualified me." On the basis of this we introduced a birthday appeals policy for people who felt unfairly treated.

Turning to the people who had had the day off and the cake I asked them if they were happy with the cake they'd received. I was flabbergasted by the response I got back. One colleague complained he'd received a £5 cake from Aldi when someone else had got a 15 quidder from Tesco with his picture on it! We then standardised the cake policy with a maximum value of £10 on the cake but seriously considered whether we should have our in-house cake makers, bearing in mind that we had about three birthdays per week. I thought this would solve our problems until I met somebody who told me they couldn't eat cake because they had coeliac disease, so they'd get a rubber plant amiably.

This is a great example of the importance of treating people as *they* would like to be treated. Keeping it simple, fair and workable is the real skill, and is never easy.

Let's spend the . . . day together

Sometimes you have to accept that you can't please everyone and a benefit just has to be scrapped. We began by having some successful colleague days out; everyone reported great feedback afterwards. But the next year, someone asked, "Could we go to Chester instead of walking in Wales?" So we ended up with two different days out, which began to undermine the main intention, which was to bring everybody together for a day so they could get to know each other. The next year some people asked if they could go to the seaside. Others asked if they could bring their children, while another group wanted to go to the races in York and we were in danger of having 170 bespoke days out. It just got ridiculous – we abolished the concept and replaced it with our two day Think-a-Thon.

It is an old, but nevertheless true, adage that if you look after your workforce, they will look after the company and the customers. It worked for Titus Salt and Lord Leverhulme a century ago and it works for Richard Branson, Julian Richer and us now. That's what all good employers should do. Most companies would never dream of putting on singing or dancing lessons because they don't understand the benefits that these would produce, corporately and personally for their colleagues. Yet many, even in the austere times we're in, will send managers to Cranfield Business School, or even Harvard, not to mention various conventions, symposia, conferences and so on, with often ill-defined benefits and huge per capita costs.

There's a well established conference circuit in the public sector and of course it's usually the top people who go. They come back stating that the conference was "very useful" "interesting" "thought provoking" etc. I've been to many a conference myself and I ask myself what impact being there has on my ability to run our company and to improve morale, colleague commitment and customer service. There's the old chestnut extolled by many that attending a conference is a great networking opportunity. Very often however, the only difference between networking and gossiping is that you can claim expenses for networking.

Make sure your policies reflect your values

The world is constantly changing and companies need to be flexible, responsive and have policies which effectively drive the business forward. None of our policies are set in concrete – over time they may less become less relevant or colleagues might question whether a policy is fair or whether it reflects our values and ethics.

As part of our healthy living programme we introduced a variety of measures to help people quit smoking. These included health and addiction advice, shock tactics (like the ghastly sight of cancerous lungs in a bell jar) and enforcement, ie. banning smoking in all cars, offices and close proximity to our building.

A colleague questioned me at one of our Gdansk meetings, and asked how I could justify giving people £300 to quit smoking, when we gave only £100 for a 20 years' long service award (which equates to a penny a week).

Smoking is a tricky one. In 2000 almost half of our colleagues smoked, some heavily, and regularly walked off the job for smoke break. Even before the smoking ban we managed to reduce smoking to less than 5% of our workforce (and not because half the workforce died). We are very keen to encourage people to give up smoking, and the £300 is a big incentive, but the policy has created resentment among people who have never smoked. On the other hand, there tends to be even more resentment against people who are allowed to nip out regularly for a 15 minute fag break. They also have higher absenteeism rates and their breath smells. Many other policies, such as childcare vouchers, will cause resentment amongst people who don't qualify. With diverse workforces, however, there has to be something for everybody.

Anarchy vs repression

Julian points out in his book *The Richer Way* that management has to strike the right balance between anarchy and repression. If you had no rules, and say a heavy metal rock god as the CEO, everyone would have a great time for a few days, but it would all quickly go pear-shaped. A highly repressive regime, headed up by President Assad of Syria on the other hand, would produce short term results, but in the long run would fail in today's world, because with no creativity, it would be unable to adapt to challenges and changes.

Moreover, modern workers are less likely to respond favourably to the authoritarian control and command structures which were the norm in many businesses during the last century. The repressive, hierarchical management structure which characterised public services when I started work in the 1980s produces poor results and is extremely wasteful and depressing to work under. Very often, layers and layers of management are created by human beings building their own power bases, demanding more staff and introducing more complexity, jargon and rules. Those lower down the hierarchy respond by building their own power bases. You end up with more and more people doing less and less.

Efficiency should not mean getting more efficient at things that don't really matter. Clockcards in local government are a classic example of non-productive, labour intensive bureaucracy which is at best ridiculous and at worst a puerile waste of time. The skill is to get the balance right, so that people have fun, whilst understanding that rules are designed to facilitate and make great things happen.

Rules need to be reasonable and they need to be clear. In many organisations they are fuzzy and not firmly enforced, which means the curve is easily pushed to the wrong side of the graph. Too many rules are as bad as too few. A bit of anarchy now and again ain't a bad thing in the workplace but, equally, sometimes there have to be heavy duty rules regarding probity, diversity and governance.

People must be treated with dignity and respect. Even when you are disciplining a colleague or making someone redundant, there are appropriate ways of doing it, in fairness to them and also so that other colleagues will realise that you have handled this decently. The same applies to numerous other conflicts that will inevitably emerge in any organisation. One of the main principles is that there must be some sense of justice amongst people in the workplace.

We have no compunction about suspending anybody who is racist, dishonest or is demonstrably behaving badly. I only wish that equally swift action could be taken against racist tenants or bad neighbours. Unfortunately this is not so and it constitutes one of the major obstacles we face in sorting out some of the problems in our neighbourhoods.

Rules need to serve, enable and facilitate rather than dominate and destroy. We need to be careful that we do not regulate out innovation and that there is ample opportunity for creativity within a business risk framework. Good ideas rarely occur in the office between 9am and 5pm. I often have my best ideas before or after work, especially after swimming my daily mile or riding my bike or out with my dogs.

Diamond Service employment

Just as we have meritocracy for customers, we also have it in the shape of Diamond employment and Standard employment for colleagues. This tiered approach has been embraced by the workforce, and we have never had any objections from our unions, because it is seen to be fair.

In 2005 we introduced a three tier, performance based, benefit and reward system for all colleagues as part of our meritocracy. The tier you are on has nothing to do with your position in the organisation: it's solely about your performance. The better you perform the more money, privileges and benefits you get. The system is unique in the housing sector, as it matches the benefits and pay that an individual colleague receives to their performance. The system moves our best performers up their salary grade in return for excellence, not length of service.

In 2012 we revised the system to make it simpler and easier to operate. We introduced significant differentials between Diamond and Standard colleagues.

BENEFIT	DIAMOND	STANDARD
25 days' leave + statutory bank holidays	X	X
ECU Allowance	X	X
Pension scheme	X	X
Refreshments	X	X
Statutory maternity/paternity leave & pay		X
Statutory redundancy		X
Sick Pay – Statutory only		X
Basic Flexitime		X
Xmas/Summer Parties	X	X
Childcare Vouchers	X	

Season ticket loan	X	
Anti-smoking incentive	X	
Non Consolidated Bonus	X	
Additional annual leave (2 days per annum)	X	
Birthday policy	X	
Buy/Sell Annual Leave	X	
Car loan	X	
Discount Car MOT/Service	X	
Career break	X	
Company Classes Massage/Health Check	X	
Consolidated Pay Rises	X	
Dental Plan	X	
DVD Library	X	
Enhanced maternity/paternity leave & pay	X	
Enhanced rudundancy	X	
Full/Super Flexitime	X	
Healthcare	X	
Monthly Raffle	X	
Sick Pay – 6 months full pay + PHI	X	
Service holidays	X	
Social events – Family Day Out etc.	X	
Support fund	X	

Each colleague's performance is assessed every six months in our coaching checks (our version of appraisals) which link directly, through competencies and personal targets, to our five zero priorities. Managers have the discretion to promote and demote at any time provided that they have a robust case to do so. There is an independent appeals policy to ensure fairness and transparency.

Our Diamond and Standard employment structure directly affects our colleagues' pay, holidays and other benefits. Its significance warrants the high level of time and energy we have put into developing it and making sure that our best performing people receive the highest rewards and the best and widest choice of benefits. Even people on Standard tier (and these are less than 2% of the workforce) have a decent deal and good levels of pay. However, they will not receive sick pay, flexitime and so on unless they improve their performance and move up to Diamond.

Accessing our Diamond employment package depends not just on performance appraisal scores but also a commitment to ensuring health and wellbeing. Our consultant physician, Dr Godfrey, is on hand to give expert medical advice to each colleague. He does not hesitate to comment on lifestyle: if he thinks that a colleague's health is suffering because they're too fat or they drink too much, he will tell them.

Colleagues who give us this commitment to maintaining their health receive enhanced benefits, six months paid sick leave, healthcare etc., and an individual health and wellbeing programme if they suffer any problems. Absences from work due to sickness will have an immediate and direct impact on the benefits they receive. Any colleagues who choose not to take on this commitment and engage with Dr Godfrey are given our standard remuneration package and lose entitlement to most of the benefits.

Appraisals OMG

We have replaced appraisals with a much more relaxed assessment which we call our coaching checks. These complement our monthly Five Time meetings.

Although these are less formal than a traditional assessment, they are a serious business. How a colleague is assessed at a coaching check fundamentally affects their fame and fortune. Our aim is for all colleagues to be performing to the highest possible standards and accessing the Diamond employment package. The coaching check is a very tricky, almost precarious, part of our business as it sits at the very heart of our meritocracy. It challenges managers to be honest, open and transparent and it charges them with the responsibility of being straight with their colleagues about performance. We have had incidences of managers over-inflating their colleagues' scores in order to ingratiate themselves, but to prevent this we correlate the designation given against the performance on measurable business critical indicators.

It is important the managers are confident and competent in their abilities and get close to their colleagues in a supportive coaching role as regularly as possible. There should be no surprises at a coaching check. We actively dissuade people from leaving any issues until there is a formal opportunity to raise them – if there is a concern, however small, it is dealt with early. Problems need to be tackled quickly in order to prevent them escalating.

We have a very high emphasis on reward, recognition and respect. Ideally our coaching checks are all about these three Rs, rather than an opportunity to empty in trays and deal with day to day matters. We also encourage people to develop personally and professionally on a daily basis and managers are empowered to recommend that somebody move from Standard to Diamond employment package or vice versa whenever they feel it's appropriate.

It is not always easy for middle managers to assess their colleagues. If a manager rates his or her colleague low, what does that say about him or her as a manager? We recognise that there will be a tendency for managers to want their teams to look better than they are, so they can boast that their whole team is on Diamond service. The organisation has to be aware of the circumstances in which a person is given a particular assessment. However, as mentioned, we look much deeper into these situations than just having a cursory glance at the scores.

A very small percentage of colleagues are on our Standard employment package. New starters, poor performers and those on disciplinaries are not permitted to enjoy anything like the same benefits that their high performing counterparts do.

New starters can be put on to Diamond service at any time by their managers. People on disciplinaries can return to Diamond service once their punishment is spent, whereas persistent poor performers are pretty much in the departure lounge. Sadly these are colleagues with bad attendance, bad attitude and bad performance. Sooner or later, in most cases, we will let them go.

We do put Standard folk on leadership and motivation courses to try to push them forward but if they don't have the right attitude their performance won't improve. Our Diamond colleagues are characterised by excellent attitude, excellent performance and whilst you might not always get excellent attendance (because of genuine illness) these are the characteristics we wish to see in our people.

No business, public service or hospital will ever be able to improve their services, cut out waste, eliminate bureaucracy and absenteeism unless they embrace the reward, respect and recognition agenda and have remuneration and benefits which reward the outcomes that they want their people to achieve. They need a meritocratic system.

When you're young, meritocracy is instituted and expected, whether it's at school, university or the cub scouts. You know that the harder you work the more you will achieve and be recognised with better marks and awards. However, most of this stops when you enter the world of work. Most public sector organisations operate a remuneration and employment package on a 'one size fits all' basis and treat everyone the same. For the public sector to be transformed, the rewards for every employee must be linked to the desired outcomes. Strong courageous leadership is needed to set the scene for a public sector performance culture. This must be backed up by a meritocratic reward system which eliminates poor performance.

Health authorities, for example, should reward GPs for the health of their constituency, not for the level of health problems. This should apply even in disadvantaged and deprived neighborhoods, where lifestyle choices and behaviour produce unhealthy people. GPs should be financially rewarded for their efforts to turn the inverse care law on its head. It is obvious that teachers who get the best results with the resources that they have should also be the highest paid.

In this chapter I have described the philosophy, policies and practices which have enabled our business to double in size in 10 years, with fewer employees than we had eight years ago, and to deliver our best ever financial and service results. Being one of the first housing associations to hit the *Sunday Times'* list of top ten best companies to work for, being inducted to the *Financial Times'* best employers hall of fame for five consecutive years and receiving national and international awards from the Chartered Institute of Housing in the UK and National Association of Housing and Redevelopment Officials (NAHRO) in the USA does not happen by accident or luck. In my view you get lucky when preparation coincides with opportunity. If I had my time again, I would focus almost all of my and my senior managers' attention on recruiting and retaining the best, cleverest, happiest people we could find, whilst ejecting average and below performers.

Our business is very simple, we have one source of income and three types of expenditure: people, maintenance and debt. It is the people who make it happen or not as the case may be. It is crucial to focus upon them and make sure they understand their roles and responsibilities.

Chapter 8

Meritocracy and its wider applicability

Our meritocratic, rewards-based approach has made us much more effective and dynamic and has brought measurable benefits and improvements to the people we work for and the people who work for us.

In 2010 we refocused and simplified our approach to ensure that we achieve the highest possible efficiencies, effectiveness and customer service. In 2011/2012 we reported our best results ever. Although we are performing much the same sorts of functions that we did 15 years ago, we are doing it so much better, with fewer people, getting greater value for money and utilising our resources to solve societal problems and challenges.

If the rewards-based approach works for us, could it work for other organisations? Is our business model and philosophy applicable widely in the post 'casino capitalist' society that we have? I believe it is. I think that this could be the key that unlocks the latent potential of local government and areas such as health, education, welfare reform and our failing prison service.

Our experiences, together with that of my friend Julian Richer, strongly suggest that the approach could be transferred to larger more complex and more diverse organisations in the country.

Having worked in local and central government, academia and the private sector, I understand that transferring our experiences would not be easy or instant. But what is important here is not an organisation's size, structure or functions, but its leadership mindset, assumptions and way of thinking. Even a small district council delivers a wide range of services which, as activities, do not have much in common – from emptying the bins to paying out housing benefit to tending the flower beds in the park. The same diversity could be said of a hospital. But as an organisation, these entities will have a culture, a way of managing themselves and an attitude towards their customers. More often than not, this is what needs to change.

I started off this book talking about the problems we have in society, and the tendency for social ills to get worse, though the action of the curve. Public services have a huge role to play in addressing the consequences of this behavioural decline in society. Revolutionary change is needed in order to equip local government and the health service to do what they are there to do, ie. support and promote a safe, decent, healthy, responsible society.

As a society we have an abundance of resources available to us: IT, knowledge, money and most importantly people. Applying our meritocratic philosophy to various public sector organisations would, I believe, yield massive productivity gains and dramatic reductions in sickness levels, foster feelings of belief and commitment, radically improve customer service and allow workers to feel more fulfilled and enlightened.

Public services in themselves can never solve all the ills of society. But they can do much to create the conditions that stop those ills arising in the first place or eradicate them whenever they arise. Over hundred years ago, big city corporations like Birmingham and Manchester transformed public health by installing clean water and proper sewage systems for their citizens, which dramatically lengthened life expectancy and improved socio-economic conditions. The same energy, innovation and vision afforded to public health reforms by the Victorians are urgently needed today.

Many public sector workers would love to do this, but are not encouraged to use their skills in such a way because of cultural and bureaucratic stagnation. GPs and nurses know full well how the people registered with their surgery could be healthier, but most of the time they are unable to give this advice because of the reactive nature of the service, health economics and performance management demands.

Happy and healthy

Could we imagine GPs being paid based on the proportion of healthy and happy patients they have in their practice, rather than ill, sad ones? There is emerging evidence from the health service that the meritocratic approach works. Locally enhanced services, whereby GPs measure and improve body mass index, blood pressure and other key indicators of health, are now being rewarded financially on the basis of the improvements they make. With over half of the UK population over weight, 30% obese and the escalating problem of child obesity, urgent action is imperative. A quantum shift in our approach to preventative healthcare would save money, improve wellbeing and allow health professionals to focus more on non-lifestyle induced illnesses.

According to paramedics, GPs and other health professionals, it is evident that a vast amount of our health expenditure goes on fixing or elevating lifestyles and behaviours which cause illness. Only proactive steps will address this: just giving the general public vague advice has not worked. Patients don't tend to approach their GP to talk about healthy living – they just want a prescription and a sick note when they fall ill.

The best social workers and teachers can do an enormous amount to improve the lives and outlook of the families and children they work with. But this is not usually what they are asked to do. Instead, they operate within a compliance culture, in which all that matters is that the right boxes are ticked (lessons plans drawn up, reports filed and so on). No-one asks them the question, what real difference have you made to people's lives? Their focus is not on tackling the root causes of problems.

In the compliance culture, fostered by the myriad of inspection regimes within which public services operate, there is little room for a meritocracy. The best GP surgeries, social workers or teachers are often deemed to be on the same level as the worst, or merely average, or satisfactory, as long as they all tick the same boxes.

The holy grail

Could you have a meritocratic workplace within an organisation such as a local authority? The answer is yes, with the right leadership, culture, determination, incentives and sanctions. At the moment however that's not how public sector workplaces are structured or operate.

I put the emphasis on reward, but the carrot is meaningless without the stick. In many public services the only carrot is that you don't get the stick. Very often there is no stick. It is almost impossible to get sacked from a local authority. Unless you commit fraud, or display violent or racist behaviour, your job is pretty much safe, no matter how mediocre, rude or lazy you are. You can get made redundant of course, but that decision is rarely made on performance grounds.

Local government is heavily unionised, with a complex system of national pay rates. There are reasons for this – and it has to be acknowledged that some of those pay rates are low – but the net result is that, up until recently, everyone has been locked into a system of regular pay increments and promotion based on length of service. There are hints of innovation, like the Agenda for Change in the NHS which seeks to promote meritocratic remuneration, but this is a new idea for the public sector. Although pay increases in local government have been low or non-existent in recent years, that hasn't really altered the general expectation that there should be increments as a matter of course. People are not surprised if they get an increment but shocked if they don't. This approach prevents motivation through pay. The best people get the same as the worst; in fact, as we've seen with the absence statistics, some people are getting paid for not showing up for work at all.

The coalition government's expenditure cuts have called a halt to pay rises. With more than 60,000 people losing their jobs in the public sector the winds of change are blowing through our town halls. But cuts do not inevitably lead to greater efficiency. Undoubtedly the events since 2010 have lowered morale and reduced productivity even further.

Local authorities have had to shed staff whether they like it or not and for the foreseeable future they will have to deliver their services with fewer employees. Doing more with less, in an incentivised culture run by courageous leaders, has never been needed so much.

All public services, quite properly, come under close scrutiny. Local authorities now have to publish any item of spending over £500. Clearly, anybody spending public money needs to be accountable; we undergo rigorous financial audits and have to report to national performance standards. This includes, for instance, recognising what is now called 'Protected Characteristics' under the Equality Act 2010, which replaces the seven strands of diversity (race, disability, gender, gender identity, age, sexual orientation and religion and belief). It is very important, however, to ask: where does this end? And what is its purpose?

This is the framework that the public sector operates in and that distinguishes it from the private sector. Like anything however, what starts out as a noble ideal can turn into a ridiculously complex system of measurement, which causes embarrassment, fear, disbelief and serves a dubious purpose. My 80 year old Auntie Beryl for example was recently asked by a council official if she was the same sexuality as she was five years ago!

Eating people is wrong

The way it's going I can imagine cannibalism being included as one of the protected characteristics for the future. After all, just because it's against the law to eat humans it doesn't mean to say that there are not practising cannibals out there in our communities who feel unloved, suppressed and discriminated against. Getting cannibals to "come out", be visible and seek help would be an important step for them and may help us understand why many people seem to mysteriously disappear every year, particularly those who abandon properties leaving large debts.

To try to understand this issue, we recently concluded our positive about cannibals project (PACP), on which I've just received an interim report. We employed three cannibals to help us understand their needs and issues and also to help us develop our business. I must say they worked their socks off and behaved impeccably for five months. But then somebody noticed that Mary, one of our cleaners, had not been turning up for work and was non-contactable. I called in Rodney, the Head Cannibal, and asked him if he had any idea as to what had happened to Mary. Looking twitchy he said: "Tom, I told the others not to eat her." I was appalled and said, "Rodney, you're joking!" But he admitted they had eaten her the previous week. I said, "Well, what do you have to say for yourself?" and he replied, "It just goes to show I was right to tell them to leave her alone. We've been eating your colleagues from finance, IT and human resources for the last five months and no-one said a dicky bird. Eat a cleaner and everybody's up in arms."

So be warned – look around your workplace and see if you can spot the early onset signs of cannibalism, like people biting their finger nails or picking their noses and eating it.

Joking aside, I believe that you could replace a lot of these complex policies and monitoring systems by simply treating people with dignity and respect and treating them as *they* would like to be treated, which would probably mean affording them no special treatment and no special mistreatment.

It is right that public services should be expected to operate to high standards of probity, transparency and fairness. The downside is that a lot of bureaucratic measuring and reporting systems have to be put in place (think of itemising all that spending above £500) and unless this is done efficiently and unobtrusively, it can get in the way of the job in hand. Recent estimates suggest that it costs almost £400 on average to respond to FOI requests. This is barmy.

The other problem is that when people are under scrutiny all the time, they play safe. They take refuge in rules, and there are a lot of rule books in public sector organisations. Every function is governed by a stack of standing orders, procedure manuals and so on. With dynamic management, this need not be an obstacle to good service delivery, but with unimaginative management, the rule book rules. We found when we took on ex-local authority employees that they were very institutionalised, virtually incapable of doing their job other than in the time-worn way they had always done it, regardless of whether or not that was a good way. I'm not saying all public sector staff are like that, but that's how people get after years of poor management and lack of challenge, working in hypocritical organisations where the bosses don't clock on and off, the councillors get free refreshments and the workers pay for their own tea fund.

Local government – the wild frontier?

Local government has the reputation of being a stable, staid place to work, but the reality is that it is a very volatile environment. Political control can change, there can often be conflicts of priority between elected members and paid officials; government policies which control local authority services also change, sometimes radically and with little warning. Budgets can drop sharply from one year to another and this is particularly true now with the public expenditure reductions scheduled to 2015.

In this fast changing environment, where people can be very unsure what they're supposed to be doing, it is tough to expect innovation and bold thinking. Taking risks in local government is hazardous; minor errors can end up blazoned over the front page of the local newspaper. People learn that risk is more likely to be punished than rewarded.

So rather than a performance culture, a herd-like survival culture emerges. People cling on to procedures, because that saves them from having to make an independent decision. Procedures become more important than performance, because to make a judgment on performance is difficult. Managers don't have the confidence to make the judgment that one member of staff is contributing more than another. They may not even be sure what it means, to do the job 'well'. In, say, a football team, it's obvious who plays well and who doesn't. But in an office there are all sorts of ways for people to hide slack performance. So unless the manager is perceptive and really focused on colleagues as individuals, it is easier for them to stick with the 'one size fits all' management approach that treats every member of the team the same, regardless of whether they are pulling their weight or not.

Taking disciplinary action against people is also very time consuming, stressful and often calls for disproportionate effort for little gain. Performance management cannot work unless you can get rid of the under performers, but this is difficult and risky for middle managers. It diverts attention from productive work and is frustrating, especially as approximately 80% of the poorly-performing culprits go off sick anyway… and still get paid.

Sick pay doesn't last for ever though. What HR people call 'the magic letter' (sent to inform people that their sick pay is about to end) triggers a recovery of Lazarus proportions in around 90% of cases. The beatification of Pope John Paul II and his eventual sanctification has to be based on hard evidence of three miracles. Personnel managers up and down the country should be sanctified on the basis of the miraculous cures effected by their letters!

The anti-performance issue extends higher up the organisation. Senior executives and politicians frequently don't want to make the judgment that a service is performing badly and not delivering what customers need. Instead they assure themselves that the service is complying with statutory requirements and can usually come up with a raft of statistics to prove that. Almost every public service can point to a survey that shows they have an 80% or so customer satisfaction rate. Customers of course have their own views.

Alongside all these factors which make public sector bodies difficult to manage, they have a high level of demand for their services and little control over that demand. Most of their services are mandatory and non-negotiable. The fire service has to be there, week in, week out, and so does refuse collection, or indeed the homelessness unit and the environmental health team.

The great thing about public services, which we all take for granted, is that they really are there, week in, week out. In emergencies – floods, terrorist attacks – they have frequently shown how good they can be.

These services are part of the fabric of society, and if their delivery could be improved, society would be enhanced. People would be more fulfilled, behave better and more likely to feel happy about paying their council tax. But currently, public sector cultures are not tuned into motivating their workforces to deliver a better service. Can that be changed?

No more 'one size fits all'

Our company operates under a strict regulatory framework. We have to answer to the Homes and Communities Agency and the Housing Ombudsman. Colleagues and myself belong to Unite, one of the main public sector unions. But we do not have the statutory responsibilities that councils have, for example to house homeless people. Furthermore, we are governed by a board, not by elected members. So in many ways we have more freedom to move than local authorities have.

Having said that, we have still gone further than many public and private bodies in making performance management a minute by minute reality. Many public sector managers are interested in performance issues. But it's difficult for them to do more than assign employees to their roles, and then apply a whole series of pressures and motivational techniques to get people to perform well in those roles.

As far as I know we're the first to instigate a performance structure which actually crystallises, in pay and conditions, the sorts of outcomes and behaviours that we want. Without this, organisations exhort people to be successful and motivated, but operate within a wage structure that pays wages and awards increments regardless of each person's outcomes. The two strands – performance and reward – never meet.

We've rejected the 'one size fits all' approach. We reward the behaviour which makes us an effective and efficient business, which takes advantage of market conditions, provides fantastic service to our customers, and which encourages people to progress, personally and professionally. We want that system of reward to be just and fair, and to demonstrate, quite simply, that the harder people work, the more they get. The less you work, the less you get and the shorter your stay with us.

When we first introduced a tiered scheme for colleagues over 10 years ago, we encountered opposition to it from outside Irwell Valley, but not from within. Unite shop stewards backed the idea. What worked to our advantage was that we'd had an informal meritocratic approach for years, giving staff awards for customer service and that kind of thing. There was a high level of trust that we were serious about this and it was not some back door ruse to sack people or pay certain favourites more.

Even though we had this backing from colleagues, devising and implementing a system that is just, fair and practicable has not been easy. We went through a long thinking process before arriving at our Diamond Employee scheme which began in 2012 and we will always be looking for ways to improve on it. I am not claiming a meritocratic system is easy, but I'm convinced it is worth the effort and that it works.

Once you start differentiating between individuals' performance, quite properly you attract scrutiny, because there is a risk of unfair discrimination. You need a system that is sophisticated enough to look at people in the round, not just tick two or three boxes against them. But the system must also be simple enough to be robust, easily understood and believed in by everybody. I think that if most managers are doing their jobs and are honest, they should be able to accurately score people's performance without relying on some 'scientific' appraisal system. It's called gut feeling or intuitive management.

Crucially, it must also produce the right results. When we display who's in the top percentile of performance, those people should not be any surprise to others in the organisation. There should be no muttering, "How come she's in the top 10? She's useless and always comes in late." The system must be fair, honest and perceived as just.

To complicate matters further, we don't just measure a colleague's performance in their job. We want to take into account what they are like as a person, what they contribute to their team, their attitude to customers. So no matter how technically competent they are, the 'thank God it's Friday, I live for my holidays' negative person, who carps at every new idea and drags everybody else down, will not be rewarded because their corrosive attitudes are unacceptable. Ideally, we don't want anybody like that in our organisation. Those who are just coasting along, with their 'not bad' attitudes, will not progress in our meritocratic remuneration scheme. Conscientious objectors, armchair quarter backs, spectator critics, player managers and the 'I hear what you say' brigade rarely survive the demands of our high performance, high reward culture.

What we want are the people who contribute much more, those who have enthusiasm and energy and are ready to embrace the culture and drive it forward. Senior managers take responsibility for creating the future, keeping things going and strengthening our culture. I know that by focusing on these important issues it will bring untold benefits to any business and its customers. One of the many things I've learnt from Julian Richer is that if you have the right people in place, with the right attitude and energy, you will be profitable and give great customer service. The challenge for every organisation is ensuring that all employees embrace this approach and that you nurture them, help motivate them and get rid of those who hold you back.

But how do you measure something intangible like attitude? We worked through a variety of different systems, culminating in a complicated scheme (with appeals) which took up an inordinate amount of time for everyone involved. As well as being unwieldy, it seemed to generate unrealistically high scores, with people scoring, say, 95% and being devastated if their score dropped to 94%. Managers had a tendency to inflate their staff's scores and were loath to mark anyone down.

In fact, as we came to realise, for a scheme to be fair and accurate, you cannot have managers appraising their own people. To take a comparison, GCSE and A level papers are not marked by the teachers who taught that class; an examining board ensures that the whole process is impartial and consistent.

Under our new scheme, we employ an independent consultant to carry out the annual performance appraisal. Each colleague will send the consultant a report of their views of what they've done and achieved during the year, with their targets alongside. They will also say something about our company, how we perform, what we are, what we do, the context we operate in and so on, to show that the person has a general understanding of the business and its raison d'etre. The colleague's manager will also give comments on the person's performance, and there will be a few words on training and development.

With this information, the independent reviewer places the employee in one of our categories of employment – Diamond or Standard service.

There is an appeals procedure, and during the course of the year, a manager has the power to move a colleague up or down a category.

As I explained in Chapter 7, the employment category a person is in fundamentally affects their pay and conditions. Standard, which is essentially for people in their first three months with the organisation, for non-performers and for people on disciplinaries, means they receive our standard terms and conditions, which are still good by comparison to the sector, but with no entitlement to sick pay or pay rises.

Diamond employment brings significant advantages such as extra holidays, six months sick pay, entrance into a monthly raffle, pay rises, super flexitime and so on.

Previously, we had four categories, but our colleagues didn't believe there was sufficient differentiation between them. Now the difference is massive and people are faced with stark choices. You're either a high performing enthusiastic member of the team or you're not. To remain in Standard employment you do have to be a poor performer, ignoring advice and persistently and wilfully behaving inappropriately. It is not one of our core values to create under performing numpties.

Ideally, every organisation would want all of its colleagues to be in the Diamond category and it is now very obvious to people why they to strive to get in and stay in our Diamond employment programme. We promote a highly aspirational system with lots and lots of winners. There's no point in having a half-hearted scheme that pretends being third class is as good as first when it simply isn't.

Having an independent adjudicator strengthens the system, just as our absence management system became more robust when we brought in a doctor to judge whether people were fit for work or not, instead of putting the decision on managers.

Supporting managers through our coaching check system takes some of the time-consuming burden off them; it also helps them to have a more positive relationship with their colleagues. Although they still sit down with each colleague periodically for a formal discussion, a manager's job is to focus on ensuring that their team members get into Diamond service and stay there. They are becoming more like coaches training athletes for a big event – measuring their performance, seeing where they need to improve, setting targets, bringing in training as necessary and above all being truthful and sincere in their relationships. This enables managers and colleagues to have an honest conversation about performance and attitude, with colleagues knowing that their manager is on their side, and wants to help them improve.

Our coaching check system will still have a large measure of subjectivity, of course, but we feel it is the fairest we can achieve. We did extensive research into this important area and concluded there is really no such thing as a totally objective, scientific, performance appraisal system, because you are dealing with human beings. Psychometric tests and box ticking will never give a true picture and can be dangerously misleading.

Tests have their place, but to be over reliant on procedures and processes can obscure reality and produce embarrassing results. I remember talking to a member of the British Medical Council after we'd spoken at a conference. He said they had seriously considered introducing a 'GP of the year' award in the 1990s and he was glad they hadn't. He felt that, had they implemented it under the monitoring and appraisal system they had at the time, it could well have been won by Dr Harold Shipman!

A meritocracy in public life

Our employment deal is our way of making a meritocratic culture a tangible reality. There is still a lot of resistance in the British psyche to meritocracy. To Americans, it is central to their culture. The US stands for a better life. We in Britain mock that sometimes, but belief in a meritocracy is what drives the US. However far away they might be from reaching the ideal of a better life, however stuck they might be at the bottom of the pile, US citizens believe they can get on and move up. There are countless examples in front of them of people who have done just that, from Barack and Michelle Obama to Oprah Winfrey, General Colin Powell and Elvis Presley.

That belief doesn't exist in the UK in the same way, even though, in practice, there is much more social mobility here than 50 years ago. Meritocracy appeals to the British sense of fairness and the UK too can point to many examples of successful people who started out right at the bottom. Nevertheless, there is a suspicion that Britain doesn't really stand for 'a better life' – more 'knowing your place'.

Why do we want a meritocracy in our public services? Because if we want good public services, we want the people working in them to be the best people – the most competent, the most friendly and the most enthusiastic about their job. Why shouldn't we have the best? Especially as we, the taxpayers and council taxpayers, are paying their wages.

The NHS, with 1.7m employees, is the largest employer in Europe and one of the largest in the world (for years only just behind the Chinese Army and Indian Railways, although in fact these days Wal Mart tops the list with more than 2m employees). Councils are very often the biggest employers in their areas, certainly in many inner cities. The quality of their staff affects us all, every day. If these public services could find a way to unlock the potential of their people and generate energy and enthusiasm, it would create a fantastic civic realm that would genuinely improve the society we live in.

There's no reason why this couldn't be done. Getting staff to perform to their full potential is nothing to do with the structure of local government or the health service, its functions or its political control. It is about leadership. If a leader (and that could be the leader of the council, the chief executive, or the head of an individual department or team) sets out to recruit and retain the best people, in order to maintain and deliver the best possible services, that's what we will get. Without leadership, it won't happen.

It might be thought that local government staff are poorly motivated because many of the jobs are low status, low paid, or downright messy. This is far from the case. The lowest paid jobs are often performed by very motivated people. Being a school dinner lady is never going to be highly paid, but you nearly always find they love their work: the hours suit them, the atmosphere is friendly and they enjoy working with the kids. Most kids love their dinner ladies and lollipop ladies.

The best job in local government I ever had was as a bin man. I had to get up at 4am, but we were finished by 12.00 each day. Our customers were happy, we completed all our rounds perfectly because we didn't want to have to go back and redo anything. Going home at 12 o clock was all the motivation we needed.

Then somebody in the council decided these hours were not acceptable. What if everyone wanted to finish work at 12.00? A timetable was introduced, we were told to slow down and make sure we finished at 3pm. We weren't happy. The customers weren't happy; people want their bins emptied early in the morning, and by cheerful Tom the bin man, not one who's resentful and bored.

It was a classic case of the local government 'one size fits all' approach being applied. No one gave any thought to the nature of the refuse collection job or how the team might best be motivated.

A willing, positive attitude does matter, especially in those jobs which have regular, day to day contact with the public – the bin men, the dinner ladies, the receptionists. It also matters for people like building inspectors and parking attendants – they are never going to be popular, maybe, but they can be courteous, fair, willing to listen and engage with the public.

From the point of view of having a decent civic society, the people in these jobs are more important than those higher up the local authority. If the bin men didn't turn up for work one morning the council phones would be ringing within hours, but I'm sorry to say if the chief executive's secretariat were kidnapped by aliens it would be a while before the public noticed.

I would guess the most poorly motivated people in local government are not the ones who have contact with the public, but those who are stuck in an office doing some sort of processing work, cogs in the big bureaucratic machine. This is where local government productivity slows to a crawl. Managers here who find their staff lack motivation should be asking themselves some questions. Is the job necessary and does it help improve society? Does the job have to be boring? Do staff feel their role is unacknowledged and their work unimportant? Is it unimportant? If so, why are they being asked to do it? We have IT to do the mindless repetitive tasks; there is no excuse for giving people work to do which does not call on their skills and talents as a human being.

The right people

Recruitment is one of the highest risks any business takes. Retaining the right people, talent spotting, fast tracking and creating the environment in which people want to come to work, enjoy it and miss their colleagues when they are away, is a major challenge for all businesses.

It all comes down to the people you take on, and how you treat them when they're with you. We've identified a range of business risks that our financial people monitor all the time. But in fact our biggest threats are just two things: recruiting and retaining the wrong people.

It takes us maybe an hour to interview and recruit someone. That hour can have huge repercussions. Equally if we house the wrong person, we quickly find out when the street descends into chaos. If we recruit the wrong people, as has happened sometimes, they undermine our culture and we end up spending an inordinate amount of time and money trying to get rid of them.

So we now spend lots of time on careful, clever recruitment and recruit for both skill and attitude. If you recruit purely for skill you sometimes get people who are technically competent, but completely at odds with your culture. Now we want people who will not only understand what we're about, but are enthusiastic about creating new futures, strengthening our culture and keeping our business efficient and effective. We have a compelling vision, we understand our social role, dedicated to improving the lives of the communities we serve, and our corporate role, providing jobs and other sorts of other ancillary businesses. There's plenty there for the right person to buy into.

Again, I've learnt from Julian Richer the importance of recruiting the right people. The reputation of his business relies on good customer service and he takes recruitment very seriously. He's not looking for hot-shot sales people; the first thing he looks for is friendliness, because that's by far the most important quality for anyone dealing with the public. Technical skills can be developed. "If you want good service, recruit the kind of people who are most likely to give it," he says in his book. "Are your staff the kind of people you would like to be served by?"

That's a simple, key principle and there's no reason why it should not be applied in public services as much as in business.

In a sense, what we look for in employees are the qualities you find in people who are happily self-employed. They know what they have to do and why they're doing it; they're engaged, well-motivated and have a strong sense of responsibility.

Of course, self-employed people have the motivation that comes from knowing that whether they earn a living or not depends entirely on their actions. If you're paid a regular wage, you haven't got that urgent motivation, so the impetus has to come from the culture of the organisation, making you feel sure your job is worth doing and that other people rely on you to do it well.

We don't want to recruit people who think it's enough to turn up, do their tasks according to the job description, and go home. We want people who want more, whether they're the cleaner or the finance director: people who want a sense of self-worth and who want to develop personal and professional skills. That's why we provide so much to aid our colleagues find and fulfil their potential – the classes, the gyms, book clubs, DVD libraries. They're fun, they help people be fitter and more relaxed, and they also help them become a more rounded person. Professional development and personal development go hand in hand, because the professional and personal are always interlinked. We have our in-house counsellors and we encourage people to come forward and talk about personal or family issues. Sooner or later personal issues will affect professional performance.

Are public service employers ready to look after their staff in this way? I would argue they have no choice.

Public services are, by their very nature, people businesses. The public sector is criticised by the private sector for being overstaffed, and maybe there has been truth in that. But on the whole, local authorities and health services are complex businesses, delivering services to people (the young, the old, the sick, the needy, often the difficult and demanding), by people; these are not jobs that can be done by some automated process.

Despite the examples of some enlightened employers, the corporate sector has also been slow to come round to the idea that its employees are its greatest asset and its key to success. The typical business instinct is 'we must look after the shareholders'. It seems to me that is the wrong way round: shareholders don't make a business successful, its people do. Look after the people and shareholders will ultimately gain because customers will be treated properly and profitability will improve.

A lot of companies still find that a radical idea. Look after the employees? We pay them their wages – isn't that enough?

No, it's not enough if you want to be really successful. The same applies even more so to public services. Their role as employer is hugely important to the communities they serve. If they can resolve to employ people who genuinely contribute to the organisation's mission, and if they can then make the working environment enjoyable and supportive, they will find that colleagues are using their imagination and energy to deliver better, meaningful services almost intuitively. Remember, if you love your work you'll never have to work a day in your life.

Chapter 9

Is our public spending effective?

I have said a lot about what has gone wrong in our society and how and why that has happened. I have also argued that public services are part of the problem, because they have actively contributed to some of our most intractable issues, both through well-meaning but misguided policies and through poor service delivery. But if we rethink our approach to public services, they can also be part of the solution.

At this point, it is worth standing back and taking a more objective look at the UK's public spending. The sums are colossal – as they are in all other Western Europe countries. The important question is whether that spending is effective. Do comparisons with our European neighbours show that we are getting excellent results from our public spending? Is it helping us to get the kind of society we want – healthy, vibrant, dynamic, educated, happy and secure?

Taxpayers need to know that their money is spent in an effective way. In the current economic climate this is more important than ever. As the Office For National Statistics observed: "given the Government's announced intention to cut government spending and given that almost everyone is a potential user of public services such as the NHS or schools, there is a particular concern about 'what we are getting for our money'." The change in demographic structure of the UK, with people living longer and therefore likely to need more intensive care later in life, will exert ever more pressure on scarce public resources and therefore increase the need to ensure value for money.

According to the Treasury, public sector spending on services accounted for almost half of GDP in 2009-10. The coalition government would like that proportion to come down, of course, and its cuts to public spending are focused on the reduction of the budget deficit. The cuts are undoubtedly having an impact, but in the longer term they may also lead to greater discipline in the way that public funds are used. This could mean an opportunity to ensure that public funds are used, not just more frugally, but more effectively – because people will want to see better quality outcomes and less wastage, from all public spending.

Understanding the effectiveness of public spending

The effectiveness of public spending can be defined in many ways. Broadly, measurement of spending and analysis of outcomes can reveal areas where expenditure is not matched by effect.

Outcomes will vary depending on the spending area under consideration. For example, healthcare outcomes may be changes in life expectancy, while in education they may be school achievement, or perhaps employment rates (though of course employment rates are linked to the state of the economy as a whole and also vary geographically).

To place such measurement and analysis into context, the UK's performance can be compared with that of other European nations, many of which faced similar fiscal challenges even before the Eurozone crises. This analysis will allow the establishment of benchmarks for the quality of outcomes which should be expected, given expenditure levels, against which future trends in spending effectiveness can be measured.

We can look here at statistics and research in four key spending areas vital to a thriving society: healthcare, education, housing and criminal justice.

Healthcare

The picture here is quite positive – the main concern is how things will develop in the future. Although the health service takes up an enormous slice of public spending in the UK, this is relatively low compared to other European countries and it yields an above average expectancy of healthy years. UK residents' downfall is their lifestyle, contributing to growing obesity and high death rates from cancer and heart disease.

There is much debate, not only in the UK, about the future for health services. *The Future of Healthcare in Europe*, a report from the Economist Intelligence Unit (sponsored by pharmaceutical company Janssen), predicts inevitable increases in cost of healthcare provision. It says the main drivers of rising healthcare costs in Europe are: ageing populations and the related rise in chronic disease; costly technological advances; patient demand, driven by increased knowledge of options and by less healthy lifestyles; legacy priorities and financing structures "that are ill-suited to today's requirements."

The report predicts that "keeping the universal healthcare model will require rationing of services and consolidation of healthcare facilities, as public resources fall short of demand."

The proportion of its GDP that the UK spends on health is close to the average for the EU (8.4% in the UK compared with 8.8% in the World Health Organisation European Region) but is less than the proportion in the most comparable countries, including France, Germany, the Netherlands and all but one of the Scandinavian countries.

Total spending on health as % of GDP by selected countries

Country	% of GDP
France	11.0
Germany	10.4
Denmark	9.8
Sweden	9.1
Norway	8.9
Netherlands	8.9
Italy	8.7
Spain	8.5
UNITED KINGDOM	8.4
Finland	8.2
Ireland	7.6

In common with most of its European neighbours, spending on health in the UK is largely publicly funded. As may be expected in a country which provides a system that is free at the point of use (rather than for example, one which makes use of a medical insurance scheme), the proportion of the UK's health spending which comes from public funds, at 81.7%, is larger than the European average of 76%.

While health spending per capita in the UK – both total and public – is well above average for the EU as a whole, it falls below that in France, Germany, the Netherlands and most of the Scandinavian countries.

Per capita public expenditure on health (US$) by selected countries

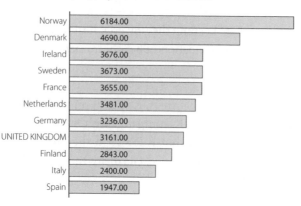

Norway	6184.00
Denmark	4690.00
Ireland	3676.00
Sweden	3673.00
France	3655.00
Netherlands	3481.00
Germany	3236.00
UNITED KINGDOM	3161.00
Finland	2843.00
Italy	2400.00
Spain	1947.00

Per capita total expenditure on health (US$) by selected countries

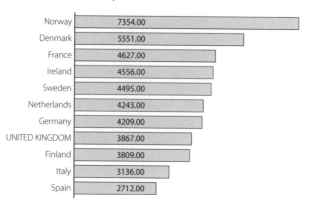

Norway	7354.00
Denmark	5551.00
France	4627.00
Ireland	4556.00
Sweden	4495.00
Netherlands	4243.00
Germany	4209.00
UNITED KINGDOM	3867.00
Finland	3809.00
Italy	3136.00
Spain	2712.00

So is the UK's spending on health producing benefits for its citizens? Raw life expectancy in the UK is around average for the EU.

However, quality of life is an important consideration and both men and women in the UK can expect to live for longer without disability or disease than the EU average (males: 64.9 years vs 61.5; females: 66.1 years vs 62.3). Healthy life years for both males and females in the UK exceed those in many comparable countries.

Male healthy life years by selected countries

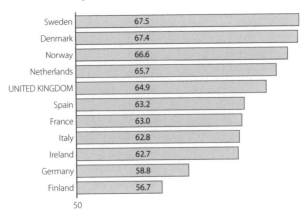

Sweden	67.5
Denmark	67.4
Norway	66.6
Netherlands	65.7
UNITED KINGDOM	64.9
Spain	63.2
France	63.0
Italy	62.8
Ireland	62.7
Germany	58.8
Finland	56.7

50

Female healthy life years by selected countries

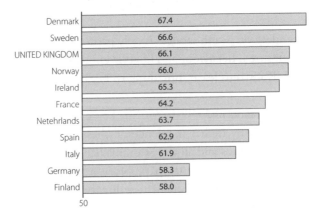

Denmark	67.4
Sweden	66.6
UNITED KINGDOM	66.1
Norway	66.0
Ireland	65.3
France	64.2
Netehrlands	63.7
Spain	62.9
Italy	61.9
Germany	58.3
Finland	58.0

50

Death rates tell a contrasting story. Indeed, proportional to population, deaths in the UK from cancer and ischaemic heart disease are significantly above the EU average.

The rates of such deaths, together with those from cerebrovascular disease, exceed those in France, Germany, Italy, Spain and Norway.

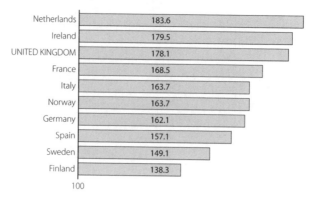

Deaths per 100,000 population
from Cancer by selected countries

Country	Deaths per 100,000
Netherlands	183.6
Ireland	179.5
UNITED KINGDOM	178.1
France	168.5
Italy	163.7
Norway	163.7
Germany	162.1
Spain	157.1
Sweden	149.1
Finland	138.3

In contrast, the UK's death rate from diabetes falls below that in several key countries, though, as has been widely reported, this is a disease which is on the increase. The UK has 6.4 deaths from diabetes per 100,000 of the population, compared with 16.7 in Italy, 14.4 in Germany and 13.6 in the Netherlands.

Of course, spending on health services is only part of what makes for a healthy population. People's own behaviour and lifestyle choices are a hugely important factor and here UK citizens leave something to be desired.

Consideration of established risk factors for key causes of death reveals that the UK has a significantly higher incidence of obesity than France, Germany, Spain, Italy, the Netherlands and all the Scandinavian countries. We have more than double the rate of obesity in Denmark, Norway, Italy and the Netherlands and more than 50% more than Ireland, where dietary habits might be expected to be similar to the UK's.

% of population obese by selected countries

UNITED KINGDOM	22.7
France	16.9
Finland	15.7
Spain	15.6
Ireland	13.0
Germany	12.9
Sweden	12.0
Denmark	11.4
Norway	10.0
Netherlands	10.0
Italy	9.8

Alcohol consumption in the UK is also higher than that in many comparable countries, although lower than in Ireland, France and Germany. Once again we come back to the issues of behaviour and personal responsibility that I have highlighted throughout this book.

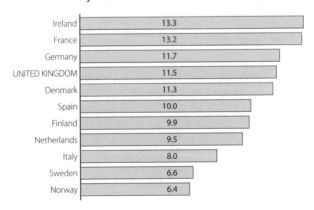

Per capita pure alcohol consumption (litres/year) by selected countries

Ireland	13.3
France	13.2
Germany	11.7
UNITED KINGDOM	11.5
Denmark	11.3
Spain	10.0
Finland	9.9
Netherlands	9.5
Italy	8.0
Sweden	6.6
Norway	6.4

Education

Here, the picture is much less positive. Despite spending levels in line with the EU average, the UK ends up with relatively low school achievement rates and high rates of youth unemployment.

The proportion of its GDP that the UK spends on education is average for the EU, falling below that in France and the Scandinavian countries, but above that in Germany, Spain, Italy and the Netherlands.

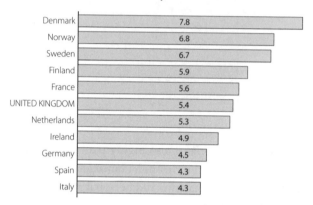

Public spending on education
as a % of GDP by selected countries

Country	% of GDP
Denmark	7.8
Norway	6.8
Sweden	6.7
Finland	5.9
France	5.6
UNITED KINGDOM	5.4
Netherlands	5.3
Ireland	4.9
Germany	4.5
Spain	4.3
Italy	4.3

However, this spending sector is not displaying good value for money. The results of the OECD's 2009 Programme for International Student Assessment reveal that British 15 year olds rank below those in France, Germany, the Netherlands and all of the Scandinavian countries for both reading and mathematics. Indeed for mathematics, the UK is outranked by Poland, the Czech Republic, Slovakia, Slovenia and Estonia.

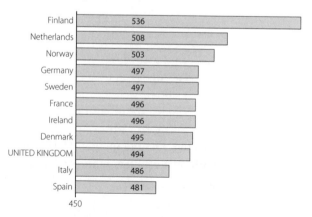

Performance of 15 years olds in reading
by selected countries

Finland	536
Netherlands	508
Norway	503
Germany	497
Sweden	497
France	496
Ireland	496
Denmark	495
UNITED KINGDOM	494
Italy	486
Spain	481

450

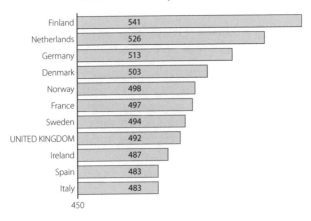

Performance of 15 years olds
in mathematics by selected countries

Finland	541
Netherlands	526
Germany	513
Denmark	503
Norway	498
France	497
Sweden	494
UNITED KINGDOM	492
Ireland	487
Spain	483
Italy	483

450

The proportion of 15-25 year olds in the UK who are not in education, employment or training is an astonishing 40.4%, meaning four in ten young people are basically seeing their lives going nowhere. This is significantly above the EU average of 33.3%, exceeding the proportions in many comparable countries – including Italy, France, Germany, the Netherlands and all of the Scandinavian countries.

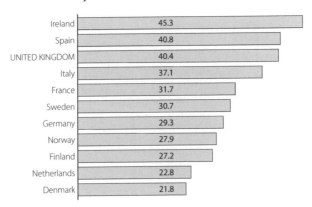

Percentage of 15-25 year olds not in
formal/non-formal education and training
by selected countries

Country	Percentage
Ireland	45.3
Spain	40.8
UNITED KINGDOM	40.4
Italy	37.1
France	31.7
Sweden	30.7
Germany	29.3
Norway	27.9
Finland	27.2
Netherlands	22.8
Denmark	21.8

In contrast, the proportion of the appropriate age group in the UK entering tertiary education is higher than in Germany, the Netherlands and the Scandinavian countries. This suggests that efforts over recent years to expand access to higher education have not been in vain, and the more motivated kids have been taking the opportunity (though there are early signs that trend could be reversing).

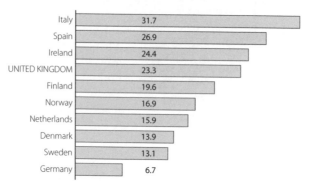

Percentage of relevant age group entering tertiary education by selected countries

Italy	31.7
Spain	26.9
Ireland	24.4
UNITED KINGDOM	23.3
Finland	19.6
Norway	16.9
Netherlands	15.9
Denmark	13.9
Sweden	13.1
Germany	6.7

Education at this level in the UK presents a brighter picture. Consideration of European university rankings shows that eleven of the top 20 are UK-based. Indeed, UK universities occupy four of the top five places, and according to the Times Higher Education World University Rankings 2010, the UK is home to the three highest ranked universities outside the USA.

Top ranking European universities

UNITED KINGDOM	1 =	University of Oxford
UNITED KINGDOM	1 =	University of Cambridge
UNITED KINGDOM	3	Imperial College London
Switzerland	4	Swiss Federal Institute of Technology, Zurich
UNITED KINGDOM	5	University College London
France	6	Ecole Polytechnique
UNITED KINGDOM	7	University of Edinburgh
France	8	Ecole Normale Superieure, Paris
Germany	9 =	University of Gottingen
Sweden	9 =	Karolinska Institute

Employment

IInterestingly, the statistics on unemployment generally are not as bad as they are for young people. The employment rate amongst the population of the UK has been above average for the EU, running at 69.9% in 2009, compared with

64.6% in Europe overall. The employment rate has been exceeding that in France, Spain and Italy though falling below that in Germany, the Netherlands and most of the Scandinavian countries.

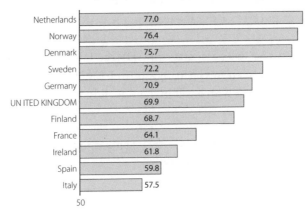

Employment rate by selected countries

Netherlands	77.0
Norway	76.4
Denmark	75.7
Sweden	72.2
Germany	70.9
UNITED KINGDOM	69.9
Finland	68.7
France	64.1
Ireland	61.8
Spain	59.8
Italy	57.5

50

The proportion of the UK's active population that is long-term unemployed is below the EU average, and markedly below the proportions in many comparable countries, including France, Germany, Spain and Italy – being more in line with rates seen in the Scandinavian countries.

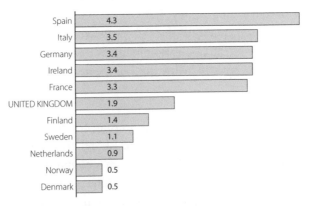

Percentage of active population who are long-trerm unemployed by selected countries

Country	Percentage
Spain	4.3
Italy	3.5
Germany	3.4
Ireland	3.4
France	3.3
UNITED KINGDOM	1.9
Finland	1.4
Sweden	1.1
Netherlands	0.9
Norway	0.5
Denmark	0.5

Housing

Investigation of the statistics for housing reveal a situation of which the UK cannot be proud. Levels of housing investment in this country are more similar to those in former eastern block countries than in the more affluent nations of north western Europe. The UK's population lives in poorer quality, more overcrowded accommodation than in many comparable countries – with a relatively high risk of poverty or social exclusion.

EU statistics show that as a percentage of GDP, the UK's investment in housing is less than half that seen in Germany, Finland, the Netherlands, Spain and France – being more in line with levels in the Czech Republic, Slovakia, Poland and the Baltic States.

Fixed capital formation in housing as % of GDP by country

Country	Value	Country	Value
Cyprus	8.0	Latvia	3.7
France	6.4	Czech Republic	3.3
Netherlands	5.9	Estonia	3.2
Spain	5.9	Lithuania	3.2
Finland	5.8	Sweden	2.9
Germany	5.6	UNITED KINGDOM	2.8
Denmark	5.1	Malta	2.8
Italy	4.7	Slovakia	2.3
Austria	4.4	Luxembourg	1.8
Greece	4.2	Ireland	0
Slovenia	4.1	Hungary	0

Comparison with the rest of the EU as a whole reveals that the UK has less of a problem of overcrowding – only 7.2% of the population living in overcrowded conditions, compared with the European average of 17.8%. When it comes to the percentage of the population living in poor quality accommodation, the UK is closer to, but still below the European average, at 14.6% compared with 15.9%.

However, it should be borne in mind that housing conditions are poor quality in many of the countries which joined the EU relatively recently, and the UK should surely be comparing itself with the richer countries like the Netherlands, Germany, France and the Scandinavian countries. The proportion of the UK population which lives in poor quality accommodation exceeds that in these countries. Overcrowding is less of a problem in the UK, as shown in the following graphs.

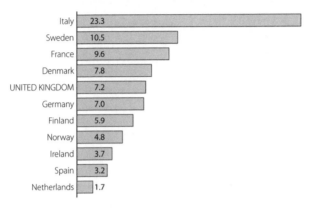

Percentage of population in overcrowded accommodation by selected countries

Italy	23.3
Sweden	10.5
France	9.6
Denmark	7.8
UNITED KINGDOM	7.2
Germany	7.0
Finland	5.9
Norway	4.8
Ireland	3.7
Spain	3.2
Netherlands	1.7

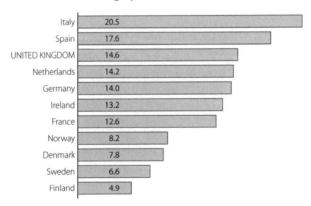

Percentage of population in non-decent housing by selected countries

Italy	20.5
Spain	17.6
UNITED KINGDOM	14.6
Netherlands	14.2
Germany	14.0
Ireland	13.2
France	12.6
Norway	8.2
Denmark	7.8
Sweden	6.6
Finland	4.9

Nearly 3% of the UK's population lives in severe housing deprivation – half the EU average.

However, this proportion is high in comparison with several key countries – notably almost six times that in the Netherlands and two to three times that in the Scandinavian countries.

Percentage of population in severe
housing deprivation by selected countries

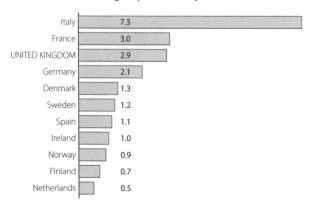

Italy	7.3
France	3.0
UNITED KINGDOM	2.9
Germany	2.1
Denmark	1.3
Sweden	1.2
Spain	1.1
Ireland	1.0
Norway	0.9
Finland	0.7
Netherlands	0.5

Welfare

Despite its huge social security bill, the UK is below the EU average when it comes to the proportion of GDP that the government spends on welfare benefits, with the UK spending 15.1%, as against the European average of 17.1%. This relatively low level of welfare spending is matched by a relatively high proportion of the British population who are at risk of poverty or social exclusion.

So if the UK's welfare benefits bill is not going to go up in future (and the government wants it to come down), it will have to be spent a lot more intelligently and effectively if it is to help lift people out of poverty and prevent more sliding into social exclusion.

The International Labour Office's Social Security Report 2010/11 concluded that welfare benefits spending can be a positive force. It said: "...contrary to earlier beliefs, no negative effects on economic growth of increased social spending during and after crises have been found. On the contrary, well-designed unemployment schemes and social assistance and public works programmes effectively prevent long-term unemployment and help shorten economic recessions."

Social benefits (other than social transfers
in kind) paid by General Government as %
of GDP by selected countries

Country	%
Italy	19.2
France	19.0
Germany	18.5
Finland	18.3
Denmark	16.8
Sweden	16.4
Ireland	15.3
UNITED KINGDOM	15.1
Spain	14.5
Norway	13.7
Netherlands	11.5

Further examination reveals that the proportion of the UK government's social protection expenditure that actually reaches households and individuals (as opposed to covering the costs of the administration and management of the scheme and so on) is in line with the European average, but lower than in Spain, Germany and the Scandinavian countries.

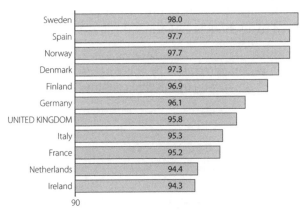

Total expenditure on social benefits as %
of total expenditure on social protection
by selected countries

Country	%
Sweden	98.0
Spain	97.7
Norway	97.7
Denmark	97.3
Finland	96.9
Germany	96.1
UNITED KINGDOM	95.8
Italy	95.3
France	95.2
Netherlands	94.4
Ireland	94.3

90

More than a fifth of the UK's population is at risk of poverty or social exclusion. Although lower than average in EU terms, this proportion exceeds that in countries whose societies are comparable to ours, such as Germany, France, the Netherlands and the Scandinavian countries.

Criminal Justice

Public order and safety make up around 5% of UK public spending, with policing, prisons and law courts accounting for the vast majority of this.

The number of police officers per 1,000 of the population is higher in the UK than in the Netherlands and the Scandinavian countries, but lower than in Spain, France, Ireland and Germany.

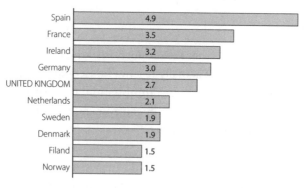

Number of police officers per 1000 of population by selected countries

Spain	4.9
France	3.5
Ireland	3.2
Germany	3.0
UNITED KINGDOM	2.7
Netherlands	2.1
Sweden	1.9
Denmark	1.9
Filand	1.5
Norway	1.5

Per 1,000 of the population, UK police record more crimes than their counterparts in many comparable countries. (Sweden seems to have a strikingly high rate – is this related to all those Scandicrime thrillers?).

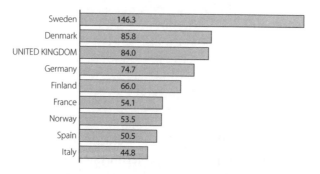

Crimes recorded by police per 1000 of population by selected countries

Sweden	146.3
Denmark	85.8
UNITED KINGDOM	84.0
Germany	74.7
Finland	66.0
France	54.1
Norway	53.5
Spain	50.5
Italy	44.8

The UK has a higher prison population (per 1,000 of the population) than many of the most comparable countries – in fact 50% or more higher than most of the countries. However, none of these approach the United States' rate of around 7.5 prisoners per 1,000 of the population.

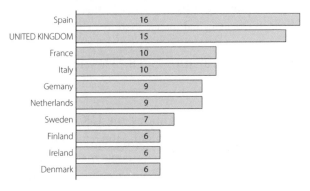

Prison population per 10,000 of population by selected countries

Spain	16
UNITED KINGDOM	15
France	10
Italy	10
Gemany	9
Netherlands	9
Sweden	7
Finland	6
Ireland	6
Denmark	6

The effectiveness or otherwise of prison is a controversial area. If prison is intended to prevent crime (through deterrence or rehabilitation) as well as punish crime, it is not doing a particularly good job. Around 40% of those prisoners released (or commencing probation) in the first quarter of 2008 went on to re-offend in the following year. Due to differences in measurements and definitions between nations, accurate European comparisons on this measure are not available. However a 2009 study by the Pompidou Group (Council of Europe, Strasbourg) showed England, Wales and Scotland to have the highest rates of recidivism amongst comparable countries.

What these statistics tell us

The overall position of the UK, in terms of its effectiveness and value for money compared with other European countries, is not great. In terms of health, the UK fares reasonably well. But the combination of an ageing population and the obesity explosion will exert heavy pressure on the state in future years. People's lifestyle choices have a major impact on public expenditure, as services struggle to rehabilitate and treat excessive Western lifestyles. Witness the £4.6 million super-size mortuary built at the coroner's court in Gloucester, which has room for 62 corpses, with larger fridges and two heavy duty trolleys which can hold bodies weighing up to 35 stone and one capable of dealing with a 50 stone corpse. The mortuary manager said: "the dimensions have got bigger because people are getting bigger."

The UK's performance in the areas of education, welfare benefits and the criminal justice system similarly fall short of the more successful European states such as the Netherlands, which operates a very intelligent and long term view to public investment with a greater emphasis on preventative measures. Britain's education outputs identified here are particularly worrying, as indeed are the findings with regard to the criminal justice system.

This chapter has dealt only with statistics. These never tell the whole story, but they can be a wake-up call.

Despite the current economic conditions, the UK is a wealthy nation. In many areas of public life, citizens are not getting the returns from their taxes that they should expect. It is time we developed strategies and tactics which seek to optimise the benefits our society should enjoy from one of the highest levels of public expenditure on the planet.

Chapter 10

Seeking the returns on society's investment

I began this book by arguing that, to move towards a better society in the UK, we need to find ways to change behaviour. As I showed in my portrayal of the curve, in chapter 2, it is easy for behaviour to deteriorate, quite rapidly in certain circumstances, and unless we act to reverse this deterioration, we will be spending more and more public money tackling more and more social problems.

I've tried to demonstrate that it is possible to change behaviour, and the way to do that is by rewarding the behaviour that you want, rather than spending enormous amounts of time and money punishing and clearing up after the behaviour you don't want.

Furthermore, the principle of actively rewarding the behaviour that you want can be used to great effect within organisations, to create a dynamic and productive culture. I believe this approach could be used within Britain's public services, (which for too long have had exactly the opposite of a dynamic and productive culture) to transform those services so that they can deliver much more, to support the kind of safe, healthy, decent society we want. Equally I believe our meritocratic business model has wider applicability in the business world.

This is not really about spending money or saving money, rather about thinking and using resources differently. But there can be no doubt, looking at the facts and figures in chapter 9, that we need to examine why we are not getting better value for money from our public spending.

It is particularly interesting to look at health and education. Both are services which touch almost everyone; the future of both is under discussion, with arguments raging about structure and funding, central control versus local independence, public funding versus private, and so on.

The international comparisons show that we get pretty good value for money from the health service. Unfortunately, this does not necessarily mean we are a healthy nation. The figures for obesity are startlingly worse than for other comparable European nations and show that more than one in five of UK citizens is obese, with all the attendant health risks. So in future, doctors could be fighting a losing battle to maintain the health of a British population intent on eating itself to death.

The statistics for education are very dispiriting. The poor performance of 15 year olds in reading and maths must inevitably follow through to the extremely high percentage of young people not in employment, education or training. Increased numbers of young people have gone to university in recent years – so these statistics must mean increased numbers at the other end of the scale are hanging round the streets or sitting at home watching (or appearing on) Jeremy Kyle.

Evidently, our education system is not teaching thousands of young people what they need to know, and society is not providing them with the channels they need to move on, move up and build an independent life.

Most British people are proud of the NHS. I would guess few (certainly in England) would claim to be proud of our education system. For all its faults, the NHS is trusted to be there when you need it, to be genuinely free at the point of delivery, and to be genuinely universal. Our class-riven education system is not universal, as everyone knows. A person from an inner city council estate, who is suffering from cancer, has every chance of being treated at a prestigious hospital, under the care of a world-class consultant. The large city hospitals are some of our best and anyone can be admitted there: they don't distinguish between 'good' or 'bad' patients from 'good' or 'bad' neighbourhoods.

Compare that with education. Will the children from that inner city estate be going to a prestigious school, taught by the best teachers? It's hardly likely.

Getting a return on society's investment

What is the most effective way to spend public money? Where will it generate the biggest benefits to society? The answer has to be education and health – especially education. As a housing professional, of course I think good housing is very important to quality of life, and certainly bad housing undermines your life chances in many ways. But good education and good health are the things that lift human beings out of poverty, dependency and restricted horizons.

In my view, education is where the game is won and lost. To compromise on education is a fatal blow to society. Of course good health is an important part of being able to live a good life, and is often undervalued by people when they are young and fit. An effective health service also allows people with disabilities or chronic illnesses (including mental illnesses) not to be prisoners of their condition, but to fulfil their potential. However, education remains paramount, because a well educated person is more likely to understand the importance of healthy diet, exercise and so on. The healthier life they lead will ultimately mean savings for the state, because they will make less call on medical services.

The biggest return on public investment will come from education, if it can produce young people who can get a good job, look after their health, contribute to their community, and don't indulge in illegal and destructive behaviour.

So when it comes to education, are we rewarding the behaviours that we want? Are we rewarding young people for pursuing their studies and are we rewarding schools for delivering good education?

The perception of young people at the moment is that, far from being rewarded, they are actually being penalised for staying in education. The prospect of being saddled with a huge burden of debt will undoubtedly deter many from going into higher education. The effect is going to be most extreme on the people from low income homes – the ones whose lives could be most transformed by higher education.

The loss of educational maintenance allowance has been perceived by young people as a blow. This was a payment which did, quite simply, reward young people for choosing to stay at school. There was criticism that EMA was too much of a blanket scheme and it's interesting that it is to be replaced by bursaries handed out by the schools and colleges themselves, with the suggestion that they will link the payments to the student's behaviour or attendance, so there is potential for some useful incentive schemes there, if handled well.

But the fact remains that a young person from a low income household who wants to pursue his or her education faces an uphill struggle. They will have to look for all sorts of routes to find funding. Their family and their friends might not be supportive.

In Britain we never seem to have moved away from the idea that all we need is a privately educated elite to run things and take all the decisions, and a population of factory fodder, who don't require much more than minimal literacy and numeracy. This way of thinking is instilled at the bottom end of society as much as at the top. In the British psyche is always this suspicion of education – that it doesn't really do you any good.

Well, there's no point in producing factory fodder because we have very few factories any more. If we are ever going to improve our economy we are going to need people with skills, motivation, imagination and the ability to think for themselves.

Education at its best, delivered by inspirational teachers, develops you as a person: it makes you stronger, more creative, more confident, better able to adapt to change, better able to cope with setbacks. It gives you a greater appetite for life and it also encourages you to carry on learning, long after you have left school or college.

The question that follows, of course is: can our education system deliver that? Do we reward schools and teachers who do deliver it?

People who work in education and education policy are well aware of these issues. But I still think the public sector 'one size fits all' approach applies all too often in state education. There is a reluctance to talk about quality. Teachers are treated as if they were all as good as one another, when every pupil knows that isn't the case. The attitude to education has become increasingly utilitarian, as if its purpose were solely to equip students for employment, and a fairly narrow definition of employment at that. Schools are judged only on what is measurable, in other words, the league tables of exam results.

It is no wonder young people feel disengaged from education. They are told that the point of it is to get a job, yet they can see few jobs out there for them, or if they can, they don't feel confident of earning enough money to warrant taking on enormous loans.

Anyone who has had a good teacher knows how education can bring its own rewards – the excitement of feeling inspired and enthused, of whole areas of knowledge opening up to you. I ask people, how many teachers did you have who made you feel special, proud of yourself, confident and made learning a dream for you? Most people have had at least one, maybe two. I say, how did you do in those subjects? They usually say they did well. And what about those teachers who were rude, uninterested, whose idea of teaching was to march into class and order you to open your books? People generally say most of their teachers were like that, and, no, they didn't do well in the lessons where they sat baffled and bored, disliking the teacher.

It's obvious really, but it's not often mentioned when people are agonising over why not enough pupils study physics or chemistry or languages. Favourite lessons are often art, music, drama – the ones which get people's emotions up and running. If you want kids to study physics and chemistry you have to find a way of teaching that enthuses them, not just hope they will be motivated by a sense of duty and the desire to pass an exam. That might work for the most conscientious or ambitious, but not for the others. Why should it?

I've benefited hugely from education. As an ordinary kid, I was fortunate enough to go to a school that taught ordinary kids well; I went to university, got a PhD. I even taught in a secondary school myself. Teaching ought to be acknowledged as one of the most important jobs in the country. It should be a job that people aspire to.

Shaping young people

What sets a young person on one road rather than another in life? If you take a handful of kids from an estate, why, a few years down the line, will some have a decent job, a happy relationship and hopes for the future, some be on benefits, and some be in prison?

There will be a host of reasons. Some will be to do with the individual's personality and intelligence. But other factors are things that society can influence and change.

I see four main influences on a child: home, school, church/mosque (or temple, chapel, synagogue) and neighbourhood.

Where we have a problem is where the home influence is weak or malign, either not imparting decent values to a child, or else actively teaching them a toxic lifestyle. But all is not lost for that child if the other influences can come into play.

Whether a young person is influenced by church or mosque partly depends on the family, but religious institutions of all sorts do a lot of outreach work with young people who may never set foot inside a religious building. Valuable work is also done by charities like The Prince's Trust, which have succeeded in transforming the life chances for many young people.

So there are people out there who are ready to help, but it is difficult for them to reach everybody and often they concentrate on those in most need – boys who have already been in trouble for anti-social behaviour, for instance.

Society needs to be sure that the values it counts as important are imparted to kids from an early age. Like home, neighbourhood can have an influence one way or another. I've described how my neighbourhood was a strong influence on me as a child. I had no doubt that values like honesty and hard work were what everyone believed in. The community I grew up in had the confidence to expect that all its young people conform to those standards. Of course you could rebel, as I did – but you knew what the values were.

Neighbourhoods rarely work in the same way in the 21st century, and if anything we are inclined to see the neighbourhood as a malign influence, particularly where gangs rule. But my work has demonstrated that it is possible to change neighbourhoods and make them places where good values apply. In fact, as I've argued, this is essential. We can't expect kids not to indulge in anti-social behaviour, vandalism and nuisance if they see people around them doing those things with impunity. Every time a child walks to school past graffiti, litter and needles they are learning something. Their view of what is 'normal' is shaped by their daily environment.

So I come back to school, which is the strongest influence, after the home, because it includes all children, from an early age, and is surely the most powerful tool society has for shaping future generations. And I'm not just talking here about how many kids pass five GCSEs A⋆ – C.

Code for success

Recently, we have carried out a programme of making grants to primary schools in our area. These are relatively small amounts – £1,500 per school, and we've been going to six different schools a year – but we get maximum effect out of it because of the way we involve the pupils themselves in deciding how to spend it.

When I visit schools I usually speak at the school assembly. I give them a story passed on to me by Bob Armstrong and I find it always captures their imagination. I say: "I've got some money with me today. This is for your school because we're a successful company and I want to tell you how to be successful." I tell them I have a "code for success" given me by a successful friend in the US.

When Bob Armstrong was seven, he was sent by his father to visit a lady called Mother Jackson, who was exactly 100 years older than Bob. She was a former slave who had learned to read or write when she was 95. Bob's father reckoned she was the wisest lady he knew.

So Bob went to see her every day and she lived to the age of 114. This was her code for success: "In order to be successful there are some things you must know. You must know how to read and write, how to add, multiply, subtract and divide." At this point I ask the kids how many can read, write, add, multiply, subtract and divide, and lots put their hands up, feeling they are well on the road to success.

Mother Jackson said: "Once you've learned to read and write you need to learn how to act and how to behave in certain circumstances, because you will never be accepted into society unless you know how to behave. You need to know how to communicate, how to talk and how to listen. If you've got good ideas, and you need help to put those ideas into practice, you need to be able to communicate with people.

"Once you can do all those things, you just need to be kind."

After that we discuss what to do with the money and how to use it in a fair way; some favour sharing it out equally between every pupil, some want to give it to charity, some want to have a lottery so that one person wins it all. No assembly that I've visited has ever agreed to give the money to their teachers.

I was particularly impressed by one school, which set up a bank account for each of its 150 pupils. They started off with £5 each, but the children quickly learned the benefit of money gaining interest and started to pay in their pocket money. Meanwhile the school is using the other £750 to set up a variety of reward schemes, such as for punctuality, being kind, improving your health and so on.

That school is a wonderful place, led by a dynamic, enthusiastic head. The pupils were from a very wide range of backgrounds and she had embraced this, making the school the centre of a mixed community. For example, when we visited, a group of Somali women were attending an English language class, held within the school. The head's motivation percolated throughout the school: the kids were chipper, articulate, full of life. I felt confident that the school could compensate to a great extent for the difficulties and disadvantages a lot of those kids had in their young lives.

There was a real contrast between this school and another we visited soon after. There, the head had forgotten we were coming and made it clear she didn't care whether we were there or not. She regarded her headship as a temporary post, though she had been there for a number of years, and was counting the days until she left. The other teachers were similarly downbeat and the children were very muted and reluctant at first to come forward with ideas. I could only hope the head left as soon as possible and somebody dynamic was put in her place, because her negativity was doing untold damage to the school and the pupils.

If we want to move the curve and improve behaviour in society, I say education is where we should be concentrating our resources. Too often the assumption is that anti-social youth can't be reached by education. The kids most in need of the education system are the quickest to leave it, and most schools are happy to see them go, because they're dragging down the league table results.

As I've seen in primary schools, in education, as in the workplace, it all comes back to leadership. You need to be a very good teacher to reach the disaffected kids, but there are people who can do that and it is up to the head to find those teachers and motivate them. It may be that those young people will never pass many exams, but what matters is their leaving school feeling that they can do something in the world, that there is more ahead of them than a life of drugs and petty crime, for the boys, or a life of babies and benefit, for the girls.

My own experience of teaching showed me the necessity of the principle I now use at work – of creating the conditions which motivate people by tapping into what's important to them, not what's important to you. In one school I was given the remedial unit. I was supposed to teach them IT and economics and it was pretty obvious my PhD wasn't going to be much help to me. The classroom was utterly chaotic. Fortunately I could convey to them that I was tough and streetwise, so I managed to impose some discipline, but that still left me with the problem of what to teach.

In the end I taught them maths by starting with darts. They didn't know what a differential equation was but they knew how a nine dart finish could be done. They could work out a "yankee bet" which is quite a complex bit of mathematics. They were great with figures when it came to that sort of thing because that was their culture: they could see the point of it, they were excited by it.

A good teacher can pitch education at people's level – not by talking down to them but by ensuring it connects to their world, and then take them forwards from there.

Where are the rewards?

How can society measure the payback from its investment in education? This question is usually discussed in economic terms, with the 'results' from education considered to be qualifications, which lead to employment and thence affect the country's economic performance.

But the returns on education are much wider and could be measurable, if we looked in the right places. Good education motivates and inspires young people, gives them strong values and leads them to fulfil their potential. Equipping young people in this way will ultimately reduce the demands on our criminal justice system, the welfare system and the health service. It is young women who can see no prospects for themselves who have a baby early, thinking it will lead to a life where they have at least some minimal status as a mother, funded by a reliable income from welfare benefits. It is young men who feel themselves at the bottom of the heap, with no chance of getting a worthwhile job, who are attracted to the overblown status and quick money of crime.

Good education always leads to more education. If you've had a positive experience at school, you can appreciate the value of going on to train as a plumber or a nurse, or going to university. You understand the rewards on offer if you put in the effort. Without education, you stay a child, constantly looking for unearned rewards and instant gratification.

Everyone loves talent shows these days. They seem to offer easy rewards. Even someone with a very second rate singing voice can attain the glamour of being on TV. We are forever being told we can achieve our dreams "as long as we believe in ourselves". So kids dream of being a footballer, boxer, pop star, dancer, but they have no grasp of the sheer hard work it takes to get there. Too many people don't find out what they could really do with their lives, so they end up with a negative attitude born of disappointment and resentment.

Society needs to think about how it can use reward to steer young people in the right direction. In fact society offers many rewards, but they are not having the effect we would like.

ASBOs were introduced in an effort to control the behaviour of anti-social youth through penalties. But young lads simply turned the penalty into a reward. An ASBO became like an MBE for the poor. You'd hear them boasting:
"I got an ASBO!"
"What's it for?"
"Bans me from two estates!"
"That's nothing. I got an ASBO Manchester!"
His ASBO bans him from entering Manchester city centre. Everyone around them is thinking admiringly, "That's cool!"

What happens to all those kids with an ASBO? The order itself does nothing and is largely unenforceable. It serves merely to make the rest of society feel something has been done. But if those young people are not to follow a bleak trajectory to organised crime and prison (each time costing public services more and more) intervention is needed.

Intervention costs money and you have to find the right people to do it –

people who understand the minds and culture of what look, to the rest of us, like a bunch of unappealing yobs. Usually, the right people are ones who have come out of that milieu themselves. In fact, the next community youth workers and community leaders should be the ex-gang members and those with anti-social behaviour orders.

I'm not saying we should be in awe of criminals, but we need to understand what is happening in communities and that does not mean sending some unsuspecting sociology graduate on to an estate as a social inclusion worker, wandering around like a zebra being watched by lions. The people who could really have an effect are the people the authorities might not want to talk to. If the country could talk to the IRA to bring about peace, we can talk to ex-gang members and people with ASBOs to help sort out inner city problems.

Stop making poverty comfortable

A lot of public resources are spent on rewarding dependency. As a landlord, we have found that unless we take active steps otherwise, we foster a dependency culture.

Some years ago I was visiting one of our estates and went to see a new tenant, who had moved into her house six weeks previously. She was a nice woman, a single parent (but, as ever, with men's clothes hanging on the line), delighted with the house, which had new central heating, double glazing, laminated floors and so on. She had installed a huge TV and better electronic equipment than I had at home. "Is everything OK?" I asked. "Fantastic. But just one thing," she said. "When are you doing me garden? The grass is getting a bit high."

I asked her where she got the idea from that we would do the gardening and she was puzzled. "I just assumed you would," she said, "you do all the repairs, the external painting and that… I thought you'd do the garden".

Of course, it was true: we did do everything else. In social housing, the landlord does a host of things that owner occupiers do for themselves as a matter of course, down to tightening the hinge on a garden gate. These all count as 'repairs' and housing associations are measured for their speed of doing repairs, and tenants' satisfaction at how well the repairs are done.

We have now taken the radical step of stating that, rather than doing more and more repairs, faster and faster, we do not want to do any at all. We have a target of zero unnecessary repairs. Major problems should be forestalled by regular maintenance and minor issues can be handled by tenants themselves. That raises all sort of things I won't go into here (to do with health and safety, liability etc) but the fact is there is much more tenants could do for themselves if they weren't locked into the dependency frame of mind.

Traditionally, tenants weren't 'allowed' to do anything themselves. On local authority estates they couldn't choose the colour of their front door. The system infantilised them. When people bought their council homes under the right to buy, the first thing they did was to fit a new front door and proudly announce to the rest of the estate: "We are owners." They exercised choice.

During one Housing Corporation inspection, a resident turned up at a meeting with the inspectors holding a jar of ants. He said: "I've been waiting for this opportunity. Here's some bloody ants from the kitchen. What do you think about that?"

I asked him if he had ordered any pesticide or fumigation. "No," he said, "I was asked to come to this group here today so I thought I'd bring the ants. These are your ants."

I made it clear that we didn't own any ants. But the point was he saw them as our problem. If I had ants in the kitchen I would go out and buy ant powder. Not him: he just complained to me.

Social housing providers have fostered that sort of attitude, always urging people to contact their housing officer about this, that and the other. In an understandable effort to provide a 'good' service (and score highly on tenant satisfaction) many providers unintentionally encourage dependency.

Indeed the very process of accessing social housing tends to reward people for being dependent. There are valid historical reasons for this, but the net result is not good for society.

Years ago, for council tenants there used to be housing visitors, who would go round to your home annually and grade you A to F. I remember my mother polishing all day when the housing visitor was due to come around. These bossy little clerks wielded an undue amount of power and it led to claims that council properties were being allocated unfairly and that tenants were being patronised.

So housing allocation was reformed and turned into an objective, points-based system, reflecting need.

This sounds fine, except that it forces low-income households into an arms race of need. Their problems become their most valuable assets. So if you have a heart problem, if your children have asthma – that's good – it means more points! You might be chain smoking 60 a day and making your family ill, but that doesn't matter.

Crucially, being a single parent gains you more points, so women are positively rewarded for not living with their partner, and children grow up without a stable male presence in the home. Plus if you count as a single parent it's a passport to help with your utility bills, council tax, TV licence and so on. The rewards continue.

Our benefits system was designed as a safety net but it has become a spider's web. It was intended to prevent families from falling into poverty during periods of ill health or unemployment. But, 60 years on, it has become a way of life, and one that's dragging down both society and individuals. The spider's web traps people: they can only crawl out of it if they put in a huge amount of effort and are prepared to lose money. The comfortable option is to stay put.

On the whole, it is pretty comfortable. In the UK, we have learnt to manage poverty as an art form. With each generation, we have employed more people to keep others comfortable in their poverty. Some families have so many professional helpers, they're like royalty in reverse. They have home makers – people to show them how to shop, how to dress, and how to decorate their home. They have housing benefit income maximisers, social security advisers and social workers. Their kids have probation officers and floating support workers. There's an army of people trying to do their best for them. But are we genuinely helping them, or incarcerating them in terminal dependency? If you make poverty comfortable, people will stay poor.

On a course once, I met a woman who introduced herself as a social inclusion co-ordinator. "What do you do, exactly"? I asked. She said: "I co-ordinate all the social inclusion workers." That is the crux of the matter. We have countless people inadvertently but, nevertheless, successfully managing poverty. Most of their jobs have 'social' in the title – social workers, social services, social security, social housing. Most of them are engaged in keeping their clients in a state of dependency, whether they understand it or not.

It's like the problem we had with empty properties, as I described in chapter 4. Empty properties had to be sheeted up, which not only made them harder to let, but meant we had void inspectors, we had to pay the sheeting contractors to fit and remove the sheets, we had to repair the window frames. We ended up with all these people working on something we didn't want in the first place. What we really needed was no empty properties, which we've now almost achieved.

Public services frequently spend their time dealing with problems that, as a society, we don't want in the first place. But once you have people regularly working on them, the problems become normal, then hard to eradicate. Instead, we should think about dealing with things before there's a problem. How could we help a child before he or she needs a social inclusion worker (who in turn needs a social inclusion co-ordinator)?

In our area there was a problem with fires in certain tower blocks. A great deal of fire prevention work was carried out, residents were given fire educational programmes, sprinklers were fitted, a fire engine was even stationed nearby. In the end, what prevented the fires breaking out was giving all the residents deep fat fryers. They stopped setting their kitchens alight and a lot of money was saved. However, perhaps a health eating programme may have been more beneficial in the long term by reducing dependency on fried foods!

Downloading help and sympathy on to people in perceived need doesn't improve their situation. They've got to stand up on their own two feet and find their own way of including themselves in society.

I saw a telling example of this in the US. With Bob Armstrong, I visited two native American reservations in Nebraska. One belonged to the Winnebago tribe. In theory, they are in charge of their own destiny there: they have their own police force, they run their own lives. In reality, the place was a tip, the buildings covered with graffiti; alcoholism and family break-up were rife. We went to see the chief who still seemed to be mourning the loss of the buffalo, a century ago. Bob said, "Who are the heroes in this tribe"? The only name people could come up with was that of the chief who had appeared in the film *Dancing with Wolves*, who died of sclerosis of the liver!

Then we went to visit the Sioux. The contrast was enormous. They didn't care about buffalo; their chief had a big Cadillac and gold rings. The Sioux went out to work – many of the construction workers on New York's classic skyscrapers were Sioux – and they had used the money to build income-generating casinos on their land. When we asked the Sioux chief who the tribe's heroes were, he reeled off a long list of footballers, sports stars, film stars and the like. The Sioux had the same resources and opportunities as the Winnebago but used them differently. They may not be living the old way of life but they've created a can-do culture of achievement within the native American traditions.

How prescriptive should we be?

As an employer, we do a lot for our colleagues. But we're not trying to molly-coddle them and make them dependent on employment with us. We're trying to create a culture of justice and opportunity, in which people will be motivated and take personal responsibility for the things they do. We pay their wages and in return we expect certain behaviour from them.

I think society can take the same approach. Some people would argue that society has no right to get involved with individuals' lifestyles, but I think it does – especially if it is paying for those lifestyles. There is no doubt that society is funding, through benefits, lifestyles of dependency, ill health and poor life-chances for children. In our well-intentioned efforts to mitigate the bad effects of these lifestyles, we just seem to make them worse. What we really need to change is the lifestyles – in other words, change behaviour.

There are examples of society doing this successfully. In 1986 around 27,000 car accidents a year involved drivers who had been drinking. With the tightening of the alcohol limit, by 2000 this figure had dropped to 19,000 a year – still high, but a substantial improvement.

That is an example of the law leading behavioural change. With compulsory seatbelts and, in recent years, bans on smoking in public places, people begin by regarding the changes in the law as an infringement of their liberties, but as the rules take effect, there is a change in attitudes and behaviour. Having 'one for the road' or smoking in a restaurant are now completely unthinkable.

So you can do all sorts of things. It depends how prescriptive you want society to be. In my view society could be much more prescriptive, in areas where there are implications for the public purse. But it needs to couple this with clever rewards to motivate people to change their behaviour, rather than instituting complicated, expensive systems of policing and penalties.

Take obesity. This is a serious problem for the UK. As is shown in chapter 9, we are outstripping other European countries in our rate of obesity and things are going to get worse. The obesity rate has more than doubled in the past 25 years and if the current trend continues, by 2050 we will truly be a nation of fatties, with 60% of men, 50% of women and 25% of children obese. It is not a pleasant prospect, and the health service will be spending huge sums of money coping with the heart disease, diabetes, stroke and other illnesses that obesity brings.

Much research is being done into this area, but on the whole, the causes of obesity (where there is not a medical condition involved at its origin) are no mystery: people eating too much, of the wrong sort of food, and not taking enough exercise.

In most cases, obesity, like smoking, is a self-inflicted health problem. To solve the problem, people need to change their behaviour and it seems to me society has a right to demand that, just as it has the right to ban smoking in public places.

The curve has been moving fast, with obesity. Social changes are a big factor. We have got used to the difference in people's body size and shape. Children who would have been considered plump in the 1960s now look normal. Our eating habits, which have never been particularly healthy in Britain, have been targeted by powerful industries intent on selling us high fat, high sugar – and highly profitable – processed food. Eating out has become affordable and, importantly, one of the ways we reward ourselves. Children are taught at an early age to regard a trip to KFC or McDonalds as a treat (with giveaway toys).

Exercise used to be something people did naturally in the course of a day, walking to work or school, carrying out manual tasks, while playing outside was kids' main source of entertainment. Now we don't live like that: most of us have to choose to exercise and have to go to the park or the gym to do it. It is hardly surprising that adults can't be bothered and children would rather stay in with their I-Pod.

In the 19ᵗʰ century, when most people didn't have a good enough diet, plumpness was a sign of wealth, but now we have the paradox that the lower your income, the more likely you are to be obese. The *Manchester Healthy Weight Strategy 2010-2013*, a joint project by the local authority and NHS in Manchester, identifies the groups most like to be obese as: adults who are un-employed or in low-paid work, children in low income households, single parents and (a shameful indictment of the care system) children in local authority care.

A number of factors are at work here. If you've got to feed a family on a small budget you go for cheap, high calorie food. Junk food is comforting as well as filling. Most of us would admit that if we are feeling stressed and fed up, chips or chocolate are a lot more appealing than a salad. Education is a factor too: clearly people aren't making the connection between the food they eat and their state of health or their children's future health.

Are we rewarding obesity? And if so, can we change that so that we reward a reduction in obesity?

We are certainly 'rewarding' high-calorie food and drink, in the sense that it is cheap to buy, yet profitable to manufacture. It could be made less profitable, through tax. However, we'd have to be sure that didn't penalise low income households by pushing up their food bill so that their children ended up with an even poorer diet.

It is not easy to change people's diet (as Jamie Oliver will attest). People will need help and guidance and this would have to be more than vague exhortations to eat 'five a day'. I would argue everyone ought to have a personal programme worked out with their GP, just as we do for our colleagues.

I would like to see everyone going for an annual health MOT with outcomes being linked to taxation levels. The doctor or practice nurse would sit down with them, assess their weight to see if obesity is an issue, find out in detail about their eating and drinking habits, their smoking, how much they exercise, and work out a programme that will improve their overall health, with weight reduction and stop smoking goals if necessary. The doctor would also be looking for undetected problems, such as mental health issues or undiagnosed medical conditions.

How could you make people attend such a health check? It could be done in conjunction with schools, if they have children. If they are claiming benefit, it should be done as a condition of their claiming. Some might already be seeing their GP regularly for a medical condition, such as asthma.

Many people will struggle to keep to their health programme and they should be able to ask for further help if, say, they haven't been able to cut down their smoking or get their children to a healthier weight after six months. The emphasis should be on helping them live a better life, not telling them off for falling short of their goals. However, a doctor's advice is a very powerful thing. It's one thing to think, "Oh I ought to lose weight." It's another thing to have your doctor tell you bluntly you need to shed pounds now or you could develop diabetes in just a few years' time. In addition, doctors should have the authority to award tax breaks for gym membership fees and to raise or lower national insurance contributions in accordance with results.

Yes, it's bossy and interventionist, but the benefits to society will be enormous. There also need to be visible rewards in place, such as tax breaks for those who can demonstrate improvements at their next health MOT. Of course there is also the personal reward that just comes from losing weight and becoming more healthy. Everyone feels better for being slimmer, fitter and having more energy. Numerous studies show that children are better behaved and concentrate better at school once their diet improves.

Public services need to be more concerned with lifestyle and health, because bad lifestyles and ill-health are costing the country a lot of money. The *Manchester Healthy Weight Strategy* reports that the cost to the NHS of dealing with obesity alone will be £3.9 billion in 2015, a rise of 70% since 2007. The cost of dealing with all the illnesses in which obesity is a factor – heart disease, stroke and so on – will be £19.5 billion nationally in 2015.

Public services have a right to intervene. GPs ought not to be content to write regular sick notes for people who simply need to change their lifestyle; perhaps employers should be able to challenge GP practices if this is a regular occurrence.

If people are claiming benefits, the DWP should have a right to make it a condition of payment that they go to their doctor and start improving their health. Why should the state just continue to download money to them, to fund a lifestyle that will ultimately cost them, and the public purse, dear? DWP figures released in April 2011 showed that 42,360 incapacity benefit claimants were on IB because they had an alcohol addiction, 37,480 were drug dependent and 1,800 were deemed unable to work because they were obese. Further break down of these figures showed that 12,800 alcoholics, 9,200 drug addicts and 600 obese people had been in this situation, funding their self-inflicted problems through welfare benefits, for more than 10 years. Surely for many of these people, public money is killing them.

Intervening in lifestyles is a controversial idea, but we could do it, as a society, if we wanted to. We would need to invest money now in order to see savings five years down the line. Interestingly, it is the sort of approach that private medical insurers take: they understand the value of prevention in order to avoid big payouts in the future.

Getting more out of the benefits system

Welfare benefits are a big cost to the UK and it is not surprising governments want to reduce the bill. But withdrawing benefits is not, in itself, going to make society a better place. All the long-term unemployed, the single mothers and people on incapacity benefit are not going to suddenly go out and find jobs. Many have a long way to go before they are in a position to enter the world of work. But I think the benefit system could be used intelligently to help us make this happen.

For example, take teenage mothers. The UK has the highest teenage pregnancy rate in Western Europe, and has both the highest birth rate and the highest abortion rate amongst teenagers. The rate of teenage births is five times that in the Netherlands, more than twice that in Germany and twice that in France. Back in 1998, the government set up a Teenage Pregnancy Unit to try to get these figures down, but the impact has been minor: by 2008 the teenage pregnancy rate had fallen by around 13%.

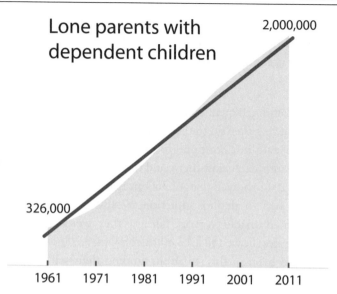

Lone parents with
dependent children

2,000,000

326,000

1961   1971   1981   1991   2001   2011

So far, no-one has found a good way of persuading teenage girls not to get pregnant. The more socially disadvantaged the girls, the more likely they are to have the babies, and to become lone mothers of several children.

As we have seen, there are tangible rewards for girls in following this path, particularly for girls who see very few other rewards within their grasp. Amid all the talk of girls outstripping boys in school performance, or of women 'having it all', we lose sight of the fact that many girls have no role models around them of women with fulfilling jobs; they are not encouraged to have any ambitions for themselves or have any thought of leading a life of their own, not dependent on either a man or the state. If they had to make their own way in the world, they wouldn't know where to start. Emotionally starved, they have no idea how to make a good relationship.

For girls who have very little, a baby gives them a lot: having a baby brings them an income, through benefits; it stands to get them a house or flat of their own; they gain status and identity as a mother; it appears to make them an adult. It also gives them someone to love and who loves them.

My grandmother brought up her children alone, when she was widowed during the war, so I would never argue that single parents can't be good parents. But being a parent is one of the hardest jobs in the world and there is no way that, as a teenager, you have the skills and life experience to do it well. The results can be seen in many ways, such as high obesity rates and low educational achievement among children of single mothers living on benefits.

We could use the benefit system here and make it a condition of claiming that lone parents follow a health programme for themselves and go on parenting courses. There are any number of rewards that could be put in place to motivate young women to learn to be better parents.

We do have to place responsibilities on people. It is not enough for them just to state the number and ages of their children and receive benefit payments accordingly. It is wrong for people to see having children and claiming benefit as a single package, a lifestyle choice, almost a career path. It does nothing for the children and, ultimately, it gives the mother nothing. Teenagers don't think that far ahead, but children grow up and the mother is left with no qualifications, no experience in the outside world, few prospects of getting a decent job – really, no independent life. It should not be surprising if many of these mothers are keen to become young grandmothers, when their own teenage daughters get pregnant.

The welfare benefit system currently requires lone mothers to look for work once their youngest child is in full time education. Unfortunately, as any parent knows, young children and work do not mix. School hours do not match with office hours, after-school cover has to be paid for and holidays are a headache. Small children are liable to fall ill without notice. On top of that (and this is a problem the government has recognised) the loss of benefits once a person enters work creates a marginal tax rate of more than 90%. In other words, a lone mother taking up a job would find herself only a few pounds better off each week, but would have all the expense of going to work, plus all the stress of making child care arrangements. Where's the reward in that?

There will be rewards if she can stick with the job, but she and her employer need help to make that happen. I would suggest, use part of the benefits the woman formerly received in order to give the employer a subsidy. This could be used to cushion the cost of a single parent having to take unforeseen time off, but also to give her the training and development she needs to move on and up.

I know there are inspiring examples of single mothers holding down two jobs and taking an Open University course at night to transform their lives, but people that motivated are few and far between. Most people need help and encouragement.

The same approach could be used to support people who get a job after being on the dole or claiming incapacity benefit for years. In most cases, they won't be able to move smoothly into work; there will be issues which emerge and which employers will have to deal with. We regularly employ people with chequered histories, including people who have been homeless or in prison, and we have always found that eventually some trauma in the past resurfaces and creates problems which we need to deal with.

I still believe work is the best way forward for those people, but employers need encouragement to take them on. Why doesn't the DWP say to an employer: if you take someone off the dole, pay them their wages and train them, we will pay you their former benefits, for a certain period? If the deal is made attractive to the employer and the employer can develop that person, in five years they might never have to be on benefit again.

Prison – rehabilitation or revolving door?

I believe that prison, the ultimate sanction available to society, should constitute both punishment and rehabilitation. Our prison population has grown exponentially since the 1950s in association with the societal deterioration we've discussed earlier.

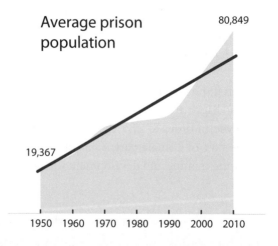

Average prison population

80,849

19,367

1950   1960   1970   1980   1990   2000   2010

With some noticeable exceptions, such as fraudulent politicians, businessmen and murderous aristocrats, the vast majority of prisoners emerge from the lower socio-economic groups in our society. Compared with the rest of the population, prisoners are far more likely to have come from chaotic families and have a complex knot of problems – drug dependency, learning disabilities and low educational achievement, debts, mental health issues and so on.

This should come as no surprise. But could anything have been done to intervene in these people's lives before they ended up in prison – the most expensive option for the taxpayer? And when they are in prison, is anything done to unpick their problems so that they can build a better life once they leave? Or does prison inevitably lead to more prison?

In December 2011 the prison population in England and Wales had reached its highest ever point at 88,179 – up 4,720 in 12 months. Heavy sentencing following the summer riots had added to the numbers in custody. "Over the past 15 years Britain has developed an expensive over-reliance on imprisonment," the Prison Reform Trust said in response to this statistic. "Our overcrowded jails increasingly act as an early port of call for the courts, expected to deter, to rehabilitate and to act as a dumping ground for all those failed by other services."

Between 1996 and 2010, the prison population in England and Wales grew by 54%. The number of prison places available failed to keep pace with this increase, so creating overcrowding in more than half of jails. The number of women in prison increased by a massive 114% over that period, although women still make up a fraction of the population behind bars, at 4,211 in December 2011.

Imprisonment is astonishingly expensive. The criminal justice system takes up 2.3% of our GDP, a higher proportion than in the US or any EU country. The average annual overall cost of a prison place in England and Wales in 2010-11 was £39,573. The cost of the crown court process of imposing a prison sentence is approximately £30,500. Between 2003 and 2009 prison expenditure increased nearly 40% in real terms.

This can't continue, of course. Following the 2010 spending review the Ministry of Justice will have to make overall resource savings of 23% in real terms by 2014-15. It is far from clear how it will achieve that, given the current trends.

As the Prison Reform Trust remarks, "Outcomes of imprisonment are poor." In itself, prison does not seem to do much to reduce reoffending: 47% of adults are reconvicted within one year of being released, and for those serving sentences of less than 12 months this increases to 57%. The more often people go to jail, the more likely they are to return: those who have served more than 10 previous custodial sentences have a reoffending rate of 66%.

The National Audit Office calculated that in 2007-08, reoffending by all recent ex-prisoners cost the economy between £9.5 billion and £13 billion.

The real question we should be asking as a society is: are we getting value for money out of our prison service? Our ultimate goal should, surely, be to have lower levels of crime. So do our prisons contribute to this or not?

Prison is a punishment, but it can help lower the crime rate in two ways: firstly by keeping the hardened criminals and psychopaths locked up and safely out of circulation. Most people would recognise this as an essential function of prison.

The second way is for prisons to help those who are not hardened criminals, but who have ended up in prison after a series of poor choices – usually by getting into drugs, falling in with a gang and so on. Many of these people would like to turn their lives around and prison could potentially give them the chance to do that, by getting them to confront their crimes and their lifestyle and – most importantly of all – giving them the opportunity to educate themselves, even learn a trade.

Nearly half of those in prison have no qualifications at all and many are barely literate: 48% of all prisoners are at, or below, the level expected of an 11 year old in reading, 65% in numeracy and 82% in writing. While it would be simplistic to claim that teaching people to read will stop them committing crimes, it is surely true that if we want people to stay within the law, get a job and build some sort of stable life, they need to be equipped with the very basics to operate in the world – a reasonable level of literacy and numeracy, freedom from drug and alcohol dependency and, ideally, some sort of skill or work experience.

Achieving these things won't be easy, and with some people it will be impossible. It will require intervention. But let's face it, prison is the ideal opportunity for that intervention.

In fact there is ample evidence that prison is a very effective environment for changing behaviour. Unfortunately, that change goes in completely the wrong direction. Our prisons are some of the most violent places in the UK. Illegal businesses flourish, as do gang cultures, gangster sub-cultures and sexual attack. Prisons are among the easiest places in the country to obtain drugs; people go in clean and come out addicted.

Clearly there are immensely difficult problems here. But I wonder why, as a nation, we do not demand better outcomes from our prison service? Are we too wedded to the idea that rehabilitation is a 'soft option'? Do we believe criminals should be locked in cells all day, not lounging around in the library? Do we think that the violence and bullying that goes on in prisons is an intrinsic part of the punishment?

These are all points of view, and the debate over the criminal justice system could fill a book in itself, but I would say we should look at what is best for society as a whole, both in terms of security on our streets and the cost to the nation. A prison service that acts to change behaviour for the better, even at the margins, has got to be preferable to one that actually makes criminal behaviour worse.

Our prison service does operate to some extent a meritocratic system. It's called parole, ie. the better behaved you are in jail the shorter the sentence you will serve. This is important but we need to stop people going to prison in the first place. Whilst we probably have to accept that the generation of convicts we have jailed and not rehabilitated are likely to be either welfare or crime dependent for the rest of their lives, we should be thinking about the large numbers of young people going to prison. What about all those rioters – will prison have set them back on the straight and narrow, or will it have pushed them to the criminal margins? Having a criminal record is a serious barrier to getting a job, which is likely to create frustration and increase people's propensity to either fund their lifestyle through crime or welfare benefits.

It is crucial that we aim to significantly reduce the number of people in prison by strategically targeting resources into those communities which are the current breeding grounds. We need to get to the point where, for young people, a job in mainstream society is valued higher than a life in the underworld economy.

The UK's spending on criminal justice and prisons is perhaps our most extreme example of negative expenditure. Of course, society needs to have a robust, fair justice system with real penalties, but far too much of this expenditure goes on maintaining a section of population as they go round the circle of under achievement–crime–prison–homelessness–joblessness–crime–back to prison and so on.

As I've argued in this book, we should be looking at areas of negative expenditure and trying to reduce them or eliminate them, not increase them. I'm not saying we can eliminate crime, but we should be wary when governments point to increased spending on prisons as evidence that they're doing a good job. In my view, high spending on prisons is evidence of failure: evidence that, as a society, we've failed to act and invest at the points where it would have made a difference to the lives of people who have ended up in prison, to the detriment of us all.

Conclusion

This book has sought to explain my philosophy and views on work and customer service. I have set out the business model I've developed in conjunction with Julian Richer, which identifies the importance of valuing people, recognising their achievements and understanding the psychological and emotional need for reward, respect and recognition.

Over the past decade I have worked in an innovative and challenging environment and have tried to bring meaning to our ideals of unlocking potential; making productivity gains; ensuring that people understand both their rights and responsibilities; and treating people with dignity, respect and trust. Having had the opportunity to work globally and in some of the toughest and most challenging neighbourhoods in the UK and America, I believe that western economies in the post casino capitalist world need to embrace business models which are ethical, believed in and supported by people.

Western nations face enormous challenges. Demographic changes, longevity, fragmenting household structures and the competitive challenges emerging from what are termed the BRIC (Brazil, Russia, India and China) economies are rapidly reducing the UK and other European nations to service and financial economies, with slow growth rates and high public expenditure as a proportion of gross domestic product.

The UK's welfare state, health service, housing, education and civil justice systems are increasingly becoming unsustainable and will continue to do so for the foreseeable future. The UK derives low productivity from most of its public expenditure compared with other economies, particularly Scandinavia and the Netherlands, and we are on a par with less developed nations, such as Greece, Turkey, Portugal and Spain when it comes to educational productivity.

In short, we must tackle the way in which public services are provided and delivered. We need revolutionary, unbridled thinking, to produce a new meritocratic paradigm which rewards the behavioural outcomes that society believes in.

This is not some sinister fascist intrusion into civil liberties and personal freedoms. It is simply a recognition that if we want a true 'reward society' we should reward and encourage thrift, hard work, good personal health and diet, limited reliance on welfare, avoidance of imprisonment, high educational achievement, low dependency on public services, neighbourliness, civic pride and tolerance.

Clearly, citizens who genuinely experience medical, social and psychological conditions should not be excluded from the reward society, but should indeed be at the heart of it. Equally, whilst we must strive to include the socially excluded, the socially excluded must also realise the importance of including themselves. The hallmark of a just society is its compassion and support for people who are genuinely unable to help themselves. Everybody would support such a notion, but where there is a growing sense of injustice, unfairness and hypocrisy, warning lights start flashing. Not only is our current level of public expenditure on the big ticket items unsustainable in the long term, it is simply not right that we should appear to reward those behaviours and actions which undermine social cohesion and a unity of purpose in UK society.

There is a whole body of respectable academic literature which explains human needs and motivation. Regrettably these findings have not featured significantly enough in the central thinking which underpins a great deal of society's policies and programmes for advancement through positive non-violent social change.

For example, it cannot be right that people can earn more through not working than working; similarly, how is it that up to two thirds of ex-prisoners return to jail; that social and nursing care is not available for people who have worked all their lives and have been law abiding contributors to society, unless they sell their homes and use up all their net of taxation savings?

Why is it that inordinate amounts of scarce public money are being spent by the National Health Service on treating illnesses which are the product of unhealthy lifestyles? Why does the housing lobby clamour for increased numbers of affordable social housing units when there are already almost half a million empty properties in the UK, when few, if any, of the housing professionals either live or aspire for their children to live in social housing and the UK already has one of the highest proportions of social housing globally? Surely, if we spent more effectively on health and education, many residents would become more successful and move out of the sector to find their own housing solution.

Is it right that obese people can be referred by their GP to a gym free of charge when others who take responsibility for their personal health pay significant amounts in gym fees net of taxation? Equally, as unbelievable as it might appear, our welfare benefit system currently rewards obese folk with higher benefit payments for food and clothing. The list is endless and engenders feelings of injustice and in some instances understandable outrage.

I have tried to avoid what might be termed fish and chip shop anecdotes in my discussions but inevitably opinions are shaped by subjective experience and perception.

Throughout my book I have tried to provide empirical evidence to support the various hypothesises I have postulated. I have demonstrated that treating people who work with you with dignity and respect, and treating them as they would like to be treated, in a meritocratic business context, produces high levels of personal happiness and productivity. In our organisation we now achieve far more, with fewer people, than we've ever done. We've reached this point largely through focusing our attention on what really matters in business, ie. income, knowing your customers, controlling your costs and getting the absolute best out of yourself and the people you work with in a truly reciprocal relationship.

As one of the highest performing housing providers in the UK, which has received over 30 national and international awards in equal numbers from public and private sector organisations, our business model has wide applicability and is particularly relevant to the challenges which our public services face now and in the foreseeable future.

We've also applied our meritocratic philosophy to social housing residents and significantly changed the nature of the landlord-tenant relationship by encouraging prompt rent payment, neighbourliness, tidiness and civic pride. Having repositioned our relationship with our customers we have experienced a dramatic change in what we do. Ten years ago 80% of our activity was devoted to reacting to problems like anti social behaviour, vandalism, rent arrears and so on. My colleagues on the front line knew the names of their worst customers, but not their best customers. The frustration which they felt was one of the driving forces behind the quiet revolution we have pioneered. Our Gold Service programme significantly helped us change behaviours and cultures, by treating customers with dignity and respect and rewarding them for responsible behaviour, whilst being sympathetic and supportive in times of trouble. We now have customers who are valued and who appreciate the products and services we provide.

Diamond Service, an innovation launched in April 2012, is the fourth generation of our meritocratic philosophy. It applies equally to customers and colleagues and seeks to encourage everyone to improve themselves and others to find and fulfil their potential.

My experience is that people understand and value meritocracy. They think it is right that honest, hard working and law abiding citizens should be rewarded for trying to live a decent, honest life, paying their dues and making a contribution to society. They do not value or understand the opposite attitude, the kind of "the world owes me a living" state of mind. Good people do not like to see others rewarded for negative behaviour.

Human beings rise to levels of expectation. We need to continuously review all of society's support and financial mechanisms to ensure that they work towards outcomes that will save the human race from its own self socio-economic and political destruction.

As Steve Jobs said: "Your time is limited, so don't waste it living someone else's life. Don't be trapped by dogma – which is the result of other peoples thinking. Don't let the noise of others' opinions drown out your own inner voice. And most important, have the courage to follow your heart and intuition. They somehow already know what you truly want to become. Everything else is secondary."